SUCCESS IS OUR PLAN

When God blesses me with the millions, billions and trillions, how will I help build the Kingdom of God?

Table of Content

Dedications

First, I would like to thank our Abba Father, Jehovah-Jireh for trusting me with His Word. I am thankful for a listening ear, as God has guided my hands in writing this book, for His Kingdom business owners. God wants the best for His people, but we must live and operate by His standards; which are all written in the Bible; and revealed to us as we mediate and study His Word; daily.

This book is dedicated to all business owners and future business owners. Success is easy, but it is everlasting when we apply God's principles and standards for building His Kingdom for greater living. Everything you need God has it.

"Seek the Kingdom of God above all else, and live righteously, and he will give you everything you need." Matthew 6:33

Thanks to my husband, Manuel; children, DeVeon, DeJyreka, and DeNaysia; family, church members, and friends for the encouragement, as I embark on this journey, as an Inspirational Author guided by God's Voice and His Promises.

I will always remember the Women that left me with much inspiration and guidance through their lives, while they were here on earth; my dearly mother, Gwendolyn, my great-grandmother, Elizabeth, great aunt, Elouise, my mother-in-law, Elease, my grand-mother Jessie Mae. You all are in Heaven, but your words have never left my spirit.

Preface

There are 2 kinds of Success:
The popular choice: The World System
God's Choice: True Success or Success His Way

God has allowed me to write many books on marriages and the anointing of our leaders in today's society, based on my experiences and deliverance route. Through trying to figure out why my marriage is still being attacked so badly, pushed me to search a little harder to why my husband and I are still having such a struggle. We are both prophets, raising other prophets, which are our children. Therefore, we hear from God; and Satan is using all his tactics to keep us from hearing from God and delivering his message to His people. The more I yearn for understanding and knowledge of this War between the Spirit, Satan and flesh, God reveals more to me. In this book we are going to go deeper back into history concerning **The Promised Land of Israel, the overtaking of 7 Nations.**

As I mature in Christ, the deeper I plow into the roots of evil spirits that are holding God's leaders down in the pit. I published a book "18-Day Challenge for Every Man and Woman". The book went into details the many addictions that we are dealing with or have dealt with. Before, I make this statement of my further research and studying, I have been delivered from alcoholism, lying, cheating, idolatry, adultery and many more additions. To add, once I completed the "18 Challenge……." The attacks became real.

In the "18-Day Challenge……", God revealed to me that "smoking" is the last addiction to be delivered from. Therefore, I wanted to search more concerning these demons and spirits. Then, God led me to the 7 evil spirits. I may relate to marriages on many occasions in this book, although, this book is for all God's children, single or married, that need more understanding on how to be "God's Success"; not man's success.

Although, marriage is a powerful cord between man and woman, we still need to tighten this bond with un-dissolvable glue, with the power of God; together, the three strands will help strengthen other marriages on this Earth. Then, we can use "two" individuals, as "one" with God's strength, with 14 times greater power, than the giants that we are about to read about, to destroy Satan tactics and forces here on Earth.

"A person standing alone can be attacked and defeated, but two can stand back-to-back and conquer. Three are even better, for a triple-braided cord is not easily broken."
Ecclesiastes 4:12, NLT

How will I help build the Kingdom of God?

Introduction

It is so important to understand why God blesses us with abundance; let us just say millions. The first thing we do is pay all our bills, purchase a home or car, travel the world, purchase expensive clothing and jewel……purchase mommy a house, provide for our grandparents and so forth. All this is good, but what about the rest of the world that need homeless shelters, homes for the orphans and the widows, food for the hunger, programs for the teenage pregnancy, jobs for people with criminal backgrounds and so forth.

When we are blessed with millions, why do we only think about ourselves and our immediate family? Why don't we think about the "hunger", "homeless", "jobless" and so forth in the economy?

When, I made millions in the family first business, all I wanted to do was "change the world". I wanted to make a "difference" in this world. Although I did make a small difference, somehow, I got side tracked as the money in the bank account increased. I began to worship the money and the material things. I was not boastful or bogus about the success; but I became careless. Over these 4 years of not making the millions, I began to ask God to show me, "me". I need to be a better person in the next business venture. I need to truly be a spokeswoman for our nation. I want to help the economy. The question: How and why should I do this? My answer: " But God!"

My first step was being delivered from the evil sins that were deeply rooted in my soul; in which are discussed in the book, "18-Day Challenge for Every Man and Woman", authored by me, Eureka A. Butler. After writing the book, God showed me how to help build the Kingdom of God by removing some mountains that are keeping God's people from being successful for the Kingdom and not successful for self or man.

Our war is against Flesh (us) and Spirit (God). Therefore, this book, "Success Is Our Plan" is about evil spirits, the demons and mountains that we must conquer in order to become "Successful" in God's Kingdom; not man's kingdom. Now, allow us to begin.

Promised Land One
Understanding the War as Christians

Evil spirits are normally viewed as "influences," and their effectiveness in the lives of people is undetected because they are not seen as real personalities that are totally and unreservedly evil. People discuss the issue of whether or not a Christian can be "possessed" by an evil or unclean spirit; all the while, these ambassadors of Satan are busy doing the thing they do best; deceiving men and women, both unsaved and believers alike. While we are judging people and wondering if Christians have evil spirits or if Christians are living a holy and righteous life; which is confusion by Satan, Satan is busy deceiving men and women.

We as Christians need to believe that no matter what our positions or titles as seen by our families, church or community; we are all inclined to sin. We need to stop the judgment against church leaders and Christians and come together to conquer these 7 mountains that are listed in this book. We Got a Fight ahead of us............and Satan is not backing down until we come together and bring Him down with the power of Jesus.

Scripture says that we are born sinners and that we are by nature sinners.

Psalm 51:5 states that we all come into the world as sinners: *"Behold, I was brought forth in iniquity, and in sin my mother conceived me."* **Ephesians 2:2** *says that all people who are not in Christ are "sons of disobedience."* **Ephesians 2:3,** *also establishes this, saying that we are all "by* **nature** *children of wrath."*

If we are all *"by nature children of wrath,"* it can only be because we are all by nature sinners; for God does not direct His wrath towards those who are not guilty. God did not create the human race sinful, but upright. But we fell into sin and became sinful due to the sin of Adam.

Also, Scripture speaks of humans as unrighteous from infancy.......... Proverbs 22:15 says *"Foolishness is bound up in the heart of a child."* Genesis 8:21 declares, ". . . *the intent of man's heart is evil from his youth. "* One commenter remarks that on this verse: "The word translated youth, signifies the whole of the former part of the age of man, which commences from the beginning of life. The word in its derivation, has reference to the birth or beginning of existence . . . so that the word here translated youth, comprehends not only what we in English most commonly call the time of youth, but also childhood and infancy."

Therefore, sin lies within our flesh. Therefore, we have to walk by Spirit daily, meaning every second of the day. *Galatians 5:16-17* *"But I say, walk by the Spirit, and you will not carry out the desire of the flesh. For the flesh sets its desire against the Spirit, and the Spirit against the flesh; for these are in opposition to one another, so that you may not do the things that you please."*

Therefore, NO ONE IS PERFECT.............No More Judgments.............Only Kingdom Building!!!!

Promised Land Two
The Seven Nations

"1 When the LORD thy God shall bring thee into the land whither thou goest to possess it, and hath cast out many nations before thee, the Hittites, and the Girgashites, and the Amorites, and the Canaanites, and the Perizzites, and the Hivites, and the Jebusites, seven nations greater and mightier than thou; 2 And when the LORD thy God shall deliver them before thee; thou shalt smite them, and utterly destroy them; thou shalt make no covenant with them, nor shew mercy unto them" **(Deuteronomy 7:1-2)**

This was part of God's instructions to the people of Israel before they could take the Promise Land. This means that, in order for each one of us, each spouses as "one", and for the Church as a whole, to enter into our spiritual inheritance, we must be able to overtake 7 nations; the mountains of **the Hittites, the Girgashites, the Amorites, the Canaanites, the Perizzites, the Hivites, and the Jebusites.** These nations, which were literal people in the past, now represent 7 "varieties" of evil spirits, which are the evil counterparts of the 7 Spirits of God (Revelation 3:1, Revelation 5:6, Zechariah 4:10).

Revelation 3:1, (GWT). *"To the messenger of the church in Sardis, write: The one who has God's seven spirits and the seven stars says: I know what you have done. You are known for being alive, but you are dead."*
Revelation 5:6, (NLT), *"Then I saw a Lamb that looked as if it had been slaughtered, but it was now standing between the throne and the four living beings and among the twenty-four elders. He had seven horns and seven eyes, which represent the sevenfold Spirit of God that is sent out into every part of the earth."*
Zechariah 4:10, (NIV) *"10 "Who despises the day of small things? Men will rejoice when they see the plumb line in the hand of Zerubbabel. "(These seven are the eyes of the LORD, which range throughout the earth.)"*

When we look at the meaning of these nations' names, we can begin to infer the types of spirits they represent:

Spirit name	Meaning of name	Abbreviated explanation of effects
Hittites	Sons of terror	Subliminal torments, phobias, terror, depression, deceit
Girgashites	Clay dwellers	Focus on earthliness, unbelief in what cannot be seen
Amorites	Mountain people; renowned	Obsession with earthly fame and glory, domineering
Canaanites	Lowlands people	Addictions, perversions, exaggerated people-pleasing
Perizzites	Belonging to a village	Limited vision, laziness, low self-esteem
Hivites	Villagers	Vision limited to enjoying an earthly inheritance, hedonism
Jebusites	Threshers	Suppression of spiritual authority in fellow believers, legalism

Promised Land Three
Marriage and Success

I am a strong believer in saving marriages for the battle field. Therefore, allow me one Promised Land to expound on the attack that marriages are having. It is so imperative to know who we are in Christ. Consequently, before two individuals vow to marriage, they will be able to understand their calling and the power of their anointing in their life, as "one". When you join together, you will have the greater power of two individuals, working as "one", to help destroy the tactics of Satan and to build-up the kingdom of God. "Success" is achievements based on a person's standards and principles.

To narrow the achievements, "Success" is based on two forms: **God's Choice**, which is true success; "Success His Way" or the **The popular choice;** which is "The World's System." It all depends on who side you are on: God or Satan, the Right or Wrong, Holy or Unholy Side.

For example, one may know that he/she is marrying a prophet. Even though, there is a certain attraction to this individual….one potential spouse is in the church, although there are some past hurt and wounds; a little partying here and there. The other potential spouse is in the middle, "straddling the fence" (as our elders would say in the church), but still living the dark side of life; drinking, smoking, and clubbing. They both choose to marry one another, not out of love, but out of a certain attraction that is drawing them to one another. Because of their child-hood's upbringing, they have already figured out that they must attend church regularly. (*In reality, this is the norm for all freshly, newly married couples.*)

Therefore, they start going to church more together because they know this is the norm; and realize there are so many attacks because "one" has decided not to leave the evil, malevolence and malicious behaviors to become Christ-like. The attacks are because the devil knows once "one" has total committed his/her life, then, the other spouse will want to change.

With both spouses becoming Christ-like this becomes a panic and terror attack to the devil. Therefore, the devil blinds the un-saved spouse with greater tactics of this world:

      a. Immorality (lust of the flesh)

      b. Materialism (lust of the eyes)

      c. Arrogance (pride of life)

The harder the saved spouse tries to bring the other spouse in, through praying, fasting, and living in holiness, the greater the attacks. Then, at hand, arguments take place, disagreements, addictions, financial woes, adultery, and sometimes the divorce. Then, the believer, the save one says," I had less problems before I became Christ-like." True, but, the believer has to understand, when we are on Jesus Christ side, the Winning side, there is a spiritual battle that has developed between Satan and the believer. Satan is not there to fight the un-believer or un-saved spouse, because he/she is where he wants him/her to be; but Satan is attacking the one who is saved and following Jesus Christ.

James 1:12 **"Blessed is the man who remains steadfast under trial, for when he has stood the test he will receive the crown of life, which God has promised to those who love him."**

While you were on Satan side, dealing with past wounds, there were no reasons for a fight. Now, since you are on the Right side, the Winning side, Satan tries to keep one spouse on his side to try to confuse the believer, the Christ-like spouse.

We come today, to give Satan the Expulsion Eviction notice, *Ephesians 6:12,* *"12 For we wrestle not against flesh and blood, but against principalities, against powers, against the rulers of the darkness of this world, against spiritual wickedness in high places."*

We must speak that **"WE ARE NO longer bound to the principalities, against powers, against the rulers of the darkness of this world, against spiritual wickedness in high places!" Therefore, we no longer fight with our spouses, the**

flesh and blood...............We have to love on our un-saved spouses more and fight with the holy spirit guiding us through prayer and fasting.

Jesus never told his followers that if they followed him, everything would be lofty or rose-colored. As he spoke to many followers in the Bible, the same applies to us that chooses to follow Him; that it will be a difficult road, but rewarding at the end; eternal life.

When, I married my husband he had many addictions and a not so pleasing lifestyle and later in my marriage I became attracted to many addictions and a not so-pleasing lifestyle. All I can say is that "Marriage" is the power of two individuals, to overcome and defeat the many obstacles that we face today, as "one". I would say look for these qualities in your mate........

1.   **Fears God.** Some of the ways you can tell if a young man or woman fears God is by his language and how he treats other people. Does he treat them with respect? If not, why not? We as human beings are made in the image of God, and respecting people ultimately shows a heart that reverences the One whom we reflect. I know of drugs dealers, alcoholics, janitors, cashiers at Wal-Mart and millionaires that go to church; some are selfish and some are nice and encouraging. Therefore, I do not judge anyone because of their status or sin, because we were all born "sinners".

However, the main question is "Do they know God and His Son Jesus?") Because of the attraction that you two have for one another, you both will not see each other faults and marry, in any case.) This question will help determine if you are ready to fight for your marriage, when you two are joined together; because the unbeliever will be enlightened by the believer and there will be a fight against Satan and the believer due to the believer winning the other spouse over to God.

Psalm 51:5 (ESV), *"Behold, I was brought forth in iniquity, and in sin did my mother conceive me."* The way I see life and marriage now, if they keep going to church, the un-saved, living with the saved spouse, will change for the Greater!

2.   **Is not afraid to love.** That may sound like a no-brainer, but a lot of young men and women today are afraid of commitment, and the young lady ends up chasing the young man. What we need today are more young men who are not afraid of being real, authentic, and committed to a young lady in a relationship. We need men who are not afraid to love. Vice versa with woman. There have been so many women, as well as men, hurt and disappointed from past relationships that they are afraid to LOVE again.

1 Corinthians 13:4-8 ESV, *"Love is patient and kind; love does not envy or boast; it is not arrogant or rude. It does not insist on its own way; it is not irritable or resentful; it does not rejoice at wrongdoing, but rejoices with the truth. Love bears all things, believes all things, hopes all things, endures all things. Love never ends. As for prophecies, they will pass away; as for tongues, they will cease; as for knowledge, it will pass away."*

3.   **Can admit his/her faults, his/her mistakes, and when he's/she's hurt you.** "A successful marriage is the union of two forgivers." The reason is because you are going to hurt one another over and over again during your lifetime together. If you do not know how to ask for forgiveness and give forgiveness, you are never going to have a successful marriage. The growth of your marriage will be underdeveloped early on.

Ephesians 4:32, (ESV), *"Be kind to one another, tenderhearted, forgiving one another, as God in Christ forgave you."*

4.   **Honors his/her parents.** In the Ten Commandments, God tells us to honor our parents so that our lives may be long and it may be well with us (Exodus 20:12). If they do not love their parents, but, you can see the potential of them forgiving them and loving once again; after you have shown them that unspeakable LOVE to them; he/she is definitely the one, but needs a little work in healing. I have heard it said "that if you want to see how a young man will treat you, see how he treats

his mother." I would take it a step further. How does he/she honor both his mother and his father? Does he/she speak well of them or is he/she angry with them? Does he/she refuse to speak about them at all? What is going on between a young man and woman and their parents is very important. We cannot and will not judge them on their past or present, but we need to know how we can help them to overcome past un-resolved issues that need some attention and healing. I always say **"Everybody needs to be Love, Why can't you be that Person to bring them to God's love?"**

Exodus 20:12 (NIV*), "Honor your father and your mother, so that you may live long in the land the LORD your God is giving you."*

5.   Is a potential leader and knows how to serve. Being the head of a home means having authority and having responsibility that demands a servant spirit and self-denial. If a young man does not know how to deny himself on behalf of another person, giving up his personal rights, goals, and dreams, I would question whether he would know how to create a family over a lifetime. You have leaders of gangs, managers of night clubs, CEO's of corporations. Their leadership role is shown by the attitudes of their peers; not the type or field of work they are in. Therefore, a person that has money in the bank or a 7 bedroom house does not make him a potential leader....but are they influencing their surroundings.

In the beginning, because we are not perfect, it does not have to be positive influence; but do they have followers? We are looking at the followers based on some type of influence; upright or inferior. Are they the leader? If someone has the skills to have someone to follow them, then, that is an advantage. Even though the influence may not be positive, they are leaders, but need to be change to God's side, the winning side....through deliverance and healing.

I must stop and say this...I am thankful for God, my father that sits high and looks low. A Great God that will give and show you wisdom as His Word states.

Success Is Our Plan

5 If any of you lacks wisdom, he should ask God, who gives generously to all without finding fault, and it will be given to him. 6 But when he asks, he must believe and not doubt, because he who doubts is like a wave of the sea, blown and tossed by the wind. (James 1:5-6)

My heart is for all marriages to survive and to continue to fight this war against our flesh and the evil spirits that lies behind "divorce." As I am researching the nations/mountains, I am writing this book. This book is not only to save marriages now; and in the future. This book is saving my marriage as I ask God, "What is it that I am not doing?" What am I missing in making my marriage stronger?" You see, I do not put blame on anyone concerning my marriage. I am not perfect and I still battle with evils spirits because of some past relationships. I am not talking about my adulterous relations in 2010, but my fornications relations in middle school, my stealing out of stores when I was young, my lying to my parents and so forth…… I need to understand these spirits that are grounded to the roots so that I may be truly and fully set free. Satan is real and powerful, but our God is more real and more powerful than Satan. But, I need God's wisdom to destroy the enemy tactics concerning my marriage and other marriages. **"Divorce Is not an Option"**………..We just need to understand the battle that our God is fighting.

Promised Land Four
The Narrow Gate, Difficult Path

In Matthew 7:13-14 we read of Jesus saying, *"Enter by the narrow gate; for wide is the gate and broad is the way that leads to destruction, and there are many who go in by it. Because narrow is the gate and difficult is the way which leads to life, and there are few who find it"*

Narrow gate, difficult path………..

A narrow gate is harder to pass through than one that is wide, and only a few people can go through a narrow gate at once. In saying "difficult is the way which leads to life," Jesus was explaining how hard being a Christian really is. Jesus understands the difficulty that we will have.

"Difficult" is from the Greek word *thlibo*, which means: "To press (as grapes), press hard upon; a compressed way; narrow straitened, contracted" (New Testament Greek Lexicon, www.bibletstudytools.com). The lexicon adds that the word can be used metaphorically to mean "trouble, afflict, distress." If Jesus wanted to draw people to follow Him, why did He tell soon-to-be disciples that doing so would bring some hesitations and doubt?

To understand what He meant, let us scrutinize a few of the passages where He seemingly discouraged people from following Him.

Luke writes of three encounters Jesus had with would-be Christians as He and His disciples were traveling. One of them made a dramatic statement of commitment, saying to Christ: *"Lord, I will follow You wherever You go"* (Luke 9:57). Jesus didn't reply, "Magnificent! Please join us!" Instead, He said something that, at the least, would have caused the man to have second thoughts and, at the most, would have turned him away completely: *"Foxes have holes and birds of the air have nests, but the Son of Man has nowhere to lay His head"* (verse 58). Jesus was expressing the uncertainty that could accompany the life of a true Christian.

Luke's narrative continues with Jesus turning to another person and telling him, *"Follow Me"* (verse 59). The man begged off, asking to be allowed to first bury his father. Since Jewish custom was to bury the dead as soon as possible, it is unlikely the man was out with the crowd around Christ with a dead father at home. The man was asking to spend whatever remaining time he might have with an aging or perhaps ill father.

Jesus responded to this man's reason to delay following Him by saying, *"Let the dead bury their own dead, but you go and preach the kingdom of God"* (verse 60). Obviously, dead people do not bury anyone. Here, Jesus was referring to those who were spiritually dead; people who had not responded to His teaching. Jesus was telling the potential Christian that his calling was very much more important.

Then a third man, who was committed to becoming a disciple, made a seemingly reasonable request to first return home to say goodbye to whoever was at his house, whether family or guests (verse 61). To this person, Jesus responded: *"No one, having put his hand to the plow, and looking back, is fit for the kingdom of God"* (verse 62). We cannot know with certainty, but this person may not have been as committed as his words make it sound. The Bible records only the personification of the exchange; what we need to know to understand the main point. All three of these responses add clarity to Christ's teaching that **"narrow is the gate."**

In this third example, the added lesson was that Christians must continue to keep their eyes on the goal, which is God's Kingdom. An experienced plowman immediately recognizes the point of this analogy. When plowing, the farmer fixes his eyes on a rock, a hill or some other marker, so that he will plow straight furrows. Although modern farmers with vast fields often use GPS equipment to accomplish this, the principle remains the same.

What is your goal for Success? Position your marker and begin the task!

Thankfully, there are many passages and verses concerning the trials and tribulations (some other words used for the trials and tribulations are "trouble," "affliction," and "oppression"). Here are some scriptures to ponder on…

John 16:33 *"I have said these things to you, that in me you may have peace. In the world you will have tribulation. But take heart; I have overcome the world."*

James 1:2 *"Count it all joy, my brothers, when you meet trials of various kinds,"*

1Peter 1:6 *"In this you rejoice, though now for a little while, if necessary, you have been grieved by various trials"*

Romans 12:12 *"Rejoice in hope, be patient in tribulation, be constant in prayer."*

Now, that we have strengthen our minds and souls with scriptures, let us research these 7 nations/mountains that have become 7 evil spirits concerning our marriages, church, schools, and community.

Promised Land Five
Church Leaders and the 7 types of Evil Spirits

When one studies the 7 types of evil spirits, it slowly becomes evident that 5 of these 7 types are related to the 5 ministries of Ephesians 4:11: *"¹¹ So Christ himself gave the apostles, the prophets, the evangelists, the pastors and teachers,"*

1. When an **apostle** is not submissive to the Spirit, he or she tends to become a **Jebusites** that makes judgments in the flesh instead of making them in the wisdom of the Spirit.

2. When a **prophet** is not submissive to the Spirit, he or she tends to become a prophet moved by **Hittites** spirits of deception and false prophecy.

3. When an **evangelist** "goes bad", he or she becomes an earthly **Amorites** king who dominates over others, instead of conquering strongholds of evil so that **God's** kingdom may be established on Earth.

4. When a **pastor** "goes bad", he or she becomes a **Canaanites** "panderer", indulges somebody's weaknesses, who condones the iniquity of those he or she cares over in a fervent or passionate desire to please them.

5. When a **teacher** "goes bad", he or she becomes a **Girgashites** who perceives the Word of God (and life in general) with his or her natural mind, becoming a "scribe" who understands the Word literally and hates all interpretations that sound too "mystical" or spiritual to his or her liking.

Now, where do our elders and deacons fall in at?

The New Testament does distinguish between the qualification between elders and deacons, although, I think the difference pertains primarily to the areas of giftedness needed for elders to be able to carry out their roles or functions as shepherds. This difference is spelled out in 1 Timothy 3 and Titus 1. Elders are to be skilled to teach, which includes both the **desire** and **ability** to study and teach. Further, Titus shows they should be those who truly know and hold fast to sound doctrine and are able to communicate the Word (Titus 1:9) in varying conditions. Hebrews 5:14, of course, is something all believers should be striving for, but certainly, this should be true in the life of those leading the church. Compare, for instance, Hebrews 13:7 and 17 and 1 Thessalonians 5:12. These verses also suggest elders should be very mature in the Word and in their walk with the Savior. While we should seek this in deacons, as well, it is a necessity for elders due to the nature of the role and function of elders as shepherds.

Concerning deacons, no passage really describes their function. They are those who serve as helpers in a variety of functions according to the need and their gifts (which should always be considered). Acts 6 and serving tables is sometimes used as a model for what deacons should be doing, and though this may give us an illustration of the kind of thing they may do, the ones chosen to take care of the widows in that passage are never officially called deacons. Of those chosen to do that work in acts, one was Philip who is later seen doing the work of an evangelist. Further, being responsible to care for the widows suggests a certain amount of oversight in an administrative capacity, and while, under the leadership of the elders, deacons may be given administrative responsibilities that include some oversight, it is probably best not to think of deacons in such a limited capacity.

Our English word *deacon* comes from the Greek *diakonos* meaning "servant," and specifically, "a table servant." In the New Testament it has a general use in which it refers to all manner of ministries (the vast majority of occurrences), and a practical or offical use. When used in the official sense of someone appointed as a "deacon," the concept of a servant is united with that of an office. The term "deacon" thus refers to an office which involves the basic duty of rendering service to others. A deacon is one who is placed in an official position for a ministry of service to benefit others in the body of Christ. We should also bear in mind that Paul defined his apostolic ministry as a servant (*diakonia*, a word derived from *diakonos*) ministry (1 Timothy 1:12; Acts 20:24; 21:19; 2 Timothy 4:11). Compare the use of *diakonos* in Colossians. 1:7, 25; 4:7; 1 Timothy 4:6.

Concerning elders and their qualifications, two specific functions are mentioned within this list of qualifications, (1) teaching (1 Timothy 3:2), and (2) management or leadership with personal care of the church (1 Timothy 3:4-5). However, no such functions are mentioned in the qualifications of the deacons and this seems to be significant. Why is there no mention of specific functions? What are the implications?

It seems Paul did not associate any fixed duties with the office of deacons. The implication is that deacons served as assistants to the overseers under their leadership and direction. They are supporting, relieving officers. Very often Acts 6:1 is used to define the function of deacons, but it is important to note that Acts 6:1 does not use either of the terms "elder" or "deacon." So we need to be careful about using this passage in such a restricted way to define the work that deacons do.

However, since the ministries of the apostles was in many ways replaced by the ministry of the elders, this passage may provide us with a good illustration of *one* of the ways deacons may relieve and help the overseers in their care of the flock of God. However, since the terms "deacon" is not used in Acts 6, it should not be used to limit the work or ministry deacons may be called on to do by the elders. They may aid in visitation, evangelism, or other spiritual duties according to their gifts and burden.

For instance, remember that Stephen and Philip were two of those chosen to aid in the task of Acts 6, but in the very next chapter we find Stephen engaged in preaching, and in chapter 8 we find Philip involved in evangelism.

Acts 6 also illustrates some other important concepts regarding not only the role of elders, but it also may illustrate something of the relationship of the elders and deacons. It teaches the concepts of: PRIORITY, FUNCTION, OVERSIGHT (or LEADERSHIP), SUPERVISION, DIRECTION, and DELEGATION. In Acts 6 we see:

(1) *The priority of the role and function of prayer and the ministry of the Word (6:4).* To carry out their primary role, elders need the aid of the entire body (Ephesians 4:11), but this includes some who are chosen to operate in an official capacity (like deacons) for special needs that arise.

(2) *The responsibility and role of oversight—planning and goal achievement, leadership and supervision, organization and control, delegation and motivation* (6:5-6). Please note that the Apostles (later to be replaced by elders) are not limited in their responsibilities to matters like teaching. They had oversight or management of all areas. Elders, then, do not do everything else, but they are responsible, are to function as overseers: make suggestions, give guidelines, make appointments, delegate responsibility, encourage, and so forth.

This concept of management of the all matters of the flock is clear not only from the illustration of Acts 6, but also from the words used to describe the office of elder, and from the functions and commands given to this group in the New Testament . With responsibility comes a certain degree of authority to see that the responsibilities are carried out, but not in an authoritative or dictatorial way.

The primary qualifications for deacons would then be godly character as set forth in, 1 Timothy 3:8-12, with a concern for the body and a desire to serve. Possessing the gifts of helps and showing mercy would obviously help one serve as a deacon, but may not be mandatory.

What are some of the implications of this in our lives as individuals and corporately as elders and deacons? Let me add the following suggestions:

(1) Elders and deacons are not two independent offices with each doing its own thing. Both are to be supportive of one another, working together to accomplish God's purposes for the church. The elders are to support the deacons through

encouragement, instruction, leadership, guidance, and proper delegation according to gifts, burden, and interests. The deacons support the elders by relieving them to carry on their primary ministry and by cooperation. Both should give input to one another concerning problems, needs, and ideas for accomplishing the goals of the church.

(2) Communication of ideas, problems, needs, concerns, and the like; along with a commitment to work together is very important to the overall ministry of both offices.

(3) Ultimately, God holds the elders responsible for the ministry of the church and this includes the deacons and the work they are asked to do. Deacons are under the leadership of the elders and the elders are responsible to see that things are done according to the principles of Scripture. If the elders make suggestions or ask for things to be done a certain way, they are not trying to interfere, they are simply doing the job God has called them to do. The elders are not to be dictators. However, deacons have the right and responsibility to evaluate the suggestions of the elders and give input. And the elders need to give serious consideration to their input.

(4) We must all evaluate our ministries, our character, our attitudes, our motives, our agendas, and our involvement in the work of the church. Are we doing all things decently and in order? Are we following through with the responsibilities given to us by God?

To conclude….An Elder and Deacon/ness do not need to take their roles lightly. Based on scripture study, when an elder goes bad he or she is operating under the Girgashites spirit because of their teacher capacity and the Canaanites spirit because of the overseer capacity. When a deacon/deaconess goes bad he or she is operating under the Canaanites spirit because of their servant and nurturing role for the church and the Amorites spirit because of the evangelism role.

Promised Land Six
The Battle is Already Won

Many times we say, "Let God Fight our Battles." This is true. Except, we have a part in this, as well. **WE** have to understand the battle so that we may know why we need to remove ourselves, meaning our flesh, from the enemy paths, so God could use us to fight the battle, with His given power, through praying and fasting.

The apostle John wrote, *"He who sins is of the devil, for the devil has sinned from the beginning. For this purpose the Son of God was manifested, that He might destroy the works of the devil" (1 John 3:8).* Notice John said that God will destroy the *works* of the devil, not the devil himself.

When writing to the Galatians, Paul spoke of the normal, natural acts of humans apart from God, called "works of the flesh": *"Now the works of the flesh are evident, which are adultery, fornication, uncleanness, lewdness [unrestrained lust], idolatry, sorcery, hatred, contentions, jealousies, outbursts of wrath, selfish ambitions, dissensions, heresies, envy, murders, drunkenness, revelries, and the like; of which I also told you in time past, that those who practice such things will not inherit the kingdom of God" (Galatians 5:19-21).* All of these evil actions characterize the works of the devil. Humans who refuse to repent of these works will be destroyed forever.

So, how is Satan destroyed? From all we have seen, both the Greek and Hebrew Scriptures reveal that Satan, as well as his demons, will be spiritually bound and constrained by God in darkness forever. Satan's influence, his deception and his evil works will be eliminated and destroyed forever. However, Satan and his demons will, as spirit beings, continue to exist, although, in a tormented state of mind; a just punishment administered by an all-powerful and righteous God.

To understand this apparent contradiction, we need to consider the contextual meaning of the Hebrew word translated "destroyed." This Hebrew word, *'abad* (Strong's #6), is commonly used in the Hebrew Scriptures and may be translated "to perish, to vanish, to destroy or to put to death" depending on the context and the verb stem in the Hebrew (*The King James Version Old Testament Hebrew Lexicon*).

In the context of this passage, Satan was *"destroyed … from the midst of the fiery stones."* The sense is that God is going to cause Satan to vanish or be removed from His presence. When we compare what is said in Ezekiel 28 with other scriptures pertaining to Satan's fate, it becomes clear that God is going to eventually bind the devil permanently, rendering him useless in terms of continuing to deceive humans.

Many centuries after Ezekiel jotted his prophecy, Paul wrote to the Corinthians about Satan, calling him *"the god of this age"* (2 Corinthians 4:4). This scripture and many others prove that the devil was alive and actively opposing God on earth during the life of Paul and the rest of the apostles. Moreover, Satan remains alive and committed to the destruction of God's Church and its saints today (1 Peter 5:8).

Even though Satan is a spirit being, God is going to "destroy" the influence and power that the devil has had over mankind. Christ's death facilitates this action. As the writer of Hebrews explains, *"Through death He [Christ] might destroy him who had the power of death, that is, the devil"* (Hebrews 2:14).

Again, the word *destroy* in this passage does not mean to destroy in the sense of do away with or make nonexistent. The word translated "destroy" is from the Greek word *katargeo*, meaning "to render idle, unemployed, inactivate, inoperative; to cause a person or thing to have no further efficiency; to deprive of force, influence, power" (*The New American Standard Greek Lexicon*).

Even though Satan will not die, God will render him useless in his efforts to deceive humans by restraining him along with his angels. As Jude confirms, *"And the angels who did not keep their proper domain [the responsibilities God originally assigned to them], but left their own abode, He [God] has reserved in everlasting chains [some spiritual means of restriction] under darkness for the judgment of the great day"* (Jude 1:6).

Promised Land Seven
Casting out Demons

Who me, can cast out the works of the flesh and the demons in
my marriage, family, church, school and community?
Yes......You and Me!!!

CASTING OUT DEMONS

Jesus cast out demons:

In the ministry of Jesus Christ, we often notice that
'healing and deliverance' went hand in hand along with preaching
and teaching. Jesus said to the Woman who had a spirit of
infirmity for eighteen years, *"Woman, you are loosed from your*
infirmity" (Luke 13:11-16) and she was delivered from the
infirmity. Jesus says that woman was a daughter of Abraham.
(vs.16) In other words, she was a believer.

We must understand and know that Jesus never sent any
one to do the work of God without giving them the authority to
cast out demons. *Jesus called His twelve disciples to Him; He*
gave them power over unclean spirits, to cast them out, and to
heal all kinds of sickness and all kinds of disease. (Matthew
10:1) *Jesus said, 'And as you go, preach, saying, The Kingdom*
of heaven is at hand...cast out demons... (Matthew 10:7,8)
Jesus said, 'All authority has been given to Me in heaven and
on earth' (Matthew 28:18)

All the above scriptures tell us clearly that Jesus gave his
disciples "power" over the enemy. Jesus has given us the
authority over "all the power of the enemy", not just some; but
all the power of the enemy. Behold, *'I give you the authority to*
trample on serpents and scorpions, and over all the power of
the enemy and nothing shall be any means hurt you' (Luke 10:
19)
"And these signs will follow those who believe: In My (Jesus)
name they will cast out demons; they will speak with new
tongues; (Mark 16:17) Here we see two manifestations of the
supernatural power which are to confirm the testimony of a

Christian believer. The casting out of demons should take place first; then speaking in tongues, our heavenly language that speaks to God. People shall first be fully delivered from demons before they seek the baptism in the spirit and speaking in new tongues.

If you have been seeking and asking God to run the devil out of your life, your marriage, your church, your school, your community, STOP! The Bible says that you are the one, who is supposed to overcome the enemy.

In order to build the Kingdom of God with the millions, trillions and billions, we, first, must be delivered and set free from the enemy's strongholds.

The Apostles cast out demons:

Peter: A multitude gathered from the surrounding cities to Jerusalem, bringing sick people and those who were tormented by unclean spirits, and they were all healed. (Acts 5:16)

Philip: For unclean spirits, crying out with a loud voice came out of many that were possessed: and many that were paralyzed and lame were healed. (Acts 8:7)

Paul: A certain slave girl possessed with a spirit of divination met Paul. Paul, greatly annoyed, turned and said to the spirit, "I command you in the name of Jesus Christ to come out of her." And he came out the very hour (Acts 16:18). Even handkerchiefs or aprons were brought from Paul's body to the sick, and the diseases left them and the evil spirits went out of them. (Acts 19:11,12)

The above examples clearly show that the apostles 'exercised the authority', which Jesus gave them. They cast out the demons in the 'name of Jesus'. They were not afraid of the devil. On the contrary, the devil was afraid of these Spirit filled men of God.

You too can cast out demons:

Do you cast out demons? If yes, thank God! If no, you have to understand that you too can drive out demons in the "name of Jesus"; if only you would **"believe."** Begin exercising the authority you have been given. You will no longer accept "defeat" in your life, marriage, family, churches, schools, and communities; nor on the job or in your business. **"Rise up"** in faith. **"Stand up"** on the Word of God and fight the enemy, with the name of Jesus, until the enemy has been defeated. **Rise up and receive the deliverance of the Lord.**

Keys for deliverance:

1. Authority in the name of Jesus:

If you have been standing there squeezing and twisting your hands and worrying about what the devil is doing, it is time for you to put the devil under your feet. You have been given the power of attorney, which is the power of "Authority" that enables you to use the powerful name of Jesus; which is *"A name" that is above every name.* (Philippians 2:9, 10) *David says, "I have pursued mine enemies, and overtaken them...they are fallen under my feet."*(Psalm 18, 37, 38) Bind the evil spirits that are trying to destroy your home, your marriage, your finances, your church, your community, your schools, and your nation with the blood of Jesus that still works after thousands of years dying on the cross.

2. Power of the Holy Spirit:

Jesus said He casts out the demons by the power of the Spirit of God... (Matthew 12:28) Jesus said, *'The Spirit of the Lord is upon Me, Because He has anointed Me To preach the gospel to the poor...to set at liberty those who are oppressed"* (Luke 4:18). God anointed Jesus of Nazareth with the Holy Spirit and with power, who went about doing good and healing all who were oppressed by the devil, for God was with Him (Acts 10:38). The '**ability**', which is the gift from God, to cast out the demons comes from the '**power**' of the Holy Spirit.

Therefore, you must be filled with the Holy Spirit in order to cast demons out.

There is no place in Scripture where you are told to pray for the filling of the Holy Spirit. You are filled by faith. However, since the object of your faith is God and His Word, I suggest that you pray to Him claiming the fullness of His Spirit as an expression of your faith in God's *command* and in His *promise*.

An important verse in understanding the filling of the Holy Spirit is John 14:16, *"And I will pray the Father, and he shall give you another Comforter, that he may abide with you for ever;"* where Jesus promised the Spirit would indwell believers and that the indwelling would be permanent. It is important to distinguish the indwelling from the filling of the Spirit. The permanent indwelling of the Spirit is not for a select few believers, but for all believers. There are a number of references in Scripture that support this conclusion. *First*, the Holy Spirit is a gift given to all believers in Jesus without exception, and no conditions are placed upon this gift except faith in Christ (John 7:37-39). *Second*, the Holy Spirit is given at the moment of salvation (Ephesians 1:13). Galatians 3:2 emphasizes this same truth, saying that the sealing and indwelling of the Spirit took place at the time of believing. *Third*, the Holy Spirit indwells believers permanently. The Holy Spirit is given to believers as a down payment, or verification of their future glorification in Christ (2 Corinthians 1:22; Ephesians 4:30).

This is in contrast to the filling of the Spirit referred to in Ephesians 5:18. We should be so completely yielded to the Holy Spirit that He can possess us fully and, in that sense, fill us. Romans 8:9 and Ephesians 1:13-14 states that He dwells within every believer, but He can be grieved (Ephesians 4:30), and His activity within us can be quenched (1 Thessalonians 5:19). When we allow this to happen, we do not experience the fullness of the Spirit's working and His power in and through us. To be filled with the Spirit implies freedom for Him to occupy every part of our lives, guiding and controlling us. Then His power can be exerted through us so that what we do is fruitful to God. The filling of the Spirit does not apply to outward acts alone; it also applies to the innermost thoughts and motives of our actions. Psalm 19:14 says, *"May the words of my mouth and the meditation of my heart be pleasing in your sight, O LORD, my Rock and my Redeemer."*

Sin is what hinders the filling of the Holy Spirit, and **obedience** to God is how the filling of the Spirit is maintained. Ephesians 5:18 commands that we be filled with the Spirit; however, it is not praying for the filling of the Holy Spirit that accomplishes the filling. Only our obedience to God's commands allows the Spirit freedom to work within us. Because we are still infected with sin, it is impossible to be filled with the Spirit all of the time. When we sin, we should immediately confess it to God and renew our commitment to being Spirit-filled and Spirit-led.

3. *The blood of Jesus, Word of our testimony and the Willingness to fight:*

"And they overcame the enemy by the blood of the Lamb, and by the word of their testimony, and they did not love their lives to the death", (Revelation 12:11). We have to plead the blood of the Lamb; Jesus, over every situation. Watch the words that come out of your mouth. You cannot talk defeat and expect victory. You should have the 'bull dog' faith.

Have you ever watched a bulldog with a bone? Once that bulldog has his mouth watering jaws wrapped around that bone, there is no way that anyone is going to get that bone out of his mouth. He has laid hold of that which he so desired to possess. That bone now belongs to him. He has written his signature on that bone with his sharp pointed teeth.

We need to be just like that ole bulldog when it comes to our faith. The bone represents the vision that God has placed deep within our hearts. Since the vision was placed inside of us by the Lord, we know that it is **His will** for the vision to be fulfilled. How will it be fulfilled? How will the vision come to pass? Answer: By faith. Bulldog faith never gives up. It lets the devil know whose boss. Bulldog faith sees by the Spirit, lays hold of what it sees by faith and causes that thing to be manifested in the natural realm. What I am saying is "**NEVER Give up.**"

4. *Faith-filled prayer and fasting:*

When a father brought his son who was an epileptic, to the disciples, they could not cure him. The boy was then brought to Jesus. Jesus rebuked the demon (vs. 18) and the boy was cured the very same hour. (Matthew 17:15-21) When asked the reason, Jesus said, ***'This kind does not go out except by prayer and fasting."*** (Vs. 21) Fasting should become your lifestyle. This passage also shows that the disciples did not have the faith. ***"Jesus says, O faithless and perverse generation"*** (vs. 17).

Okay…...Now, we understand the power within us through the Holy Spirit. Let us receive the Wisdom of God to understand the battle that is being fought…………..……..

***"1 When the LORD thy God shall bring thee into the land whither thou goest to possess it, and hath cast out many nations before thee, the Hittites, and the Girgashites, and the Amorites, and the Canaanites, and the Perizzites, and the Hivites, and the Jebusites, seven nations greater and mightier than thou; 2 And when the LORD thy God shall deliver them before thee; thou shalt smite them, and utterly destroy them; thou shalt make no covenant with them, nor shew mercy unto them"* (Deuteronomy 7:1-2)**

Once we understand the marriage and the commitment we have with God, then we can understand that we can no longer commit adultery (covenant broken against God first, then his/her mate) or idolatry in serving other gods. Just as a marriage is successful without an adulterous act, a marriage without idolatry is successful with God.

*Isaiah 54:5 , **"For your Maker is your husband, the Lord of hosts is his name; and the Holy One of Israel is your Redeemer, the God of the whole earth he is called."***

2 Corinthians 11:2, **"For I feel a divine jealousy for you, since I betrothed you to one husband, to present you as a pure virgin to Christ."**

Revelation 19:7-9 **" Let us rejoice and exult and give him the glory, for the marriage of the Lamb has come, and his Bride has made herself ready; it was granted her to clothe herself with fine linen, bright and pure"— for the fine linen is the righteous deeds of the saints. And the angel said to me, "Write this: Blessed are those who are invited to the marriage supper of the Lamb." And he said to me, "These are the true words of God."**

Promised Land Eight
The Origin of the 7 evil spirits

Genesis 10:15, **_15Canaan became the father of Sidon, his firstborn, and Heth 16and the Jebusite and the Amorite and the Girgashite 17and the Hivite and the Arkite and the Sinite 18and the Arvadite and the Zemarite and the Hamathite; and afterward the families of the Canaanite were spread abroad. 19The territory of the Canaanite extended from Sidon as you go toward Gerar, as far as Gaza; as you go toward Sodom and Gomorrah and Admah and Zeboiim, as far as Lasha. 20These are the sons of Ham, according to their families, according to their languages, by their lands, by their nations. 21Also to Shem, the father of all the children of Eber, and the older brother of Japheth, children were born. 22The sons of Shem were Elam and Asshur and Arpachshad and Lud and Aram. 23The sons of Aram were Uz and Hul and Gether and Mash. 24Arpachshad became the father of Shelah; and Shelah became the father of Eber. 25Two sons were born to Eber; the name of the one was Peleg, for in his days the earth was divided; and his brother's name was Joktan. 26Joktan became the father of Almodad and Sheleph and Hazarmaveth and Jerah 27and Hadoram and Uzal and Diklah 28and Obal and Abimael and Sheba 29and Ophir and Havilah and Jobab; all these were the sons of Joktan. 30Now their settlement extended from Mesha as you go toward Sephar, the hill country of the east. 31These are the sons of Shem, according to their families, according to their languages, by their lands, according to their nations. 32These are the families of the sons of Noah, according to their genealogies, by their nations; and out of these the nations were separated on the earth after the flood."_**

Noah had three sons: They were Shem, forefather of the middle peoples (Semitic Arabian), Ham, forefather of the southern peoples (Hamitic North/North East African), Japheth, forefather of the northern peoples (Japhetic Eurasian).

Six of the evil spirits came originated from Noah's son, Ham:

- Canaan, son of Ham.
- Sidon, firstborn son of Canaan
- Heth, son of Canaan, described in Genesis as the ancestor of the "Biblical Hittites", a people of Canaan.
- "the Jebusite", offspring of Canaan, a tribe that lived around Jerusalem, that was formerly known as *Jebus* according to the Books of Chronicles.(1Chronicles 11:4).
- "the Amorite", offspring of Canaan.
- "the Girgasites", offspring of Canaan.
- "the Hivite", offspring of Canaan.
- "the Arkite", offspring of Canaan.
- "the Sinite", offspring of Canaan.
- "the Arvadite", offspring of Canaan.
- "the Zemarite", offspring of Canaan.
- "the Hamathite", offspring of Canaan.

The Canaanites name already includes the other tribes written in Exodus 3:8, (except the Perizzites) which are namely the Hittites-Heth, the Amorites, the Hivites, and the Jebusites. The territory of the Canaanites included much of the boundaries that would later define the nation of Israel. The Perizzites are of another "kind" or "class". The Perizzites are written in association with the Rephaim-Giants, (ha-Rapha'). In Genesis 9 Ham "fathers" Canaan because Canaan is spiritual-supernal in meaning. Ham sees Noah uncovered and this is when he "fathers" or begets the demon seed of the Canaanites in the iniquity of his heart and mind. In the Genesis 10 genealogy this is evidenced by the fact that Canaan is NOT the first born son of Ham. When the Genesis 9 transgression occurred Canaan had not yet even been born in the flesh. Therefore the name Canaan is employed as the typological framework lay out through the Scripture of the consequences of the transgression which Ham committed against his father Noah.

The sons of Ham are four and Canaan is born Fourth Generation....

Promised Land Nine
Characteristics of the 7 Evil Spirits

The Hittites (The Mountain of Media)....................

Hittites mean broken or terror. So the first one of the emotions we are to "drive out and destroy" is fear.

Hittites, being spirits of terror, are stealth operators. Stealth is a secret, quiet, and clever way of moving or behaving. The Hittites spirits with sneakiness, slyness and craftiness attacks the emotions. Also, they are the spirits behind nightmares and non-rational phobias such as claustrophobia (fear of having no escape and being in closed or small spaces or rooms), agoraphobia, exaggerated fear of dogs, and fear of being in the dark. As anyone who has suffered from a phobia can testify, terror produces a sense of deep emotional despair and torment, and causes a desire not to live anymore. Hittite spirits, therefore, are also behind suicides. Moreover, phobias are panic "attacks.
To add, claustrophobia is typically thought to have two key symptoms: fear of restriction and fear of suffocation. A typical claustrophobic will fear restriction in at least one, if not several, of the following areas: small rooms, locked rooms, cars, airplanes, trains, tunnels, cellars, elevators, and caves.
Additionally, the fear of restriction can cause some claustrophobia to fear trivial matters such as sitting in a haircutter's chair or waiting in line at a grocery store simply out of a fear of confinement to a single space.
Another possible site for claustrophobic attacks is a dentist's chair, particularly during dental surgery; in that scenario, the fear is not of pain, but of being confined.
Agoraphobia is a condition where the sufferer becomes anxious in environments that are unfamiliar or where he or she perceives that they have little control. Triggers for this anxiety may include wide open spaces, crowds (social anxiety), or traveling (even short distances). Agoraphobia is often, but not always, compounded by a fear of social embarrassment, as the agoraphobic fears the onset of a panic attack and appearing

distraught in public. This is also sometimes called 'social agoraphobia' which may be a type of social anxiety disorder also sometimes called "social phobia".

I used to be terrified of dogs; until my understanding has been enlightened. I remember when I was child, my grandparents family dog chased me around the entire family property....this was acres of land. I ran for my life. I was crying and screaming. No one came out to help me. My sister and cousins were laughing. All I can remember is that the dog got tired and stopped chasing me. Every since then, it can be a 1 lb dog and I will run. Until, now after researching these evil spirits, I no longer will or have to fear dogs. I will bind and rebuke the Hittite spirit that has tormented my life for so many years.

Also, I used to be very scary; especially of the dark....In the last years of being delivered from sins and healed from some pain and wounds, I have become less scared of the dark and being alone at night. My daughter is the same way; afraid of the dark. Although, I know the anointing that is on our lives, now I understand why the Hittites spirit torments us so badly.

Hittites spirit we give you your Eviction Notice Today:

Prayer:
In the name of Jesus, on behalf of myself, my family, and the People of our Nation, I divorce the Hittite spirit. I sever and break all soul ties with the Hittite spirit. I cast away the Hittite spirit in the name of the Lord. I renounce the works of the Hittite spirit in the lives of the family, in the marriage, the church, the community, the schools, on the streets, the men of the household, and the church leaders. In the name of Jesus, I pull down every stronghold and every altar the spirit of Hittite has established in our hearts and minds. In the name of Jesus, I bind the Hittite spirit and place it under the feet of Jesus. In the name of Jesus, I bind every demonic spirit connected to / or working with the Hittite spirit and place it under the feet of Jesus. In the name of Jesus, I renew our vows with the One and True Bridegroom, our Lord, Jesus Christ. Amen.

The Girgashites (The Mountain of Government)......

The **Girgashites** means *dense*. Here it means a denseness of thought; a thought that is bound in materialism (preoccupation with or emphasis on <u>material</u> objects, comforts, and considerations, with a disinterest in or rejection of spiritual, intellectual, or cultural values.)

"Girgashites" means, "clay dweller", which refers to "dwelling on **earthliness**". This type of spirit promotes a focus on earthly, **temporal**, secular things; and produces a disdain for things that are "spiritual" and **eternal.** They tend to focus on things that are **visible**. The Greek word translated as "seen" in the passage above is *blepo*, which means, "to discern mentally, to understand, to set the mind's thoughts on a thing, to consider".

Girgashites are very **analytical** (questioning, curious, inquiring) people who base their life's decisions on the pros and cons that their minds are able to perceive. Non-Girgashites believers are not easily distracted by what their minds can see, but, instead, focus on what **God wants** for their lives. <u>Non-Girgashites</u> believers are focused on the things that cannot be seen; the things that cannot be discerned with the natural mind, and, at times, they might make decisions that sound completely illogical and non-sensical to fellow believers and family members who are Girgashites in their hearts:

Girgashites spirit we give you your Eviction Notice Today:

Prayer:

My Heavenly Father, I pray every evil done in muddy and clay places against me and by witches backfire in Jesus' name. I command, every creature that is not of God to come out of the muddy and clay places in Jesus' name. I see myself beyond the family house or shrine or even town or village that was built partly of clay and partly of cement. I heap fire on every figurine (sigidi) molded as my image, break in pieces in Jesus' name. Oh God, my father, destroy the Girgashites spirit in me and my family life... go out by fire, go out by sword, everything hidden in clayey places and in clay things, including pots and jars. I command everyone gathering in clay and muddy places that plan and/or execute evil against me, my family, the church, the community, and the schools be scattered by fire. In the mighty name of Jesus and with the Power of the Holy Spirit, I command every evil work done inside clay bricks and kiln working against me, backfire in Jesus' name and backfire on the doers of the Girgashites spirit; in Jesus' name. Amen

Jeremiah 43:9, ***"Take some large stones in your hands and hide them in the mortar in the brick terrace which is at the entrance of Pharaoh's palace in Tahpanhes, in the sight of some of the Jews;***

The **Amorites (The Mountain of Education)**....................

       The Amorites means *mountaineer*, which indicates the generative function and has to do with lust, people who **want their name uttered** or mentioned. Amorites are **fame-seekers**, seekers of human glory and greatness. The Amorites spirit affects all people. It is a less hostile spirit but subtle and it has the same purpose as all evil spirits; it comes to steal, rob and kill. **It steals a man's purity before God. It robs a man of his inheritance. It kills a man's relationship with the Lord and with his fellow man.** The word "Amorite" means to speak, to speak against and to boast of "self." Every person, at some time in his/her life, been bothered by the speech of another, passing on gossip, saying the wrong thing or just thinking/speaking a careless and thoughtless word. Therefore, the Amorites spirit seduces believers to sin and encourages others to talk negative about them.

Amorites spirit we give you your Eviction Notice Today:

Prayer:
       You Amorites spirit, I bind you and your power from operating against me and causing me to slander or to entice me to babble and rebel and talk about other people, in Jesus' name. You will cease and desist from sowing thoughts of discord and division into my mind. You will not bring condemnation to

paralyze me in Jesus' name. I am free from your slander, from your babbling and talking and rebelling and bitterness and division and sowing discord, in Jesus' Name. Amen.

The Canaanites (The Mountain of Economy)............

The first enemy were the Canaanites and their name means "merchandizing" spirits; addictions, perversions, exaggerated people-pleasing. Canaanites were traffickers who groveled themselves for wealth. Canaanites means 'merchant, or trafficker'. Canaanites is translated, "zealous, a merchant, or trader." The spirits of Canaanites are traffickers in the minds, self-wills, thoughts, senses, imaginations, and affections. The trafficking is carried through buyers and sellers of the market. The spirits enter into the temple of the soul and are control through money and betrayal. (Joshua 7:18-21). 2 Kings 5:20-27

The **Canaanites** is translated as *one who exists for material things*. Canaanites mean, "lowlands people". Since the word "land" is related to the concept of "earth" or "ground", the "lowlands" refer to **low earthly passions**. Canaanites spirits are the legion spirits behind **addictions and sexual perversions.**

Canaanites spirit we give you your Eviction Notice Today:

Prayer:

Abba Father, that sits high and looks low. I thank you for covering me and my family in the Blood of Jesus. I speak to the Canaanites spirit that is trying to reside in my heart, soul, and mind. I dispose every curse of merchandizing, addictions, perversions, and people-pleasing over my life, my spouse, my children, my church, the schools and communities, in Jesus name. I close every door of disobedience, rejection that has allowed self-wills, thoughts, senses, imaginations, and affections that are not of You, to enter. I am claiming deliverance in every area of Satan bound addictions (drugs, alcohol, smoking, homosexuality, sexuality immortality, the works of the flesh and alike) over my life. I am claiming Heavenly passions. I have been set free of the Canaanites spirit and live and operate in the

Holy Spirit through the Blood of Jesus Christ. I accept Christ as my protector and mind regulator. I worship you Lord, God, our Heavenly King and Redeemer, in Jesus name, Amen.

The Perizzites (The Mountain of Religion) ....

The **Perizzites** means *rustic* or *countryman*, the lower levels of consciousness, strongly entrenched in the senses; "belonging to a village". Villages (rural community, town, or parish) have a connotation of "smallness". People who grow up in villages are exposed to very limited opportunities for growth; educational, cultural, and entertainment opportunities are scarce. If not careful, people who grow up in villages can develop a very **limited vision** of life. Dreams are easily spawned in an environment that stimulates people with options and opportunities; since these are limited in a village, villagers are very **likely not to dream of great things**, and the few who do, dream of making it out of the village in order to succeed in the big cities.

Perizzites spirit we give you your Eviction Notice today:

Prayer:
Father in the name of Jesus, I cut off every Perizzites family spirit in my family bloodline. I renounce every ancestral evil spirit, every covenant made between my bloodline and Satanic strongholds in the form of poverty, scarcity, shortage, hardship, neediness, and misery, in Jesus name. I renounce every mermaid spirit, spirit of the tree, the skull, the dead, the river and the forest. Every totem spirit in my life and my family, I renounce you. I revoke the covenant with Satan and I cut off every oath spoken against me. I acknowledge the blood of Jesus Christ in my spirit and I cut off every link, contact, or communication with Satan and his tactics. I command you evil spirits of the devil to come out of my life right now. I cut off your privileges and benefits of the Perizzites spirit; my portion is my covenant with Jesus Christ, in Jesus name. Amen.

The Hivites (The Mountain of Celebration) ….....…...

The **Hivites** are similar to the Perizzites, they are villagers, and they have limited vision and love to "live it up", on material wealth. We must now ask ourselves the following: what does all of the above mentioned have to do with being a "villager"? The answer is simple, if you observe Hivites carefully. Because of all the abundance and grace that surrounds them; they limit the vision of their lives to merely enjoying the wealth and fame built up by their parents (or even themselves). Hivites turn into people with few ambitions in life; all they want to do is to travel around the world and have a "good time". Such people are prone to believe that they have nothing else to do in life but relax and enjoy the wealth they have accumulated during their lives:

Hivites spirit we give you your Eviction Notice Today:

Prayer:

El Olam , The God Of Eternity, I thank you for unlimited opportunities to serve You in Your Kingdom. Through the Blood of Jesus, I cast away every abomination of the eyes. I cast away every idol of abundance and wealth that has me and my family in bondage. I thank you for opening my eyes to the will of Your visions; not Satan vision. I am truly a warrior for Christ and speak God's unlimited vision in my eyesight; which is to build the Kingdom of God with witty and sharp ideas through the Holy Spirit and guidance of the Voice of God; in Jesus name. Amen.

The Jebusites (The Mountain of Family)..........................

The **Jebusites**, which translates as *trodden down* or *polluted,* are to be driven out and destroyed. To add, Jebusites are spirits that tread or "stomp" on other people. People whose hearts are "infected" by Jebusites spirits tend to be people who do not hesitate to **put down** and **humiliate** others. By stomping on people, Jebusites make a concerted effort to prevent them from growing taller. They like to **make people feel small**, and deliberately put them down any time they see these "small" people trying to establish their authority. Jebusites believe that certain people are inherently inferior, without a right to manifest any kind of authority. According to Jebusites, "small" people should just shut up and concede, because they are nobodies who will never amount to much. As some of you might already be thinking, the spirit of racism is a Jebusite spirit. Jebusites are **enforcers of social castes**; witch are social groups of the same characteristics shared by members of a group that include the same interests, values, representations, ethnic or social background.

Jebusites spirit we give you your Eviction Notice Today!!

Prophetic Scripture:

2 Samuel 5:7-8 – "Nevertheless, David took the stronghold of Zion: the same is the city of David. And David said on that day, Whosoever getteth up to the gutter, and smiteth the Jebusites, and the lame and the blind, that are hated of David's soul, he shall be chief and captain..."

The devil has a determination to keep God's people feeling trodden down and on the defense. However, you do not have to be the devil's punching bag. When David came against the stronghold of Zion in the verse above, the Jebusites mocked his effort by saying, ***"even our blind and lame people could defeat you!"*** This same type of "Jebusites spirit" has mocked the warfare of many Christians. The Hebrew meaning of "Jebusites" is trodden down and polluted. This is an area where the Body of Christ must **pull the curtain back on the devil**! Trying to keep us feeling discouraged by repeated or seeming failure; these Jebusites spirits have mocked our purpose. It is time for us to expose them and fight with the Power of Jesus that is on the inside of us! Speak to those evil spirits in your life and command them to stop their works against you, your family, your church, the community and the schools. Decree prophetically, like David, that you will smite them and stand as a chief commander of the Lord's army from this day on! You have been anointed for this time, so step out and escape the spirit of the Jebusites!

Prayer:

I prophecy against every evil Jebusites spirit in the Name of Jesus! I command the works of the Jesusites spirit and their plans to be pull down and I place them under the feet of Jesus. I command the spirit of Jebusites that is part of my destiny and the destiny of the Body of Christ, my marriage, my children, business, church, school, and community to be exposed and stopped; immediately.. I decree and declare that every evil word set against me and my surroundings be silenced right now. Father, I thank You that I have an anointing like David to finish every assignment given to me by the Holy spirit. I am strong and free! In Jesus' Name, AMEN.

When you understand what all of these "people mountains" really represent, it is not so difficult to understand why we are told to destroy their influences, with the power of the name Jesus. These evil spirits are not part of the spiritually enlightened person we are trying to become. WE, as God kingdom people need to not judge one another; but enlightened non-believers of their God's given power through His Son, Jesus Christ. God's kingdom building is about building "people". To the "Believers", we will meet all kinds of people in this world with different characteristics. But, we must have the LOVE of Christ to win them over to the Winning Side, which is God's side. Many Christians find themselves defeated by the most psychological weapon that

Satan uses against them. This weapon has the effectiveness of a deadly missile; low self-esteem and self-will. Satan's greatest psychological weapon is a char level feeling of inferiority, inadequacy, and low self-worth. This feeling shackles many Christians, in spite of wonderful spiritual experiences and knowledge of God's Word. Although, we may understand our position as sons and daughters of God, we are somehow still tied up in knots, bound by a terrible feeling of inferiority, and chained to a deep sense of worthlessness. But, through the knowledge and understanding the 7 mountains, the deep sense of worthlessness will be removed from our spirit-being. We will begin to walk as Conquerors of the Universe destroying and cutting off every people mountains that is set before us.

Promised Land Ten
Breaking the Bondage in the Mind

1. Hittites - spirit of anger and violence
2. Girgashites — spirit of idolatry
3. Amorites - spirit of pride and boasting
4. Caananites - spirit of depression
5. Perizzites - spirit of apathy
6. Hivites - spirit of control
7. Jebusites - spirit of weariness

How can we win the battle of our minds?

1. We are to live our lives from the inside out.

"Do not conform any longer to the pattern of this world, but be transformed by the renewing of your mind." Romans 12:2

2. We are to prepare our minds for action.

"Therefore, prepare your minds for actions; be self-controlled; set your hope fully on the grace to be given you when Jesus Christ is revealed." 1 Peter 1:13

3. We are to take every thought captive in obedience to Christ.

"We demolish arguments and every pretension that sets itself up against the knowledge of God, and we take captive every thought to make it obedient to Christ." 2 Corinthians 10:5

"And if any place will not welcome you or listen to you, shake the dust off your feet when you leave, as a testimony against them." Mark 6:11

"They make their tongues as sharp as a serpent's the poison of vipers is on their lips" Psalms 140:3

"No weapon forged against you will prevail, and you will refute every tongue that accuses you." Isaiah 54:17

"He who rejects you rejects me." Luke 10:16

4. We are to turn to God in prayer

"Do not be anxious about anything, but in everything, by prayer and petition, with thanksgiving, present your requests to God. And the peace of God, which transcends all understanding, will guard your hearts and your minds in Christ Jesus. Finally, brothers, whatever is true, whatever is noble, whatever is right, whatever is pure, whatever is lovely, whatever is admirable - if anything is excellent or praiseworthy - think about such things." Philippians 4:6, 7

Promised Land Eleven
Seven (7) Things that God Abominates

In the following passage, the Lord lists 7 things that He hates:

"¹⁶These six things doth the LORD hate: yea, seven are an abomination unto him: ¹⁷A proud look, a lying tongue, and hands that shed innocent blood, ¹⁸An heart that deviseth wicked imaginations, feet that be swift in running to mischief, ¹⁹A false witness that speaketh lies, and he that soweth discord among brethren." **(Proverbs 6:16-19)**

[In verse 17, the word "look" was translated from the Hebrew word *ayin*, which literally means "eye" or "spring, fountain". The word "lying" was translated from the word *sheqer,* which literally means "deception". Therefore, verse 17 is translated as, *"A proud eye, a tongue of deception, and hands that shed innocent blood"*.

In verse 18, the word "wicked" was translated from the Hebrew word *aven*, which is better translated as "iniquity" or "vanity". The word "imaginations" was translated from the Hebrew word *machashabah*, which literally means "thought, device, plan, and invention". The word "mischief" was translated from the Hebrew word *ra*, which is better translated as "evil" or "affliction". Therefore, verse 18 is translated as, *"A heart that devises plans of iniquity, feet that make haste to run to affliction"*.

In verse 19, the word "false" was translated from the Hebrew word *sheqer*, which literally means "lie, deception". The word "speaketh" was translated from the Hebrew word *puwach*, which literally means "to breathe out, blow". The word "lies" was translated from the Hebrew word *kazab*, which literally means "lie, untruth". The word "soweth" was translated from the Hebrew word *shalach*, which literally means "to send forth, send away"; out of the 847 times that this word appears, the KJV translators chose to translate this word as "soweth" on 3 isolated occasions, and this passage is one of them. The word "discord" was translated from the word *medan*, which literally means "contention", and is derived from the word *diyn* meaning "to judge". Therefore, verse 19 is translated as, "*A witness of deception that breathes out untruth*".

This is a list of the 7 things mentioned above:
1.   A proud eye
2.   A tongue of deception
3.   Hands that shed innocent blood
4.   A heart that devises plans of iniquity
5.   Feet that make haste to run to affliction
6.   A witness of deception that breathes out untruth
7.   He who sends away contention among brothers

A closer look reveals that each of these 7 things corresponds to each of the 7 evil spirits of Deuteronomy 7:1-2 that we have examined:

"1 When the LORD thy God shall bring thee into the land whither thou goest to possess it, and hath cast out many nations before thee, the Hittites, and the Girgashites, and the Amorites, and the Canaanites, and the Perizzites, and the Hivites, and the Jebusites, seven nations greater and mightier than thou; 2 And when the LORD thy God shall deliver them before thee; thou shalt smite them, and utterly destroy them; thou shalt make no covenant with them, nor shew mercy unto them" **(Deuteronomy 7:1-2)**

1.   **A proud eye.**

As we have seen before, the Amorites spirit is the spirit of **pride and self-exaltation**. Therefore, this evil characteristic is related to the Amorites spirit. As we have seen before, the "eye" is spiritually related to the making of **judgments**. Therefore, the Lord is saying that Amorites have a tendency to "look down their nose" at others, belittling and ignoring anyone who looks "small" and "insignificant" to the natural eye. Amorites are so self-aggrandized (boastful) that they are quick to mock little people in a "dismissive" way. They are quick to **judge** them as "irrelevant" and "worthless":

"⁴²And when the Philistine looked about, and saw David, he disdained him: for he was but a youth, and ruddy, and of a fair countenance. ⁴³And the Philistine said unto David, Am I a dog, that thou comest to me with staves? And the Philistine cursed David by his gods. ⁴⁴And the Philistine said to David, Come to me, and I will give thy flesh unto the fowls of the air, and to the beasts of the field." (1 Samuel 17:42-44)

Just as it happened with David and the <u>giant</u> Goliath, the "little" people whom the Amorites disdain are the very people who shall bring them down (<u>Zechariah 4:6-10</u>). God shall bring down the Amorites in the Family, Church, the Schools, the Community, and the World through a weak-looking David remnant that will shake the nations of the Earth unto God.

2. A tongue of deception.

Tongues are used to "communicate" with others. Therefore, they are a figure of "soul communion", which points to the Canaanites spirit. As we have said before, Canaanites are anti-judgmental and they like to fashion golden calves to suit their souls' desires. They like to twist the truth to make it fit around their emotions, which turns them into **"sentimentalist judges"** who immediately reject things that make them "feel bad". Whatever causes pain or destroys "emotional unity" is immediately proclaimed as "wrong" and "unrighteous". Canaanites tongues are willing to sacrifice the truth for the sake of emotional unity. This is why they are "tongues of deception". As we have said before, Canaanites make a covenant with Hittites spirit of deceit from Sheol in order to adulterously possess people (Isaiah 28:14-19). They are tongues of deception that promote soul communion without a covenant foundation of righteousness.

While the Old Testament writings describe Sheol as the place of the dead, in the Second Temple period (roughly 500

BC–70 AD) a more diverse set of ideas developed. In some texts, Sheol is considered to be the home of both the righteous and the wicked, separated into respective compartments; in others, it was considered a place of punishment, meant for the wicked dead alone. When the Hebrew scriptures were translated into Greek in ancient Alexandria around 200 BC, the word "Hades" (the Greek underworld) was substituted for Sheol, and this is reflected in the New Testament where Hades is both the underworld of the dead and the personification of the evil it represents

Nehemiah 9:16–21, *"But they, our ancestors, became arrogant and stiff-necked, and they did not obey your commands. They refused to listen and failed to remember the miracles you performed among them. They became stiff-necked and in their rebellion appointed a leader in order to return to their slavery. But you are a forgiving God, gracious and compassionate, slow to anger and abounding in love. Therefore you did not desert them, even when they cast for themselves an image of a calf and said, 'This is your god, who brought you up out of Egypt,' or when they committed awful blasphemies. "Because of your great compassion you did not abandon them in the wilderness. By day the pillar of cloud did not fail to guide them on their path, nor the pillar of fire by night to shine on the way they were to take. You gave your good Spirit to instruct them. You did not withhold your manna from their mouths, and you gave them water for their thirst. For forty years you sustained them in the wilderness; they lacked nothing, their clothes did not wear out nor did their feet become swollen."*

3.   Hands that shed innocent blood.

As we have said before, Jebusites are murderers who don't think twice about shedding innocent blood in order to enforce the laws of their Amorites masters. Jebusites are judges who do not value the people whom they judge. They do not realize that the purpose of judgments is to manifest the inherent value and potential in others. Therefore, hands that shed innocent blood are Jebusites' hands.

Deuteronomy 19:10, *"So innocent blood will not be shed in the midst of your land which the LORD your God gives you as an inheritance, and bloodguiltiness be on you."*

4.   A heart that devises plans of iniquity

This speaks of a "scheming" heart. Of all the evil spirits, the one that prompts people to come up with "evil schemes" to get things from others is the Hivites spirit. The Hivites came up with a clever scheme to prevent the Israelites from destroying them in the desert (Joshua 9:1-23). In Genesis 34, Hamor the Hivite and his son Shechem tried to lure the Israelites into a deal where Shechem would get what he wanted (Dinah, the daughter of Jacob). In that case, however, the "scheme" blew up in their faces.

Workers of iniquity and wickedness, try to obtain blessings while bypassing God's righteousness and judgments. Hivites, therefore, are "get-rich-quick" schemers who try to get all the blessings they can from others without the necessary sacrifice. Hivites believe in the right to indulge in "inherited grace". Therefore, they see everyone around them in terms of what they can get out of them, and they will be constantly scheming to get what they want from others as "easily" as possible.

Psalms 21:11, *"Though they intended evil against You And devised a plot, They will not succeed."*

5.   Feet that make haste to run to affliction.

Girgashites **afflict** themselves and others under oppressive methods that are based on human effort. As they run through life without considering God's invisible purposes and will, they turn into pigs that run hastily down an incline to drown themselves in the sea (Matthew 8:28-34), and they do what they can to drag others along with them into the sea. Therefore, the feet that "haste to run to affliction" are Girgashites' feet.

Isaiah 52:12, *"For you shall not go out in haste, and you shall not go in flight, for the LORD will go before you, and the God of Israel will be your rear guard."*

6.   A witness of deception that breathes out untruth.

The ministry most related with being a "witness" is the prophetic ministry, and the prophetic anointing makes us sensitive to the blow of the **"wind** of the Spirit" (John 3:8). As we have also said before, prophets turn into Hittites when they go astray, and Hittites spirits are spirits of deception. Therefore, the "witness of deception that breathes out untruth" is a Hittites witness. Hittites witnesses create deceiving "jet streams" that sway people towards purposelessness.

Galatians 6:7-8, *"Do not be deceived: God is not mocked, for whatever one sows, that will he also reap. For the one who sows to his own flesh will from the flesh reap corruption, but the one who sows to the Spirit will from the Spirit reap eternal life."*

7.   He who sends away contention among brothers.

The word *shalach* here means "to send away". Therefore, Proverbs 6:19 is speaking about people who **"throw out"** contention among brothers, people who are quick to dismiss anything that may create a **debate** among brethren.

Debates are caused by differences that are often understated in nature. This means that debates are fostered in an atmosphere where people see the importance of clever differences and where people believe in their authority to make judgments. Therefore, those who "throw out" contentions among brothers are people with a simplistic spirit who are not too interested in finding the deep wisdom of God. The Perizzites spirit is a simplistic spirit that dismisses the importance of understated details.

Also, the Perizzites spirit cripples people into thinking they are too "insignificant" to make judgments. In a Perizzite atmosphere, any "small" person who dares to make a subtle distinction or judgment is immediately seen as "audacious" and "arrogant". As a result, Perizzites disable contention that leads to a deeper understanding of the truth, which in turn leads to a stagnant and limited environment of spiritual (and literal) poverty.

A summarized list of the 7 things which God abominates and the evil spirit they are each related to:

Things the Lord abominates	Evil Spirit	Sin
A proud eye	Amorite	Proud disdain of others
A tongue of deception	Canaanite	Soul communion that distorts the truth
Hands that shed innocent blood	Jebusite	Legalistic imposition without valuing others
A heart that devises plans of iniquity	Hivite	Scheming to extract "blessings" from others
Feet that haste to run to affliction	Girgashite	Living without considering God's invisible purposes
A witness of deception that breathes out untruth	Hittite	Allowing yourself to be a channel of deceptive currents
He who sends away contention among brothers	Perizzite	Oversimplified judgments

Promised Land Twelve
Female and Male Ministries

Before we go any further, (as in one church I attended would say), let us do some "house-cleaning." Next I will discuss the 7 evils spirits as the 7 mountains on this earth. Before, I do this, I need to talk about male and female ministries so that you may clearly understand how these 7 mountains are operating here on this earth.

Samuel's five siblings

"And the LORD visited Hannah, so that she conceived, and bare three sons and two daughters. And the child Samuel grew before the LORD" (1 Samuel 2:21)

The scripture says that the Lord visited Hannah after she gave Samuel over to the Lord at the temple, and that she conceived and gave birth to 3 sons and 2 daughters. It is interesting to note that the Bible never mentions these 5 siblings of Samuel ever again. Why, then, would the Holy Spirit inspire the writer of 1 Samuel to record this in Scripture? They are there as a figure of the fivefold ministry in Ephesians 4:11:

"And he gave some, apostles; and some, prophets; and some, evangelists; and some, pastors and teachers" (Ephesians 4:11)

Samuel's 5 siblings are a prophetic figure of the restoration of all 5 ministries in the latter days, since Samuel himself is a prophetic figure of the remnant Church that the Lord will raise up in these latter days to manifest the latter-rain glory. Why are there 3 **male** siblings and 2 **female** siblings? Which of the 5 ministries have a "male" functionality and which have a "female" functionality?

"Male" and "female" functionality

Let us ask ourselves the following question, "In a traditional couple, what is the role of the man and the woman?" The man's traditional role is generally to go out and work and attain provisions for the family, while the woman's traditional role is generally to stay home and to administer and nurture that which the man has gone out to attain. The man's role in a figurative sense, of course, is a role of "outward projection" and of "bringing home things", while the traditional woman's role would be one of "staying home" and of "nurturing and administering".

Please do not misunderstand or misread me when I speak of a woman's role in this sense. There is prophetic Word in the Scriptures that shows that God will restore the ministry of women in these days; and that He will elevate mighty female apostles, prophets, evangelists, pastors, and teachers. Galatians 3:28, *"There is neither Jew nor Gentile, neither slave nor free, nor is there male and female, for you are all one in Christ Jesus."*, clearly declares that, in Christ, "Anointed One", there is neither male nor female. In other words, when a person moves in the Anointing, he or she moves in the authority of the Spirit, and there is no difference between male and female.

Allow me to refer to the *typical functionality, purpose, or task* of the male and female, by nature, is most adapted to in the natural realm, as God designed it. Fathers tend to be good providers for their children, but tend to be bad "nurturers", whereas mothers tend to be great "nurturers" and **administrators** of the resources that men bring home. When we use the terms "male" and "female", therefore, we are not speaking of literal men and women. We are speaking about functionality. A literal "female" believer can be called by the Lord to perform a "male" ministry, and a literal "male" believer can be called by the Lord to perform a "female" ministry.

If the "male functionality" is one of "outward projection", which 3 of the 5 ministries are "projected out"? And, if the "female functionality" is one of "staying home to nurture", which 2 of the 5 ministries are called to "stay home to nurture"? To answer this, we have to analyze each ministry briefly.

The role of an apostle

To understand the role of the apostolic anointing in every believer, we have to look at the following passages of Scripture:

"For we stretch not ourselves beyond our measure, as though we reached not unto you: for we are come as far as to you also in preaching the gospel of Christ: Not boasting of things without our measure, that is, of other men's labours; but having hope, when your faith is increased, that we shall be enlarged by you according to our rule abundantly, To preach the gospel in the regions beyond you, and not to boast in another man's line of things made ready to our hand."
(2 Corinthians 10:14-16)

"Yea, so have I strived to preach the gospel, not where Christ was named, lest I should build upon another man's foundation: But as it is written, To whom he was not spoken of, they shall see: and they that have not heard shall understand."
(Romans 15:20-21)

In these passages, the Holy Spirit is revealing the Apostle Paul's natural tendency to go to new territories. Apostles, by nature, are **"trail blazers"** who have an innate desire to "break new ground", to go into spheres of spiritual influence where others have not gone before.

Apostolic ministries such as Paul's tend to be gifted with a **special wisdom** from the Lord that gives apostles a special revelation anointing in various spiritual arenas. Galatians 1:11-17 shows how the Lord gave Paul a special revelation over the Gospel of grace that he was called to preach to the Gentiles. Considering that the Greek word *apostolos* means "one sent", apostles are messengers sent by God with a special message, and it generally is a message that has not been heard before.

Apostles are many times sent into hostile territories, as Paul usually was, to announce revelation that defies the mental paradigms or standards that are accepted in those places. It is no wonder that the Lord said in Luke 11:49 that prophets and apostles are murdered and persecuted. As 1 Corinthians 4:9-13 shows, apostles are called by God to **pay a price so that they can pave the way for others**. They are called to suffer and travail so that others coming after them can receive the benefits of the path that God has opened through them. In that sense, John the Baptist was an apostle, since he was *sent* (Malachi 4:5, Matthew 17:10-13) to prepare the way for the Lord (Luke 3:4).

Apostles **generally do not win over a great number of converts**. When the apostles Paul and Silas went to Philippi and were whipped, beaten and jailed; God used their suffering to break the spiritual stronghold of Satan in that region, but Acts 16 only records the conversion of the jail keeper and his family, and of Lydia and her family. The church of Philippi, however, was born there, and the Lord made it to grow and prosper after Paul and Silas' departure.

David Livingston is another example of an apostle who broke new spiritual ground in Africa, even though he did not win over a great deal of converts, but brothers such as Reinhardt Bonke are now reaping the harvest that was sown through the life of David Livingston. As the following passage shows, some are called to sow while others are called to harvest:

"And herein is that saying true, One soweth, and another reapeth. I sent you to reap that whereon ye bestowed no labour: other men laboured, and ye are entered into their labours."
(John 4:37-38)

Apostles are generally given **special revelation over specific spiritual areas**. Jesse Duplantis, for example, is called the "apostle of joy", because God has given him special revelation that others do not have over the joy of our relationship with the Lord. Kathryn Kuhlman is an example of an "apostle of the Holy Spirit", because the Lord gave her special revelation over our relationship with the Holy Spirit. Kenneth Copeland is an apostle to whom the Lord has given special revelation over our divine nature and God's calling for us to be One with Him, just as the Lord Jesus and the Father are One (*ehad* in Hebrew).

When the Lord anoints an apostle with a special wisdom revelation, he calls him or her to go out into hostile territory to defy human wisdom so that others may share in that revelation. This usually implies a great deal of suffering, since most religious minds will generally reject and attack apostolic wisdom, just as the Pharisees and Sadducees so often did during the Lord's ministry on Earth. All of this, therefore, shows how the apostolic ministry is an "outward projection" ministry, qualifying it as a "male" ministry. This, then, is Samuel's first male sibling.

God does not place apostles into the Body of Christ so that they will be worshipped and revered as an idol by awe-struck believers, but rather as fellow co-laborers who will impart the apostolic anointing that has been given to them upon their fellow brothers and sisters, empowering them to move in the same anointing (Matthew 10:8). **Every** believer in the Body (not just an "apostle") is called to move in an apostolic anointing that opens up a channel of wisdom revelation into his or her mind and that births in him or her a deep desire to suffer and to pay a price so that others may enter into new revelation and knowledge of God (Ephesians 1:15-22).

The role of a prophet

To understand the role of the prophetic anointing in every believer, we have to look at the following passages of Scripture:

"Can two walk together, except they be agreed?" (Amos 3:3)

"Surely the Lord GOD will do nothing, but he revealeth his secret unto his servants the prophets." (Amos 3:7)

Verse 7 of Amos 3 is a very well known passage, but most believers do not notice what the Lord says 4 verses earlier in verse 3. What is the relationship between these two verses and why are they so close together? The clue to understanding this is in the following scripture:

"The heaven, even the heavens, are the LORD'S: but the earth hath he given to the children of men" (Psalms 115:16)

This scripture means that God's sovereign "**will**" is done in Heaven, but that what happens on Earth is conditioned on what men are willing to allow to happen. God has given this mighty privilege and responsibility to the sons of men. There are so many wonderful and mighty things that God wants to do on Earth, but He must wait for one of us or a group of church leaders to lift up his/her eyes and see His vision for the Earth. When one of us does this and believes the vision, coming to agreement with it, Amos 3:3 is fulfilled, and two begin to walk together: God and the prophet who sees and believes the vision. That is the reason why God does not do anything without first revealing it to His servants the prophets.

When one of us comes in agreement with His vision and begins to declare it prophetically on Earth, the vision begins to manifest itself. That is why the Lord told Ezekiel to prophesy over the dry bones in Ezekiel 37 (verse 4 and 9). Why would God need Ezekiel, a *"son of man"* as He calls him in verse 3, to prophesy over the bones when He could have done it Himself? Because He has given the authority over what happens on Earth over to the sons of men, as Psalms 115:16 declares. This is why the emphasis in the Lord's prayer is not over asking for our personal needs but for *God's will to be done on Earth, as it is done in Heaven* (Matthew 6:10). **God wants sons and daughters whose whole ambition and whose whole desire in life is to see the fulfillment of the Father's will on Earth. God's eyes are searching out for men and women who are willing to lift up their prophetic eyes and see God's vision for these latter days, so that they may come in agreement with Him and declare the vision** prophetically so that the vision will be manifested on Earth.

We can see, therefore, that the prophet's main duty is to see God's vision for the Earth. This is why 1 Samuel 9:9 declares that prophets used to be called *"seers"* in Israel. If a person wants to know if it will rain later in the day, he must go outside his house and see if rain clouds are coming. You cannot see the vision of what the Lord wants to bring about by staying "home".

This shows, therefore, that the prophetic ministry is an "outward projection" ministry. It goes out of the house, so to speak, to see the vision, and comes back inside to declare it. While the apostle anointing brings to the Church a provision of wisdom and revelation, the prophet's provision for the Church is **vision**. The apostle shows God's children *who they are* in Christ. The prophet tells them *where they are going*.

In conclusion, the apostolic ministry is Samuel's first male sibling, and the prophetic ministry is the second male sibling. Both ministries tend to work together and are ministries very much related to suffering and sacrifice, as the next passages show:

"Now therefore ye are no more strangers and foreigners, but fellowcitizens with the saints, and of the household of God; And are built upon the foundation of the apostles and prophets, Jesus Christ himself being the chief corner stone" (Ephesians 2:19-20)

"Therefore also said the wisdom of God, I will send them prophets and apostles, and some of them they shall slay and persecute" (Luke 11:49)

"After these things the Lord appointed other seventy also, and sent them two and two before his face into every city and place, whither he himself would come" (Luke 10:1)

The role of an evangelist

To understand the role of the evangelist, we have to look at 1 Samuel 17 more closely. When David went to fight Goliath, verse 40 declares that David chose 5 smooth stones out of the brook. These 5 stones represent the fivefold ministry of Ephesians 4:11. In verse 49, however, the Word declares that David used only one of those five stones to defeat Goliath. If each of the 5 stones represents a ministry, which ministry did the stone that David threw represent? To answer this, we have to look at what David spoke to Goliath before hurling the stone at him:

"This day will the LORD deliver thee into mine hand; and I will smite thee, and take thine head from thee; and I will give the carcases of the host of the Philistines this day unto the fowls of the air, and to the wild beasts of the earth; that all the earth may know that there is a God in Israel. And all this assembly shall know that the LORD saveth not with sword and spear: for the battle is the LORD'S, and he will give you into our hands." (1 Samuel 17:46-47)

Here, David does two things:

1. He **prophesies** to Goliath that he will smite him and cut off his head
2. He declares that it will be *known* that there is a God in Israel and that God does not save with sword and spear; this is a **declaration of wisdom**, since wisdom reveals spiritual principles and increases one's knowledge of the inner workings and nature of ourselves and of things around us. As we mentioned before, wisdom is the gift most related to the apostolic ministry, so we can conclude that David gave Goliath apostolic word here.

This means, therefore, that David "threw" *prophetic word* and *apostolic word* at Goliath before attacking him with a literal stone. Since the literal stone was **projected** towards Goliath, it cannot represent one of the two "maternal" or "female" ministries, leaving the three "paternal" or "male" ministries as the only options. However, since David threw the prophetic stone and the apostolic stone, not literally, but figuratively, in verses 46 and 47, we can only conclude that the stone that David threw represents the third "male" ministry.

Ephesians 2:20 declares that apostles and prophets lay the foundation. Their work, in many senses is invisible, and is done through intercession, suffering, isolation, and rejection. This is why the stones that represented these two ministries were not thrown literally but figuratively. Through the work of the **apostles** and the **prophets**, however, the foundation is laid for the **evangelistic ministry** to come and bring down Goliaths and all spirits of self-exaltation in the heavens. Evangelists are therefore "giant-killers" that destroy spiritual strongholds so that people can be converted to God's truths in great numbers. In Luke 10, the Lord sends 70 disciples in pairs to every city and town that He Himself would later go into. These pairs represent the apostolic and the prophetic ministries laying the foundation for the manifestation of the Lord through the evangelistic ministry. In Luke 10:18-20, the Lord declares that He saw Satan falling like lightning from the heavens, representing the fall of the spiritual Goliaths that try to establish their names in high places.

In chapters 1 and 2 of the book of Acts, we see the same principle at work. The disciples gathered to pray in the Upper Room, and, by doing so, they were living out the following prophetic word in Joel:

"Therefore also now, saith the LORD, turn ye even to me with all your heart, and with fasting, and with weeping, and with mourning: And rend your heart, and not your garments, and turn unto the LORD your God: for he is gracious and merciful, slow to anger, and of great kindness, and repenteth him of the evil. Who knoweth if he will return and repent, and leave a blessing behind him; even a meat offering and a drink offering unto the LORD your God? Blow the trumpet in Zion, sanctify a fast, call a solemn assembly: Gather the people, sanctify the congregation, assemble the elders, gather the children, and those that suck the breasts: let the bridegroom go forth of his chamber, and the bride out of her closet. Let the priests, the ministers of the LORD, weep between the porch and the altar, and let them say, Spare thy people, O LORD, and give not thine heritage to reproach, that the heathen should rule over them: wherefore should they say among the people, Where is their God?" (Joel 2:12-17)

Through this intercession, the Word that comes 11 verses later was fulfilled:

"And it shall come to pass afterward, that I will pour out my spirit upon all flesh; and your sons and your daughters shall prophesy, your old men shall dream dreams, your young men shall see visions: And also upon the servants and upon the handmaids in those days will I pour out my spirit. And I will shew wonders in the heavens and in the earth, blood, and fire, and pillars of smoke" (Joel 2:28-30)

We can see from this that the Upper-Room 10-day intercession of Acts 1 was done with a strong prophetic anointing. There is also a strong apostolic anointing in this intercession because the Lord **sent** the disciples to pray (Acts 1:4-8), and, as we mentioned earlier, the word "apostle" comes from the Greek word *apostolos*, which means "one sent". It was also during these 10 days of intercession that the apostles found a replacement for Judas, which is a figure of the restoration of the *true* apostolic ministry in the latter days, one not based on human prestige and a message of earthly prosperity but rather on the grace of God because of a spirit of integrity and righteousness (Acts 1:15-26).

After their 10 days of intercession, the Spirit burst upon them and they were baptized with the Holy Spirit. Peter then began to preach to the people of Jerusalem who witnessed the event and 3,000 souls were added to the Body of Christ in one day (Acts 2:14-41). There is a spiritual reason why Peter was the one appointed by the Holy Spirit to speak that day, and it is because he had a calling as an *evangelist*; when he was called by the Lord, the Lord told Peter that he would be a "fisher of men" (Luke 5:10). We can see therefore, how, after an imbuing of apostolic and prophetic anointing during 10 days of "invisible" prayer, an evangelist was the one sent forth by the Holy Spirit to win a great number of souls for the Lord. As we read the words that Peter spoke that day (Acts 2:14-40), we can see a strong prophetic and apostolic anointing upon him; he refers to the prophetic word in Joel and in Isaiah, and reveals the spiritual meaning of passages in Psalms 16, 89, and 110, thereby showing an anointing of apostolic wisdom upon his life. This is the reason why most modern-day evangelists do not manifest the power and the anointing of the Spirit and why so few are converted to the Lord: there is no apostolic and prophetic anointing upon their lives. An evangelist instilled with apostolic and prophetic anointing is a giant-killer, a mighty man or woman of God that can tear down principalities and powers in the air and build the kingdom of God on Earth. *"The days will come", says the Lord, "when I will raise up a mighty Church of evangelists, mighty men and women with heavy apostolic and prophetic anointing on their lives. They will be My Sons and My daughters, and they shall manifest My Glory on Earth".*

Summarizing, we can say that the evangelistic ministry is an "outward projection" ministry that goes out to bring down spiritual giants in order to turn large numbers of hearts unto the Lord. It is when evangelists behead or decapitate giants, when total victory over the enemy can be achieved and spoils can be taken (1 Sam 17:51-53).

Therefore, the three "male" ministries are: apostles, prophets, and evangelists.

The role of pastors and teachers

There is a reason why we study the roles of pastors and teachers together rather than separately, as we have done for the other ministries. If one looks closely at Ephesians 4:11, we can note an interesting detail:

"And he gave some, apostles; and some, prophets; and some, evangelists; and some, pastors and teachers" (Ephesians 4:11)

Notice how the first three ministries are listed separately "some, apostles", "some, prophets", and "some, evangelists", whereas the remaining two are mentioned together "some, pastors and teachers". The reason for this is, first of all, as a delicate way of confirming that the first 3 ministries are "male" ministries of outward projection while the other 2 tend to stay "home", which is inside the house of God and work together to nurture and grow up what the other ministries have brought "home". A second and similar reason is the fact that the 5 ministries mentioned in this verse correspond to the 4 faces of the living creatures mentioned in Ezekiel 1 and Revelation 4. Since there are 5 ministries and only 4 faces, two ministries have to correspond to a single face.

To understand the combined role of both of these "female" ministries, we have to look first at the three components of our souls. The first commandment, according to the Lord, is the following:

"Jesus said unto him, Thou shalt love the Lord thy God with all thy heart, and with all thy soul, and with all thy mind."
(Matthew 22:37)

This passage and other passages in the Scripture show that our soul is comprised of three parts:

The heart: According to Ephesians 6:6, the heart is where our **"will"** resides. This is the part of the soul that makes decisions.

The emotions: This is the most predominant part of the soul, and this is the reason why it is simply referred to as the "soul" in Matthew 22:37. This is similar to the situation with "New York City" and "New York State". When people say "New York", they can be referring to the state or to the most famous part of the state, which is New York City. In the same way, when the Bible refers to the "soul", it at times refers to the entire soul ("New York state"), and at times it refers to the most predominant part of the soul, the emotions ("New York City").

Contrary to popular belief, the heart is not the same as "emotions", even though they are very closely related. The heart is the impartial decision-maker in our souls, and it many times uses the emotions as "sensors" to detect information that the logical mind cannot pick up. When women talk about using their "woman's intuition", they are talking about making decisions based on what their emotions "hear". Here, the heart is working in conjunction with the emotions. Based on the Scriptures, we can say that the heart must learn to "hear" with the emotions and to "see" with the mind. A heart that only "hears" its emotions and ignores the mind is easily deceived, and a heart that only "sees" with the mind and ignores "hearing" becomes materialistic and faithless.

The mind: This is the center of our thoughts and logic. Judgments are made through the moral laws and principles that are stored in our mind.

Whereas the male ministries are designed to feed the authority of the spirit, the female ministries are designed to nourish the soul. Teachers are designed by God to "feed" the mind by teaching the wisdom revelation received through the apostolic anointing in the Church. This means that the male ministry of "apostle" brings to the Church wisdom revelation and the female ministry of "teacher" cultivates and reinforces this wisdom in the minds of fellow believers.

While teachers are designed for the mind, pastors are designed to nourish and strengthen the remaining parts of the soul, the heart and the emotions. Since the Greek word for pastor used in the New Testament literally means "shepherd", we can say that pastors are placed by God into the Body of Christ to ensure that the hearts of fellow believers are always "steered" towards God's will and that the emotions of fellow believers do not "stray" from God's vision and purpose.

The male ministry of "evangelist" brings to the Church converted hearts, and the female ministry of "pastor" nourishes and strengthens these converted hearts, making sure that they are always focused on God's will. Likewise, the male ministry, of "prophet", brings to the Church the vision and purpose of God, causing believers to "fall in love" with the Lord's vision. Of the 3 male ministries, the Scripture shows the **"prophet" to be the most "emotional" of the three**. The prophetic ministry is designed to channel the power of our emotions towards the vision of God. The female ministry of "pastor" then comes along to nourish and strengthen the emotions of fellow believers to make sure that they stay channeled towards the vision and purpose revealed through the prophetic anointing.

The teaching ministry alone is not designed to produce spiritual revelation, because revelation comes through the apostolic anointing, because of the Bible that holds mighty secrets and spiritual principles. Likewise, the pastoral ministry is not designed to receive prophetic vision or to tear down spiritual giants. This is why there are so many **weak** churches wandering in the desert without vision, because they are led by pastors that have kicked the prophetic anointing out of their congregations in order to pursue a human vision that does not come from God, lording themselves over God's heritage (1 Peter 5:3).

Promised Land Thirteen
The Triangle of Evil

Now, that we have a little background of the 7 evil spirits: Amorites, Hittites, Jebusites, Canaanites, Hivites, Perizzites and Girgashites. How does these mountains spirits effect the people, society, civilization, culture, social order, humanity, the population, citizens of the world, groups, unions, federations, organizations, institutes, the lower, middle, and upper class, and many other identities on this earth.

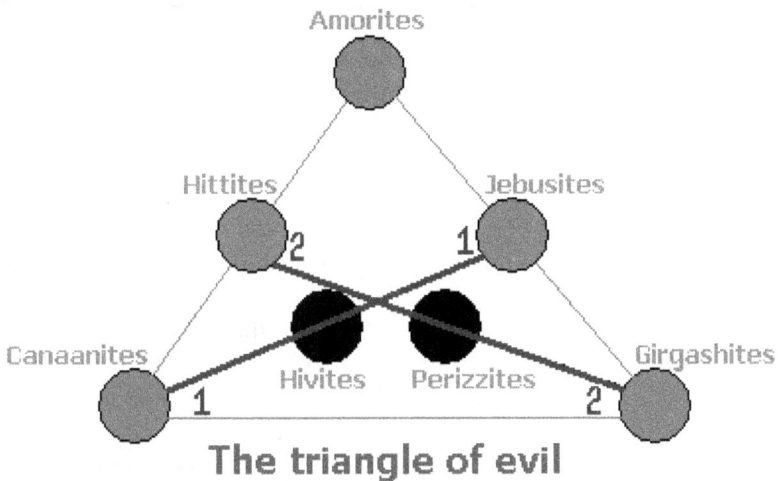

The triangle of evil

"16 There are six things the LORD hates, seven that are detestable to him: 17 haughty eyes, a lying tongue, hands that shed innocent blood,18 a heart that devises wicked schemes, feet that are quick to rush into evil, 19 a false witness who pours out lies and a man who stirs up dissension among brothers." Proverbs 6:16-19

Notice that the first evil spirit that appears in Proverbs 6:16-19 is the Amorites spirit, which is the spirit at the "height" of the triangle. After that, two "groups of 3" are formed:

Triplet #1: The **Canaanites**, the Jebusites, and the Hivites.

Triplet #2: The **Girgashites**, the Hittites, and the Perizzites

Triplet #	Evil spirit at the BASE of the triangle	Evil spirit in the MIDDLE TIER of the triangle	Evil spirit INSIDE the triangle
1	Canaanites	Jebusites	Hivites
2	Girgashites	Hittites	Perizzites

Notice that these 2 triplets start with a spirit at the foundation of the triangle (the Canaanites in triplet #1 and the Girgashites in triplet #2); they then cut across the triangle to the opposite side (the Jebusites in triplet #1 and the Hittites in triplet #2), and they end with a "village" spirit (the Hivites in triplet #1 and the Perizzites in triplet #2). In each case, the "village" spirit is right in the middle of the other two spirits in the triplet. What does all of this mean?

The fact that the first evil spirit is the **Amorites** spirit means that Proverbs 6:16-19 is speaking about men, as well as, women who are trying to establish their own earthly kingdom, in an effort to take over God's legitimate Kingship. The fact that triplet #1 starts with the **Canaanites** spirit points to the pastoral ministry, since Canaanites are "pastors gone bad". Therefore, Proverbs 6:16-19 is speaking of Amorites who try to establish earthly kingdoms ruled by the pastoral matriarchy.

Since the Canaanites spirit is "left-handed", it becomes necessary to introduce a "right-handed" spirit to enforce the rule of the Amorite. This is where the **Jebusites** spirit comes in. Under the influence of the Canaanites, Jebusites come in to place emotional; and distressing and heartrending pressure on people so that they will abide by the Amorite's decrees. Jebusites create a sense of guilt and shameful accusation around the idea of questioning the Amorite's pastoral ways. Since Jebusites lack a solid Scriptural foundation of Godly judgments that can back the Amorite's decrees, they are forced to "create" human laws of their own, disguising them as "laws from God above".

Through Jebusites pressure and shaming, the Canaanites spirit consolidates itself in the Amorite's kingdom, and the way is paved for the **Hivites** spirit to come in. Canaanites slowly wear away any interest in God's righteous judgments (Amos 5:7-10), which leads to Hivites schemers who are constantly trying to indulge in grace that they "inherit" from others through clever covenants. Once the Canaanites, the Jebusites, and the Hivites spirits settle in, the spirit of Jezebel becomes deep-rooted in the Amorite's kingdom (1 Kings 21:1-16).

As you read earlier, the Hivites spirit is a "village" spirit that limits people's vision to the self-indulgent search for "grace" and pleasure. Therefore, triplet #1 cunningly and deviously traps believers in a world where the main focus is on **false** grace.

Once believers are trapped in the Hivites village, Amorites launch triplet #2, which begins with **Girgashites** teachers. These teachers indoctrinate believers with human methods and regulations that provide a "solid structure of support and stability" for the Amorite's kingdom. Since Girgashites are anti-prophetic, their teachings slowly drain away all the prophetic anointing, which leads to an atmosphere of **Hittites** purposelessness and emptiness where God's prophetic fullness and sense of prophetic purpose are no longer present. As this Hittites purposelessness sets in, people stop "dreaming great things", and the way is paved for **Perizzites** spirits to predominate or prevail. The Perizzites spirit leads people with a very self-limiting view of life that traps them in an "I'm-too-insignificant" attitude.

Notice, therefore, that each triplet of evil spirits works to trap people inside the Amorite's little kingdom. Triplet #1 traps them in Hivites villages of self-indulgence, and triplet #2 traps them in Perizzites villages, of low spiritual self-worth. Both triplets are "initiated" by each of the two "female" ministries. Triplet #1 is initiated by **Canaanites pastors**, and triplet #2 is initiated by **Girgashites teachers**. Through each triplet, believers are **fenced in** by the Hivites spirit on the left side and by the Perizzites spirit on the right side. A crisscross fence is created around the Amorite's little kingdom. This crisscross fence is founded on the matriarchy of the 2 "female" ministries over the Church.

6 vs. 7

If you go back to Proverbs 6:16 (quoted above), you will notice that it speaks of **6** things that God **hates** and 7 things that are an **abomination** to Him. Why doesn't it simply say, "There are 7 things that are abominable to Him"? To answer that, we must go to the following verse:

"At the end of seven years let ye go every man his brother an Hebrew, which hath been sold unto thee; and when he hath served thee six years, thou shalt let him go free from thee: but your fathers hearkened not unto me, neither inclined their ear." (Jeremiah 34:14)

The number "6" is a number of "human weakness", and it points to the **temporary** tabernacles of our earthly vessels; on the other hand, the number "7" is a number of "perfection" or "completion", which points to our **eternal** tabernacles (2 Corinthians 5:1-11). This takes us to the following passage:

"¹Now I say, That the heir, as long as he is a child, differeth nothing from a servant, though he be lord of all; ²But is under tutors and governors until the time appointed of the father. ³Even so we, when we were children, were in bondage under the elements of the world: ⁴But when the fulness of the time was come, God sent forth his Son, made of a woman, made under the law, ⁵To redeem them that were under the law, that we might receive the adoption of sons. ⁶And because ye are sons, God hath sent forth the Spirit of his Son into your hearts, crying, Abba, Father. ⁷Wherefore thou art no more a servant, but a son; and if a son, then an heir of God through Christ." (Galatians 4:1-7) [The word "servant" in verse 1 was translated from the Greek word *doulos*, which literally means "slave"]

Notice that we are **temporarily** placed under "tutors and governors" until "the time appointed of the Father", after which we are no longer to depend upon them but walk on our own; humanly speaking. This means that the number "6" speaks of our time of temporary dependence on others, while the number "7" speaks of our independence from other men in order to depend upon God and God alone. This is why Jeremiah 34:14, quoted above, speaks of a Hebrew being 6 years under the slavery of another Hebrew. Upon the 7th year, the Hebrew slave was to be set free in order to live on his own. In a sense, the number "6" can be taken to represent the structures of the Old Covenant with its intermediaries, while the number "7" represents our direct, New-Covenant relationship with God.

During our "childhood" stage, we are temporarily dependent on human caretakers assigned by God to help and enable us. As we grow older, we are called to become independent in order to walk on our own. Therefore, the reference to "**6** things that God **hates**" in Proverbs 6:16 speaks of our condition when we are still under the bondage of the "elements of the world" (Galatians 4:3). When we are under such a bondage, God **hates** our actions, but He knows that we are trapped and "blinded" by our circumstances. However, once He sets us free from that bondage, His measuring standard for us is elevated. If we go back to the same 7 sins of Proverbs 6:16-19 after we have come to know Him directly, His reaction goes from "hatred" to "**abomination**", because we become all the more accountable for our actions.

When a 7-year-old boy throws a temper tantrum at a shopping mall, his young age "palliates", (to cover his behavior with accuses or apologies) the accountability of his offense. When a 27-year-old man throws the same temper tantrum, his older age makes his offense all the more condemnable.

"⁸Howbeit then, when ye knew not God, ye did service unto them which by nature are no gods. ⁹But now, after that ye have known God, or rather are known of God, how turn ye again to the weak and beggarly elements, whereunto ye desire again to be in bondage? ¹⁰Ye observe days, and months, and times, and years. ¹¹I am afraid of you, lest I have bestowed upon you labour in vain." **(Galatians 4:8-11)**

When we were born again, we were redeemed from the slavery of Pharaoh (Satan). If, after being free, we willingly go back to the "comfort" of slavery under the Amorites; our actions become a complete abomination unto the Lord.

"⁴For it is impossible for those who were once enlightened, and have tasted of the heavenly gift, and were made partakers of the Holy Ghost, ⁵And have tasted the good word of God, and the powers of the world to come, ⁶If they shall fall away, to renew them again unto repentance; seeing they crucify to themselves the Son of God afresh, and put him to an open shame. ⁷For the earth which drinketh in the rain that cometh oft upon it, and bringeth forth herbs meet for them by whom it is dressed, receiveth blessing from God: ⁸But that which beareth thorns and briers is rejected, and is nigh unto cursing; whose end is to be burned." (Hebrews 6:4-8)

After listing **6** sins, Proverbs 6:16-19 lists a **7**th sin ("sending away contention among brethren"), which is related to the Perizzites spirit. This spirit motivates us to accept the "crippledness", the permanent dependence on others. When we willingly accept this 7th sin, our actions go from being **hated** ("6") to being **abominated** ("7") by the Lord. When we willingly accept this 7th sin, we are becoming voluntary slaves inside the Amorite's crisscross fence.

"I tell you the truth, you can say to this mountain, 'May you be lifted up and thrown into the sea,' and it will happen. But you must really believe it will happen and have no doubt in your heart." Mark 11:23

The mountains in Mark 11:23 are greater than moving the "mountain of debt," "mountain of worry," "mountain of problems," "mountain of sickness," and so forth...........It is moving the mountains of the 7 nations to receive the Promised Land. Let us look at these mountains and put our faith, praying and fasting to Work.

Promised Land Fourteen
The Amorites
The Mountain of Education

It was not surprising to me at all that the Amorites were at the top of the triangle. Education is powerful. We hear many quotes about Education. Some of my famous quotes are:

"Education is the most powerful weapon which you can use to change the world." – Nelson Mandela

"Education, then, beyond all other devices of human origin, is the great equalizer of the conditions of man." – Horace Mann

" Education is the movement from darkness to light." -Allan Bloom

"Children must be taught how to think, not what to think."
— Margaret Mead

The Amorites Mountain has to be Cast Away. The Amorites spirit uses its mouth and tongue to speak evil or condemnation against all people. The spirit comes in a form of coarse jokes, swearing, blasphemy, grumbling, slander, gossip, angry speech, lies, exaggerations, boasting, speaking sarcastically, and degrading one another. The loud talking and over-speaking; not allowing someone to get a word in, are the most noticeable characteristics of them all.

The Amorites spirit enters one's soul by murmuring and complaining. Therefore, we need to cease, immediately, all murmuring and complaining; no matter what we are going through. The storms of life may be painful, distressing, heartrending, but we have to count it all "Joy" as we "go through" and finish to the end.

"Dear brothers and sisters, when troubles come your way, consider it an opportunity for great joy." James 1:2

At this point, allow us look at some history of education. "Education" is knowledge or skills obtained or developed by a learning process. The original intent of education was to serve as a place of training and admonition in the fear of God. Every early public school had ministers as headmasters. Reading, writing, and arithmetic were always secondary.

1. The 1ˢᵗ public school was founded by a Puritan minister John Cotton.

John Cotton (1585-1652), noted Puritan minister was responsible for establishing the first public school in America. Cotton himself, was a learned man, having graduated from Cambridge, and been elected a Fellow of Trinity College. During this period, he was not particularly religious in his beliefs or his teachings. Although he would later become head lecturer, dean, and catechist at Emmanuel College, the cradle of Puritanism, he himself was rather a free thinker, lecturing more often on one's self, than one's relationship with God.

When he did convert, it was with a whole-hearted enthusiasm, if somewhat non-conformist leanings. Where once he lectured at school and at home on the fields of learning, he now preached the Word and love of God to all and diverse; and with great frequency.

John Cotton was called to serve in the parish of Boston, Lincolnshire. Cotton held the usual weekly services as well as additional ones three times a week, and daily lectures for students; altogether, all this, in addition to his six daily hours of prayer and study. It was during his tenure in Boston, that he came to extol the virtue of church rule by the congregation. Eventually, his unacceptable arguments and exhortations led to his conviction for "unreformed evil" by the Church of England.

As a result, that is when a call came from the High Court of Commission; he resigned and fled to the New World, and what we now know as New England. The year was 1633. Cotton continued his teachings in Boston, Massachusetts as a firm believer in the right of a congregational minister to direct his flock, and gained widespread fame and respect for his treatises on the subject. In 1635 he established the first public school, the Boston Latin School, modeled on the Free Grammar School in Boston, England, which taught Greek and Latin. It was built on the ancient Greek premise that the only good things are the goods of the soul.

When Edmund Burke referred to America as being the model for "dissidence of the dissent" more than 100 years later, he might have been speaking referring to the Boston Latin School, founded by one of the earliest dissidents in the nation. To this day, it teaches and encourages, dissent/opposition with responsibility. Five of the 56 signers of the declaration of Independence were students of the Boston school: John Hancock, William Hooper, Samuel Adams, Benjamin Franklin and Robert Treat Paine.

The building of Boston Latin School pre-dated Harvard College by a year. It was supported by public funds, and began without a formal building, holding classes in the home of headmaster Philemon Pormort.

Harvard was founded in 1636 by general vote of the Massachusetts Bay Colony, and was often referred to as "the school of the prophets" for its focus on theology. The college awarded its first professorship, in Divinity in 1721, making it the oldest endowment in America. In later years the college would become Harvard University.

Who were the Pilgrims and Puritans?..............

Puritan in modern usage, the word "puritan" is often used to describe someone who adheres to strict moral or religious principles. The Pilgrims started in the 1620s. They were followed by thousands of Puritans in the 1630s, and these Puritans left their mark on their new land, becoming the most dynamic Christian force in the American colonies. Back in England, the Puritans had been people of means and political influence, but King Charles would not tolerate their attempts to reform the Church of England. Therefore, persecution mounted. Too many there seemed no hope but to leave England. Perhaps in America they could establish a colony whose government, society, and church were all based upon the Bible.

"Puritans" had been a name of ridicule first used during the reign of Queen Elizabeth. These were Christians who wanted the Church of England purified of any liturgy, ceremony, or practices which were not found in Scripture. The Bible was their sole authority, and they believed it applied to every area and level of life.

A fortuitous, convenient and unexpected loophole............

When King Charles granted a colonial charter to the Massachusetts Bay Company, the document failed to specify that the governor and officers of the company had to remain in England. The Puritan stockholders took advantage of this silence and agreed to move the company and the whole government of the colony to America. There they would try to establish a biblical community, a holy commonwealth, as an example to England and the World.

New England: A new way..........................

In the mother country, every Englishman was part of the national Church of England. In New England, only the converted, transformed and renewed were members of the church. Only those individuals whose lives had been changed by belief in the gospel of Christ were accepted into the church. Men who were church members were given the right to vote in the colony. They were expected to establish rules for a godly social order, a society which would glorify God. As the Mosaic Law had regulated Israel's society in Old Testament days, so the church under the Scripture's authority would regulate New England's society. There was no place for toleration in Puritan America. Those not in accords with the lofty spiritual aims of the colony could move elsewhere.

Although they were individuals of strong faith and conviction, the Puritans were not individualists. They came to America in groups, not as individual settlers. Often entire congregations, led by their ministers, left England and settled together in the new land. They organized their settlements into towns, with their meeting house or church at the center of town. The church was the center of their community, providing purpose and direction to their lives.

Honor the Lord's Day.................................

The Puritans believed God and His worship were important enough to reserve at least one full day out of the week, and the original Puritan settlers joyfully devoted Sunday to the Lord. Sermons were central to the intellectual life of the Puritans, and they rarely were less than an hour in length. Times of prayer could also be as long. Hymns were not allowed in the earliest Puritan worship; only psalms or paraphrases of other Scriptures were sung. The first book printed in America was the Whole Book of Psalms (or Bay Psalm Book), a metrical version of David's psalms printed in 1640.

The mind as well as the soul........................

The instruction and training of children were considered heavy responsibilities, and parents prayed that children would become a source of glory to their Lord.

Within five years after its founding, Massachusetts established schools for children. Every child should learn to read so he could read the Bible. As one Massachusetts law stated, "It being one chief project of that old deluder, Satan, to keep men from the knowledge of the Scriptures...schools should be established." In 1636 the colony established Harvard College, especially to train ministers. The earliest rules for Harvard testify to the Christian commitment expected: *Let every student be plainly instructed and earnestly pressed to consider well the main end of his life and studies is,... to know God, and Jesus Christ which is eternal life (John 17:3).* And therefore to lay Christ in the bottom is the only foundation of all sound knowledge and learning.

"And this is the way to have eternal life--to know you, the only true God, and Jesus Christ, the one you sent to earth." (John 17:3)

All is the Lord's.......................

In keeping with their belief that every area of life should be molded by Christian principles, the Puritans saw all honorable work as a means of glorifying God. All of life was God's, and there was no distinction between secular and sacred work. God calls each person to a particular vocation or occupation, and the Christian should act as a careful steward of the talents and gifts God has given him. Working in one's calling or vocation was a means of serving God and men. Idleness was considered a great sin; diligence in one's calling was a virtue.

Shaping America...............................
The Puritans who settled in New England laid a foundation for a nation unique in world history. They also had a most significant influence on the subsequent development of America. A large portion of later pioneers and westward settlers were descendants of these early Puritans. Their values and principles, though sometimes secularized and removed from their religious foundations, continued to mold American thought and practices in the next centuries.

> Organized like a miniature church............
> The family was the most basic institution in Puritan society and was organized like a miniature church. Established by God before all other institutions and before man's fall, the family was considered the foundation of all civil, social, and ecclesiastical life. In the morning and evening the family assembled together for worship, and on Sunday the family joined other families in worship.

2.   Harvard was founded in 1636 by clergyman John Harvard. John Harvard was an English minister in America, known as "a godly gentleman and a lover of learning". One of the founders of the most prestigious educational institutions in the world in training and releasing into society clergyman and scholars with Puritan values. Eight presidents graduated from Harvard: John Adams, John Quincy Adams, Theodore Roosevelt, Franklin D. Roosevelt, John F. Kennedy; **Law School:** Rutherford B. Hayes, Barack Obama; **Business School:** George W. Bush.

Harvard, what was originally styled *Harvard College*, founded 1636 in Cambridge, Massachusetts, and around which

Harvard University eventually grew, is the oldest institution of higher learning in the United States. For centuries its graduates dominated Massachusetts' clerical and civil ranks. Beginning in the 19th century, its stature became national, and then international, as a dozen graduates and professional schools were formed alongside the nucleus undergraduate College.
Historically influential in national roles are the schools of medicine (1782), law (1817) and business (1908) as well as the Harvard Graduate School of Arts and Sciences (1890). Since the late 19th century, Harvard has been one of the most prestigious schools in the world. Its library system and financial endowment are larger than those of any other.

3.   William and Mary College of 1693. The second oldest college in American was an Anglican School

The **College of William & Mary in Virginia** (also known as **William & Mary** or **W&M**) is a public research university located in Williamsburg, Virginia, United States. Privately founded in 1693 by letters patent issued by King William III and Queen Mary II, it is the second-oldest institution of higher education in the United States after Harvard University. William & Mary is considered one of the original "Public Ivies," a publicly funded university providing a quality of education claimed to be comparable to that available in the Ivy League.
William & Mary educated U.S. Presidents Thomas Jefferson, James Monroe, and John Tyler as well as other key figures important to the development of the nation, including U.S. Supreme Court Chief Justice John Marshall, Speaker of the House Henry Clay, and 16 signers of the Declaration of Independence. W&M founded the Phi Beta Kappa academic honor society in 1776 and was the first school of higher education in the United States to install an honor code of conduct for students. The establishment of graduate programs in law and medicine in 1779 makes it one of the first universities in the United States.
In addition to its undergraduate program, which includes an international joint degree program with the University of St. Andrews and a joint engineering program with Columbia

University, W&M is home to several graduate and professional schools, including law, business, public policy, education, marine science and colonial history.

The doctrine of the Anglican Church is an interesting mix of Catholicism and Protestant Reformation theology. The Apostles' Creed and Nicene Creed are authoritative declarations of belief for the Anglican Church and are typically recited in worship services. Interestingly, the church does not require individuals to agree with or accept all the statements of those creeds but encourages its members to join in the process of discovery. The 39 Articles, developed in the reign of Elizabeth I, laid out the Protestant doctrine and practice of the Anglican Church, but were deliberately written to be so vague that they were open to various interpretations by Protestants and Catholics. As in the Catholic Church, the celebration of the Eucharist is central to the worship service, along with the communal offering of prayer and praise through the recitation of the liturgy. In all liturgical churches, there is a danger of allowing the form of religious ceremony (Isaiah 29:13) to replace the personal application of faith (Psalm 51:16-17). This was a key point of contention by the Puritans and others who ultimately left the Anglican Church.

Thomas Shepherd, who was expelled from the Anglican Church in 1630 for non-conformity, was a spiritual giant who was concerned that people distinguish between the work of grace in genuine conversion and the religious pretense that was common within the church. Shepherd was one of the pivotal men in the founding of Harvard College and became a mentor of Jonathan Edwards, who was mightily used of God in the Great Awakening.

The Anglican Communion has 80 million members worldwide in 38 different church organizations, including the Episcopal Church. The Archbishop of Canterbury is the recognized spiritual head of the church, though each church organization is self-governing under its own archbishop. In addition to those churches, the Continuing Anglican Communion, established in 1977, is composed of churches which share the historic Anglican faith, but reject the changes in the Episcopal Book of Common Prayer, as well as the ordination of women and gays/lesbians to the clergy, and have thus severed their ties with the main church.

The term *Ivy League* has connotations of academic excellence, selectivity in admissions, and social elitism.

4.   Yale University

Yale University is a private Ivy League research university in New Haven, Connecticut. Founded in 1701 as the "Collegiate School" by a group of Congregationalist ministers and chartered by the Colony of Connecticut, the university is the third-oldest institution of higher education in the United States. In 1718, the school was renamed "Yale College" in recognition of a gift from Elihu Yale, a governor of the British East India Company.

Established to train Connecticut ministers in theology and sacred languages, by 1777 the school's curriculum began to incorporate humanities and sciences. During the 19th century Yale gradually incorporated graduate and professional instruction, awarding the first Ph.D. in the United States in 1861 and organizing as a university in 1887.

Yale is organized into twelve constituent schools: the original undergraduate college, the Graduate School of Arts & Sciences, and ten professional schools. While the university is governed by the Yale Corporation, each school's faculty oversees its curriculum and degree programs. In addition to a central campus in downtown New Haven, the University owns athletic facilities in Western New Haven, including the Yale Bowl, a campus in West Haven, Connecticut, and forest and nature preserves throughout New England. The University's assets include an endowment valued at $23.9 billion as of September 27, 2014.

Yale College undergraduates follow a liberal arts curriculum with departmental majors and are organized into a system of residential colleges. The Yale University Library, serving all twelve schools, holds more than 15 million volumes and is the third-largest academic library in the United States. Almost all faculties teach undergraduate courses, more than 2,000 of which are offered annually. Students compete inter-collegiately as the Yale Bulldogs in the NCAA Division I Ivy League.

Yale has graduated many notable alumni, including five U.S. Presidents, 19 U.S. Supreme Court Justices, 13 living billionaires and many foreign heads of state. In addition, Yale has graduated hundreds of members of Congress and many high-level U.S. diplomats, including former U.S. Secretary of State Hillary Clinton and current Secretary of State John Kerry. Fifty-two Nobel laureates have been affiliated with the University as students, faculty, or staff, and 230 Rhodes Scholars, the second most in the United States, graduated from the University.

- Presidents that graduated from Yale Law School: Gerald Ford and Bill Clinton and other graduates of Yale are: William Howard Taft, George H. W. Bush, George W. Bush

Curriculum

Yale was swept up by the great intellectual movements of the period, the Great Awakening and the Enlightenment, thanks to the religious and scientific interests of presidents Thomas Clap and Ezra Stiles. They were both instrumental in developing the scientific curriculum at Yale, while dealing with wars, student tumults, graffiti, "irrelevance" of curricula, desperate need for endowment, and fights with the Connecticut legislature.

Serious American students of theology and divinity, particularly in New England, regarded Hebrew as a classical language, along with Greek and Latin, and essential for study of the Old Testament in the original words. The Reverend Ezra Stiles, president of the College from 1778 to 1795, brought with him his interest in the Hebrew language as a vehicle for studying ancient Biblical texts in their original language, as was common in other schools, requiring all freshmen to study Hebrew (in contrast to Harvard, where only upperclassmen were required to study the language) and is responsible for the Hebrew phrase אורים ותמים (Urim and Thummim) on the Yale seal. Stiles' greatest challenge occurred in July 1779 when hostile British forces occupied New Haven and threatened to raze the College.

However, Yale graduate Edmund Fanning, Secretary to the British General in command of the occupation, interceded and the College was saved. Fanning later was granted an honorary degree LL.D., at 1803, for his efforts.

Students

As the only college in Connecticut, Yale educated the sons of the elite. Offenses for which students were punished included card playing, tavern-going, destruction of college property, and acts of disobedience to college authorities. During the period, Harvard was distinctive for the stability and maturity of its tutor corps, while Yale had youth and zeal on its side.

The emphasis on classics gave rise to a number of private student societies, open only by invitation, which arose primarily as forums for discussions of modern scholarship, literature and politics. The first such organizations were debating societies: Crotonia in 1738, Linonia in 1753, and Brothers in Unity in 1768.

5. **Princeton University** founded in 1746. The 4th Oldest University.

New Light Presbyterians founded the **College of New Jersey**, later Princeton University, in 1746 in order to train ministers. The college was the educational and religious capital of Scots-Irish America. In 1756, the college moved to Princeton, New Jersey. Its home in Princeton was Nassau Hall, named for the royal house of William III of England.

Following the untimely deaths of Princeton's first five presidents, John Witherspoon became president in 1768 and remained in that office until his death in 1794. During his presidency, Witherspoon shifted the college's focus from training ministers to preparing a new generation for leadership in the new American nation. To this end, he tightened academic standards and solicited investment in the college. Witherspoon's presidency constituted a long period of stability for the college, interrupted by the American Revolution and particularly the Battle of Princeton, during which British soldiers briefly occupied Nassau Hall; American forces, led by George Washington, fired cannon on the building to rout them from it.

First Indian Prime Minister Jawaharlal Nehru graduated from Princeton University in 1949. Thomas Mann graduated from Princeton in 1938.

In 1812, the eighth president of Princeton (still the College of New Jersey), Ashbel Green (1812–23), helped establish a theological seminary next door. The plan to extend the theological curriculum met with "enthusiastic approval on the part of the authorities at the College of New Jersey". Today, Princeton University and Princeton Theological Seminary maintain separate institutions with ties that include services such as cross-registration and mutual library access.

"Under God's Power She Flourishes"

Presidents that attended Princeton University: John F. Kennedy (transferred to Harvard University), James Madison, Woodrow Wilson

Who are the Presbyterians? Presbyterians distinguish themselves from other denominations by doctrine, institutional organization (or "church order") and worship; often using a "Book of Order" to regulate common practice and order. The origins of the Presbyterian churches are in Calvinism. Many branches of Presbyterianism are remnants of previous splits from larger groups. Some of the splits have been due to doctrinal controversy, while some have been caused by disagreement concerning the degree to which those ordained to church office should be required to agree with the Westminster Confession of Faith, which historically serves as an important confessional document; second only to the Bible, yet directing particularities in the standardization and translation of the Bible, in Presbyterian churches.

Presbyterians place great importance upon education and lifelong learning. Continuous study of the scriptures, theological writings, and understanding and interpretation of church doctrine are embodied in several statements of faith and catechisms formally adopted by various branches of the church, often referred to as "subordinate standards". It is generally considered that the point of such learning is to enable one to put one's faith into practice; some Presbyterians generally exhibit their faith in action as well as words, by generosity, hospitality, and the constant pursuit of social justice and reform, as well as proclaiming the gospel of Christ.

Now, we have read that the early schools of education were led by Puritans, Anglicans, and Presbyterians. They all started out based on Biblical Scriptures, but somehow and somewhere compromised.........but not by a "Christian" group of people.............. **WE Have Work To Do Christians!!!!**

What is Education?

The goal of education is to inspire a lifetime of a **love** to learn. Education is an on-going process. Education should be geared and focused on God and learning His principles to conquer sin and the evilness of this world; instead of focusing on degrees and titles that will keep us in high paying jobs and positions here on earth. Education is:

A love to learn
Character
Natural talent
Competitiveness
Ability to process knowledge
Knowing how to learn
Organizing skills
Self-esteem, pride
Motivation, desires
Persistence
Vision, goals
Ambition
Attitudes
Leadership
Responsibility
Research and analytical skills
Instinctive ability
Perceptive insight
Integrity
Bounce back from failure
Willingness to take risk
Creativity, visionary

Fear control, courage
Communication skills
Reasoning
Decision-making
Problem solving
Time management
Applying technology
Acquire & evaluate information
Ability to get jobs done

The Education Mountain targets the Universities. The early universities had the foundation of Scriptures. Somehow, through pride and greed, we have allowed the Amorites spirit to come into our Universities, colleges, and schools to destroy the foundation of Christianity. We have to put the fear of God back into our educational programs. In today's society, our universities have adopted a curriculum based on liberalism and humanism.

--*Liberalism* is a movement in modern Protestantism that emphasizes freedom from tradition and authority, the adjustment of religious beliefs to scientific conceptions, and the development of spiritual capacities.
--*Humanism* is in the form of philosophy, is a variety of ethical theory and practice that emphasizes reason, scientific inquiry, and human fulfillment in the natural world and often rejects the importance of belief in God.

Our universities are based more on liberalism and humanism; instead of Kingdom influences. Our universities displaces God with philosophy, in which, Man is the center; and not God.

WE need to continuously speak and pray that "the Amorites will no longer rule over the Education department in this earth." With the Power of Jesus we will cast this mountain into the sea... *In the mighty name of Jesus, we break the curses of the Amorites, ruler of the Mountain of Education; we destroy every spirit of murmuring and complaining that has destroyed God's influence in education. WE speak now, that leaders are anointed and equipped with spiritual powers and wisdom to tear down the Amorites spirit in the schools, colleges, and university of this world. WE ask, in the name of Jehovah Jireh, to restore the Christian foundations back into Harvard, Yale, and Princeton University, in Jesus name. Amen!*

We, as Kingdom Builders, have to pay attention to our schools curriculums and foundations. Let us examine and analyze the mission statements of our schools and research the roots and backgrounds of their school mottos. These spirits come in all shapes, symbols and figures. The Kings of the Amorites are shown in statements or words that end in –ism from atheism, liberalism, rationalism, humanism, in which, are a form of demonic principalities and powers of spiritual wickedness in high places.

The King of the Amorites is Beelzebub and Baal is the chief lieutenant of Lucifer, "Lord of the flies"

In our education system, administration, teachers, professors, janitors, food service, and so forth must be Holy Ghost empowered. It is imperative that we have biblical roles in position to instruct the ways of the Lord. When prayer was taken out of school, we should have been setting up prayer groups all over the world in the mornings, in the midnight hours, at homes, churches, and community centers before things became frenzied. It is never too late, but we must move quickly and powerful without fear to conquer and defeat this rapid movement of Satan. WE must have Biblical role models that influence the certification process and the curriculum.

"Right now in the mighty name of Jesus, we thank you for placing the Anointed of your chosen school administrators in the areas of the teacher's certification process and the curriculum development. We thank you, Lord; in advance for spiritually, powerful-filled Anointed Jesus Christ followers to rule over the Education department on this earth. We thank you for your rapid movement of the Holy Spirit in the atmosphere of every school,

college, university, job training schools throughout the earth. We thank you God; in Jesus name. Amen.

What can we do as Jesus disciples?

We need an Elijah revolutionary to overtake this Mountain of Education. Intercessors need to invade with prayers. Prophets need to speak and release the future. Apostles need to camp outside the spiritual walls of the education departments, systems, buildings and grounds until the walls fall and crumble.

1 Thessalonians 5:16-18 (ESV), [16] Rejoice always, [17] pray without ceasing, [18] give thanks in all circumstances; for this is the will of God in Christ Jesus for you.

Public education is universally available, with control and funding coming from the state, local, and federal government. Public school curricula, funding, teaching, employment, and other policies are set through locally elected school boards, who have jurisdiction over individual school districts. State governments set educational standards and mandate standardized tests for public school systems.

We, as God-Kingdom builders, need to pray without ceasing. Apostles, prophets and intercessors need to stand in positions at the student level; in the classrooms or internet based classrooms, at the faculty level in the teacher's certification process and at the curriculum level at the Board of Education for Public, University and College.

The Elijah Revolution........................

Elijah Revolution is a gathering of young people seeking to be equipped for purity, passion, and prayer. The future of America is in the hands of the righteous who pray....

THE GREAT REVOLUTION
In "The Harvest," Rick Joyner disclosed that in the forthcoming revolution an "army" will remove those, labeled stumbling blocks, who refuse the unity teachings of the modern

prophets. According to Joyner, ". . .to remove the stumbling blocks . . . a great company of prophets, teachers, pastors and apostles will be raised up with the spirit of Phinehas." After this revolution in the Church, "very young Christians will be pastoring large bodies of believers"

> *They yoked themselves to the Baal of Peor and ate sacrifices offered to lifeless gods; they aroused the Lord 's anger by their wicked deeds, and a plague broke out among them. But Phinehas stood up and intervened, and the plague was checked. This was credited to him as righteousness for endless generations to come. - Psalm 106: 28-31 (NIV)*

". . .Some pastors and leaders who continue to resist this tide of unity will be removed from their place. Some will become so hardened they will become combaters and disputers; and resist God to the end. Most will be changed and will repent of their resistance. . . . There will be many 'stumbling blocks' circulating in the Church that will cause confusion and some destruction from time to time. They will perceive themselves as prophets sent to judge and deliver. Those serving in leadership must trust their discernment and remove the stumbling blocks."

"To be distinguished from the 'stumbling blocks,' a great company of prophets, teachers, pastors and apostles will be raised up with the spirit of Phinehas. Just as the son of Eleazar could not tolerate iniquity in the camp of the Lord, this 'ministry of Phinehas' will save congregations, and at times even whole nations from the plagues that will be sweeping the earth. They will be moved by the jealousy of the Lord for the purity of His people. They will be sent to save and preserve the work of the Lord, not tear down, as the stumbling blocks do. . . Huge masses of people will be streaming to the Lord, the inflow so great in places that **very young Christians will be pastoring large bodies of believers.** Arenas and stadiums will overflow nightly as the believers come together to hear the apostles and teachers."

". . . **Extraordinary miracles will be common** while those considered great today will be performed almost without notice by **young believers. Angelic appearances** will be common to the saints and a visible glory of the Lord will appear upon some for extended periods of time as power flows through them. "

Those in leadership will be the most humble of all. When anyone presumes leadership without a calling of God, it will be apparent to all. "This harvest will be so great that no one will look back at the early Church as a standard; all will be saying that the Lord has certainly saved His best wine for last. The early Church was a first-fruits offering; truly this will be a harvest! It was said of the Apostle Paul that he was turning the world upside down; it will be said of the **apostles soon to be anointed** that they have turned an upside down world right side up. **Nations will tremble at the mention of their names**."

The Amorites are mountain people. The Amorites are described tall and impressive land massive that dominate over valleys. Amorites loves to be "kings", dominate and give orders.

God is the Amorites greatest competition.

Removing mountains not only mean removing big problems, but uprooting of spiritual powers in high places.....In Matthew 1, *"19 Then the disciples came to Jesus in private and asked, "Why couldn't we drive it out?" 20 He replied, "Because you have so little faith. I tell you the truth, if you have faith as small as a mustard seed, you can say to this mountain, 'Move from here to there' and it will move. Nothing will be impossible for you. "*

We need the faith that is greater than a mustard seed to move these mountains. The more we now about God and His Power; the greater and firm our faith will be in moving these 7 nations' mountains.

Before we can reach the Mountain of Education we must deal with the Amorites spirit in the churches. Amorites love to oppress and put fear in people they want to rule over.

1.   In churches, we have many pastors that want their flock to submit to them. For example, Pastor telling another member that they will pray for them because they may not hear from God correctly or the way I do….. *"26 But you do not believe because you are not of My sheep. 27"My sheep hear My voice, and I know them, and they follow Me; 28and I give eternal life to them, and they will never perish; and no one will snatch them out of My hand…." John 10:26-28.*
        If you **"Believe"**, that Jesus died on the cross for our sins and that Jesus is the Son of God; then, You are His sheep, therefore, we will and can hear His voice without man's help.

2.   Christians provoke shame and question the other person's spirit authority. I know a true Christian by his **"Love"** and **"Giving"** characteristics. We all have sinned and fell short, therefore, judgment and criticism should be nowhere in our mind. Let us stop the "tearing down" and begin "building up" one another. We have forces that are greater and mightier that we have to conquer and defeat; than being critical and hurtful to one another.

3.   The Amorites spirit carries a spirit of slapping and hitting out of anger. Also, this is in the form of domestic violence and physical abuse to one another. If anyone has slapped someone growing up. Repent to be loose from the Amorite Spirit. If anyone has slapped you, forgive them so you may loose the spirit of the Amorites…Let us exercise Forgiveness on a daily basis. The Amorites has taken control of many of us through un-forgiveness. Since we are not forgiving, we are tearing each other down by downgrading one another, talking badly about one another; and so forth. Let us stop this type of behavior so that we may move forward to do God's work.

4.   Amorites are territorial spirits. They love to rule and dominate over great number of souls. They have the "Roosters over chickens" syndrome. Some churches have a large congregation and some small congregations. Let us not have a

dominate pride spirit because one's church is larger than the other. All churches need to come together to help one another; and to come together as one....We are all God's children; His sheep. Let us combine our resources to build greater spiritual communities for the schools, colleges, and universities, as well as, Trade and Technical schools.

"21 Israel sent messengers to say to Sihon king of the Amorites: 22 "Let us pass through your country. We will not turn aside into any field or vineyard, or drink water from any well. We will travel along the king's highway until we have passed through your territory." 23 But Sihon would not let Israel pass through his territory. He mustered his entire army and marched out into the desert against Israel. When he reached Jahaz, he fought with Israel." Numbers 21:21-23

Amorites High priest, Annas, stopped Peter at the Door.........

John 18:15-18 (NIV), Peter's First Denial, 15 Simon Peter and another disciple were following Jesus. Because this disciple was known to the high priest, he went with Jesus into the high priest's courtyard, 16 but Peter had to wait outside at the door. The other disciple, who was known to the high priest, came back, spoke to the servant girl on duty there and brought Peter in. 17 "You aren't one of this man's disciples too, are you?" she asked Peter. He replied, "I am not." 18 It was cold, and the servants and officials stood around a fire they had made to keep warm. Peter also was standing with them, warming himself."

Matthew 26:57-75, (NASB)

Jesus before Caiaphas

57 Those who had seized Jesus led Him away to Caiaphas, the high priest, where the scribes and the elders were gathered together. 58 But Peter was following Him at a distance as far as the courtyard of the high priest, and entered in, and sat down with the officers to see the outcome. 59 Now the chief priests *and the whole Council kept trying to obtain false testimony against Jesus, so that they might put Him to death. [60] They did not find any, even though many false witnesses came forward. But later on two came forward, [61] and said, "This man stated, 'I am able to destroy the temple of God and to rebuild it in three days.'" [62] The high priest stood up and said to Him, "Do You not answer? What is it that these men are testifying against You?" [63] But Jesus kept silent. And the high priest said to Him, "I adjure You by the living God, that You tell us whether You are the Christ, the Son of God." [64] Jesus *said to him, "You have said it yourself; nevertheless I tell you, hereafter you will see THE SON OF MAN SITTING AT THE RIGHT HAND OF POWER, and COMING ON THE CLOUDS OF HEAVEN." [65] Then the high priest tore his robes and said, "He has blasphemed! What further need do we have of witnesses? Behold, you have now heard the blasphemy; [66] what do you think?" They answered, "He deserves death!" [67] Then they spat in His face and beat Him with their fists; and others slapped Him, [68] and said, "Prophesy to us, You Christ; who is the one who hit You?"*

Peter's Denials

[69] Now Peter was sitting outside in the courtyard, and a servant-girl came to him and said, "You too were with Jesus the Galilean." [70] But he denied it before them all, saying, "I do not know what you are talking about." [71] When he had gone out to the gateway, another servant-girl saw him and *said to those who were there, "This man was with Jesus of Nazareth." [72] And again he denied it with an oath, "I do not know the man." [73] A little later the bystanders came up and said to Peter, "Surely you too are one of them; for even the way you talk gives you away." [74] Then he began to curse and swear, "I do not know the man!" And immediately a rooster crowed. [75] And Peter remembered the word which Jesus had said, "Before a rooster crows, you will deny Me three times." And he went out and wept bitterly.

Peter's 1st Denial cost him his Apostolic Anointing
Peter's 2nd Denial cost him his Prophetic Anointing

Success Is Our Plan

Peter's 3rd Denial cost him his Evangelistic Anointing; (the Girgashites spirit was broken off by Jesus).

The Amorites Spirit manifested through the high priest in **John 18:19-23, (ESV)**

The High Priest Questions Jesus

19 The high priest then questioned Jesus about his disciples and his teaching. 20 Jesus answered him, "I have spoken openly to the world. I have always taught in synagogues and in the temple, where all Jews come together. I have said nothing in secret. 21 Why do you ask me? Ask those who have heard me what I said to them; they know what I said." 22 When he had said these things, one of the officers standing by struck Jesus with his hand, saying, "Is that how you answer the high priest?" 23 Jesus answered him, "If what I said is wrong, bear witness about the wrong; but if what I said is right, why do you strike me?"

If the Amorites spirits can dominate the high priests that were anointed, why can't they dominate the churches and schools? The high priests were designed to be different and peculiar in beauty, in strength, in wisdom, and in richness...

"The priest who is chief among his brothers, on whose head the anointing oil is poured and who has been consecrated to wear the garments, shall not let the hair of his head hang loose nor tear his clothes." (Leviticus 21:10, ESV)

God can bestow authority upon a person, but he or she has the prerogative to either exercise that authority under God's anointing or to exercise it in his or her flesh. God's promoted authority spreads God's Kingdom. Man's promoted authority will spread the Amorites' kingdom.

Now, we see the Amorites Spirit is not a today Spirit, this is a generational curse (spirit) that needs to be destroyed.

Review of the Education Mountain:

Enemy of the Mountain----Amorites (humanism and liberalism)
Principality of the Mountain----Beelzebub(lies)
Significant Displacing Authority----Teachers and Professors
Basic Mission----Bring in new fear-of-God based curriculum
Revelation 5:12 Key: Wisdom

When God blesses us with the millions, trillions, and billions, how will I help build the Kingdom of God concerning "Education"?

"And the LORD answered me: "Write the vision; make it plain on tablets, so he may run who reads it." Habakkuk 2:2, ESV

Promised Land Fifteen
The Canaanites
The Mountain of Economy

The Canaanites have the characteristics of greed/poverty. This Mountain enslaves people into poverty. Where God blesses people with abundance, the Canaanites' spirit twists abundance into greed for more. The Mountain principality is Mammon or Babylon. The Canaanites have a lying spirit to deceit people that money is the true source of provision.

Canaan means "merchant or trader". The Canaanites are spiritual Canaanites that use merchants and traders in occupying our Promised Land.

"For our struggle is not against flesh and blood, but against the rulers, against the authorities, against the powers of this dark world and against the spiritual forces of evil in the heavenly realms." (Ephesians 6:12, NIV)

The Canaanites steal from ignorant and powerless people and sell to the covenant slaves, who will sell their souls to vanity. The devil has nothing. I mean nothing of his own. The devil has to take from God's Promised Land and give to his followers. Satan uses the Canaanites spiritual forces to <u>steal</u> away stars, favors, success, money, and so forth and give to his followers.

How can Satan do this when everything belongs to God?

The Canaanites spirit puts fear in our hearts by keeping us under a constant stressor of needing more and more without ever being content............or setting up circumstances where survival is endangered.

WE, as powerful, spiritual filled Christians have to Dispose of this Canaanites Spirit.......*I dispose every spiritual trader trading in my destiny and stealing from my destiny, to be scattered by brimstones and fire; by the Holy Ghost. In the mighty name of El HaKadosh, the Canaanites mountain must restore everything that has been stolen from my life, my husband life, my children life, my extended family life, my church life, and my community life, in Jesus name Amen.*

Once we dispose the Canaanites spirit; and remain delivered and free of the Canaanites fear, then we can educate our loves ones, as well as, the church and community, the importance of "true success" and "true abundance" with riches/wealth through God; not man.........not earthly wealth, but heavenly wealth.

"The blessing of the LORD makes a person rich, and he adds no sorrow with it." Proverbs 10:22 (NLT)

"Moreover, when God gives someone wealth and possessions, and the ability to enjoy them, to accept their lot and be happy in their toil--this is a gift of God." Ecclesiastes 5:19 (NIV)

Now, allow us to look at the economy. **What is Economy?**

From Wikipedia, the free encyclopedia, economy is describe as an **economy** or economic system that consists of the production, distribution or trade, and consumption of limited goods and services by different agents in a given geographical location. The economic agents can be individuals, businesses, organizations, or governments. Transactions occur when two parties agree to the value or price of the transacted good or service, commonly expressed in a certain currency.

In the past, economic activity was theorized to be bounded by natural resources, labor, and capital. This view ignores the value of technology; automation, accelerator of process, reduction of cost functions, and innovation of new products, services, processes, new markets, expands markets, diversification of markets, niche markets, increased revenue functions; especially that which produces intellectual property.

A given economy is the result of a set of processes that involves its culture, values, education, technological evolution, history, social organization, political structure and legal systems, as well as its geography, natural resource endowment, and ecology, as the main factors. These factors give context, content, and set the conditions and parameters in which an economy functions. **The largest national economy in the Americas is the United States, Germany in Europe, Nigeria in Africa and China in Asia.**

"Right now, with the power of the Holy Spirit, I dispose of every Canaanitse spirit that is operating in the Americas in the United States, Germany in Europe, Nigeria in Africa and China in Asia; market trades. We take hold of our possessions from the Promised Land, for the building of God's Kingdom; in Jesus name. Amen."

A market-based economy is where goods and services are produced without obstruction or interference, and exchanged according to demand and supply between participants, economic agents, by barter or a medium of exchange with a credit or debit value accepted within the network, such as a unit of currency and at some free market or market clearing price. Capital and labor can move freely to any area of emerging shortage, signaled by rising price, and thus dynamically and automatically relieve any such threat. Market based economies require transparency on information, such as true prices, to work, and may include various kinds of immaterial production, such as affective labor that describes work carried out that is intended to produce or modify emotional experiences in people, but does not have a tangible, physical product as a result.

A command-based economy is where a central political agent commands what is produced and how it is sold and distributed. Shortages are common problems with a command-based economy, as there is no mechanism to manage the information (prices) about the systems natural supply and demand dynamics.

A green economy is low-carbon, resource efficient, and socially inclusive. In a green economy, growth in income and employment are driven by public and private investments that reduce carbon emissions and pollution, enhance energy and resource efficiency, and prevent the loss of biodiversity and ecosystem services.

Who are and what are the world money traders or world traders and how does this effect families, business, jobs, churches and the communities?

In short, economy is a system of production, distribution and consumption. The economy is the proper flow and balance of the production of resources, the distributions of resources, and the consumption of resources.

World money traders create economic realities…more than a billion dollars are traded each day. It is a game of buying strong currencies and selling weak currencies. Trading on Wall Street through stocks/shares affect the economy by **speculations** on the value of a company's stock based on report. The economy is based on the spending of the economy, which are based on reports and future speculations of spending and buying. In terms, many corporations, businesses, families and individual lives are controlled by the stock market; instead of God, Jehovah-Jireh, the provider of all things.

World traders control the Canaanites Mountain of Economy; not by strategy, plans or guidelines; however, primarily through fears, rumors and confidences in poverty.

1 Timothy 6:17 (AMP) *"¹⁷ As for the rich in this world, charge them not to be proud and arrogant and contemptuous of others, nor to set their hopes on uncertain riches, but on God, Who richly and ceaselessly provides us with everything for [our] enjoyment."*

The Canaanites Mountain operates on supply/demand. For a market economy to function, producers must supply the goods that consumers want. This is known as the law of supply and demand. "Supply" refers to the amount of goods a market can produce, while "demand" refers to the amount of goods consumers are willing to buy. Together, these two powerful market forces form the main principle that underlies all economic theory.

The law of supply and demand explains how prices are set for the sale of goods. The process starts with consumers demanding goods. When demand is high, producers can charge high prices for goods. The promise of earning large profits from high prices inspires producers to manufacture goods to meet the demand. However, the law of demand states that if prices are too high, only a few consumers will purchase the goods and demand will go unmet. To fully meet demand, producers must charge a price that will result in the required amount of sales while still generating profits for themselves.

For example, assume that a cell phone manufacturing company perceives demand for new cell phones. The company invests in market research to produce the exact cell phone that consumers want. The company then produces 5,000 units and puts them up for sale at $300 each. Consumers who find the phone to be valuable pay the full $300, and half of the units are soon sold.

Because of the high price, however, sales gradually begin to drop off. Many consumers still want the phone, but are unwilling or unable to pay $300 for one. Because the cell phone company loses money on unsold products, it reduces the phone's price to $250 in hopes of increasing sales. Consumers begin buying again. The process continues until a price is reached that will both meet demand and maximize the company's profits. That price is known as the "market-clearing price."

When supply becomes balanced with demand, the market is said to have reached equilibrium. At equilibrium, resources are used at their maximum efficiency. The study of economics is largely a study in how market economies can best achieve equilibrium, which is why economists spend a great deal of time analyzing the relationship between supply and demand to control spending.

The law of supply and demand explains why people behave in certain ways within a market economy, and can even be used to predict behavior and, thereby, economic outcomes. Manufacturers, who want the highest price possible for their products, utilize inventory management protocols and invest in advertising to encourage consumers to buy. Consumers who value a low price over the quality or popularity of a product shop at outlets and discount stores, while those who favor popularity over price purchase goods from retail stores at the height of the market.

The law of supply and demand is not just limited to the sale of products; however, it can be used to explain almost any economic phenomenon, such as a rise or drop in employment, increased or decreased enrollment in colleges, the expansion or shrinking of government programs, and increases or reductions in available resources. Therefore, the law of supply and demand is not only vital to economic theory; it is the foundation of economics itself.

Also, the Canaanites means "to be humbled", "to be brought low", or "to be under subjection." Canaan means "zealous", in which, greed/poverty are the decisions that are made under this mountain. The enemy tries to convince people to be more zealous in the trading/trafficking or subject to poverty….Based on the Canaanites' spirit, either you are in greed or in poverty; instead of Living in Abundance in God's provision; not the stock market.

The Economy Mountain direct enemy is Jehovah Jireh, "The Lord My Provider." When greed/poverty tries to stricken your spirit or mind…speak "Jehovah Jireh" loudly because He is Your Provider and Sustainer!!!

Canaanites live under the banner of financial hopelessness/financial euphoria………………..**Jehovah Jireh lives under the banner of the Lord's provision.**

It is the zeal for the resources of more money, wealth, possessions and wanting less of God, which the Canaanites receive its power to rule over the lives of God's people. We have to break the "zeal" by wanting less of possessions and wanting more and more and more of God.

Matthew 5:6, *"Blessed are those who hunger and thirst for righteousness, for they will be filled."*

Luke 1:53, *"He has filled the hungry with good things but has sent the rich away empty."*

Psalm 34:10, *"The lions may grow weak and hungry, but those who seek the LORD lack no good thing."*

Why do we want the millions? Is it for fame or to purchase more possessions or to build for the kingdom of God?

The King of the Canaanites is Mammon. The word mammon comes from the Greek word *mammonas*. Similar root words exist in Hebrew, Latin, Aramaic, Chaldean and Syriac. They all translate to "money, wealth, and material possessions."

In biblical culture the word mammon often carried a negative connotation. It was sometimes used to describe all lusts and excesses: gluttony, greed, and dishonest worldly gain. Ultimately, mammon described as an idol of materialism, which many trusted as a foundation for their world and philosophy. While the King James Version retains the term Mammon in Matthew 6:24, other versions translate the Greek as "money," "wealth," or "riches."

The city of Babylon (Revelation 18), with all its avarice and greed, is a description of a world given over to the spirit of Mammon. Some scholars cite Mammon as the name of a Syrian and Chaldean god, similar to the Greek god of wealth, Plutus.

Just as "Wisdom" is personified in Proverbs 1:21–33, Mammon is personified in Matthew 6:24 and Luke 16:13. Jesus' words here show a powerful contrast between the worship of the material world and the worship of God. Later, writers such as Augustine, Danté (The Divine Comedy), Milton (Paradise Lost), and Spenser (The Faerie Queene) used personifications of Mammon to show the insidious nature of materialism and its seduction of humanity.

Worship of mammon can show up in many ways. It isn't always through a continual lust for more money. When we envy others' wealth, are anxious over potentially unmet needs, disobey God's directives about the use of wealth, or fail to trust God's love and faithfulness; our thinking, then, becomes out of balance concerning material wealth.

In the Sermon on the Mount, Jesus teaches about our relationship to material goods. He says, *"Do not store up for yourselves treasures on earth. . . . But store up for yourselves treasures in heaven. . . . For where your treasure is, there your heart will be also. . . . No one can serve two masters. Either you will hate the one and love the other, or you will be devoted to the one and despise the other. You cannot serve both God and money [mammon]"* (Matthew 6:19–24).

The apostle Paul writes of the godly perspective toward mammon: *"godliness with contentment is great gain. For we brought nothing into the world, and we can take nothing out of it. But if we have food and clothing, we will be content with that. Those who want to get rich fall into temptation and a trap and into many foolish and harmful desires that plunge people into ruin and destruction. For the love of money is a root of all kinds of evil. Some people, eager for money, have wandered from the faith and pierced themselves with many griefs"*
(1 Timothy 6: 6–10).

Solomon writes of the futility of chasing after mammon: *"Whoever loves money never has enough; whoever loves wealth is never satisfied with their income. This too is meaningless"* (Ecclesiastes 5:10). Lust of any kind is insatiable, no matter how much time or effort is poured into the pursuit of the object of lust.

In Luke 16:14–15, Jesus rebukes those who refused to hear His admonition to choose God over mammon: *"The Pharisees, who loved money, heard all this and were sneering at Jesus. He said to them, 'You are the ones who justify yourselves in the eyes of others, but God knows your hearts. What people value highly is detestable in God's sight.'"*

The parable of the rich fool (Luke 12:13–21) is the story of a man who lives to increase his wealth yet in the end he loses his soul because he *"is not rich toward God"* (verse 21). Mark 4:19 warns of the deceitfulness of mammon and its ability to *"choke the Word, making it unfruitful."*
Mammon cannot produce peace in us, and it certainly cannot produce righteousness. A love of money shows we are out of balance in our relationship to God. Proverbs 8:18 speaks of true,

lasting riches: *"With me [Wisdom] are riches and honor, enduring wealth and prosperity."* Jesus teaches us in Matthew 6:19–34 to not worry about our physical needs, about houses or clothes or food, but to *"seek first his kingdom and his righteousness, and all these things will be given to you as well"* (verse 33).

To add, Mammon wrestles for God's seat in our life; Mammon says he is our source, Mammon is deceptive and Mammon influence is an excessive desire for money and wealth. You must dispose this mountain in your life in order to overtake the mountain. If you are in the money making business then you are under the influence.....Ask yourself daily, Money or God? Write down each day for 30 days, as you awake to go to work or to your business, your answer to why you work?.......Which one that is written down the most is who you will serve..........Mammon(Money) or God?

I did not know that I had made millions in my first business, in 2010, as a business owner. Money was not my precedence, helping people was the priority. It was until I had gotten under the idolatry and adultery influence when my eyes were open to buying cars, clothes, traveling; instead of loving my God, my family, the church, the community and others. The wanting/desire for millions of dollars will bring this Economy Mountain to your front doorstep. One has to understand the strongholds of the Canaanite Mountain of Economy, before asking for any type of large amount of money, from hundreds, thousands to millions; and keep it under the submission of the Blood of Jesus and His authority; in the name of Jesus.

When, you look at anything other than God as your source and your provider; you commit fornication with Mammon.

"Lord, Jehovah-Jireh, I come before you to destroy the mammon's generational curse through my bloodline and my husband/wife bloodline in Jesus name. I break the mammon curse over of my children lives, the church, and the community and in the schools; in Jesus name. I bind and loose the spirit of mammon over my job and businesses and other businesses, in Jesus name. I am no longer bound to mammon, but bound to

*Jesus, my Lord and Savior...the Provider and the Waymaker; in
Jesus Name. Amen."*

**Review of the Canaanite Mountain (represent love of the
money):**

Enemy of the Canaanite Mountain---Jehovah Jireh
Principality of the Mountain----Mammon(greed)
Significant Displacing Authority---- Prophets
Basic Mission----Stock Market, Traders, Buyers and Sellers
     Discover and transfer wealth into kingdom
purposes....Babylon will be shaken until it collapses, but those
who trust I the Lord will suffer no lack!

When God blesses us with the millions, trillions, and billions, how will I help build the Kingdom of God concerning "The Economy"?

"And the LORD answered me: "Write the vision; make it plain on tablets, so he may run who reads it." Habakkuk 2:2, ESV

Promised Land Sixteen
Jebusites
The Mountain of Family

As powerful Christian believers, we have to come together and "throw down" the Jebusites' spirit with the force of God. Jebusites are spiritually speaking "giants" of the Goliath type. They try to trample upon family lives and destinies. They try to keep families away from "possessing their possessions."

The Law of the Goliath is "let us fight just one battle and the looser surrenders all to the winner." Interpretation is to Sin. If you are defeated in one "sin", then you are guilty of all sin....If you commit fornication, then you have committed adultery ...and so forth.

Jebusites are the "giants" of sin. They are the spiritual strongholds of compromises in the lives of believers, churches, families, communities, workplace and schools; within the nation. Jebusites are the sins that pull you down in the form of addictions; such as drunkenness, drugs, sex, pornography, homosexuality, and so forth.

Our faith must win the war against the Goliath sin in order to be delivered from any other demonic stronghold that is connected to the Jebusites mountain. WE must grow stronger in Faith, Grow in Consecration and Sanctification, and Resist sin unto the Blood of Jesus.

Goliath – Who He Is?

The name Goliath means "great." Goliath was a famous giant from the Philistine city of Gath. For 40 days, he openly defied the armies of Israel, challenging them to send a man out to fight him. He was killed by the shepherd boy, David, with a single shot of a stone from his sling (1 Samuel 17:4). His height was "six cubits and a span;" taking the cubit at 21 inches, that's 10-1/2 feet tall. He had four brothers. David picked up five stones for his slingshot when he confronted Goliath. David cut off Goliath's head and carried it to Jerusalem; he hung Goliath's weapons in his own tent (1 Samuel 17:51, 53). Goliath's sword was later preserved at Nob as a religious trophy (1 Samuel 21:9). David's victory over Goliath was a turning point in his life.

Goliath – Part He Plays in the Bible?

Goliath represents the many obstacles and pitfalls we encounter in life, whether they are spiritual or physical. While we may never encounter giants in the flesh as physical enemies, we do encounter symbolic giants that can confront us in the spiritual and physical realm. These Goliaths will try to win over us, but, like David, we have the grace of God on our side; and God will empower us to confront and conquer those enormous giants. Like David, we can use the least of our weaponry to defeat them. We do not need heavy artillery for the job; all we need is the Power of prayer, the Word of God, the Strength to Fast, and God's grace to defeat whatever we encounter that keeps us fearful.

Goliath – Our Own Goliaths?

What are some of the Goliaths we face in life?

Intimidation. Unfortunately, the Israelites were dismayed and terrified (1 Samuel 17:11). Yet David, a young boy, faced the enemy with confidence. David trusted God because he had a relationship with Him, so he could stand up to any intimidation.

The Unbelieving World. The unbeliever is happy if the Christian is ineffective. But if you share the Gospel and tell people about God's wrath and judgment of sin, you may experience an intense hatred from the unbelieving world. Still, it is our duty to Christ, as Christians, to preach the truth, no matter what the cost may be, and to help fulfill The Great Commission.

Ignorance of Our Weapons. To fight the enemies of our world, we must learn to use the spiritual weapons within our reach. David's victory had more to do with his spiritual weapons than his skills with a slingshot. When we study God's Word, we put on a vital part of *"the full armor of God"* (Ephesians 6:11). We are challenged to *"stand firm then, with the belt of truth buckled around our waist, with the breastplate of righteousness in place, and with our feet fitted with the readiness that comes from the gospel of peace. In addition to all this, we have to take up the shield of faith, with which we can extinguish all the flaming arrows of the evil one. Take the helmet of salvation and the sword of the Spirit, which is the word of God"* (verses 14-17).

Believing You Are Alone in the Battle. Hebrews 13:5-6 assures us, *"'Never will I leave you, never will I forsake you.' So we say with confidence, "The Lord is my helper; I will not be afraid. What can man do to me?"'*

Not Exercising Faith. Faith is a powerful weapon against the enemy, and exercising that faith, whether small or large, will bring you great rewards. *"This is the victory that has overcome the world, even our faith. Who is it that overcomes the world? Only he who believes that Jesus is the Son of God"* (1 John 5:4-5).

Always remember with the Jebusites, no matter how holy, innocent, or anointed you may be, if you are not ready for combat, if you will not rise and defy them, subsequently, they will bring you down under their feet…and you will not be able to possess the Land that God promised to you, your family, your church, or your community.

The Family Role………..

"He will turn the hearts of the parents to their children, and the hearts of the children to their parents; or else I will come and strike the land with total destruction." (Malachi 4:6, NIV)

(Commentary) clause:
and the heart of the children to their fathers; or "with" their fathers; that is, both fathers and children: the meaning is, that

John the Baptist should be an instrument of converting many of
the Jews, both fathers and children, and bringing them to the
knowledge and faith of the true Messiah; and reconcile them
together who were divided by the schools of Hillell and
Shammai, and by the sects of the Sadducees and Pharisees, and
bring them to be of one mind, judgment, and faith, and to have a
hearty love to one another, and the Lord Christ. (Matthew 3:5
Matthew 3:6 Luke 1:17).

Hillel and Shammai

Hillel and Shammai were two leading sages, two individuals
of profound wisdom of the last 1st century BCE and the early 1st
century CE, who founded opposing schools of Jewish thought,
known as the House of Hillel and House of Shammai. The
debate between these schools on matters of ritual practice, ethics,
and theology was critical for the shaping of the Oral Law and
Judaism as it is today.

The people put more of their trust in Houses of Shammai and
Hillel; than in God. This is why it is so important to read the
Word of God; be **Still** until He reveals the secrets of the
Scriptures; while you are studying His Word and waiting for the
answers to your prayers. Some of our answers may not come
overnight; although, the answer will come at the right time.

God reveals His answers through many ways.......through a
vision, during a church sermon, through a co-worker, through a
stranger, through Bible reading, and so forth.

For example, I can remember someone ask me about a
certain necklace that I had purchase. I had my doubts, but I
didn't get a clear answer, from God, if the necklace had some
type of witchcraft symbol. I purchased the necklace and wore it
to church. A church member asked me what the necklace
represents. I told her, "I am very careful about what I purchase
because I do not want to purchase anything that holds an evil
symbolic." Eventually, I responded, "I am really not sure." The
look on her face made me wondered. (Warning sign 1). A week
later, a stranger approaches me and said your necklace look like
a "......" It was something that represented evil. My answer
came from a stranger at a store, actually, the store where I

purchased the necklace from. I took it off and tossed it in the trash. Your answers are all around you, but you have to be "quiet" and "still" enough to listen and take heed.

Despite the many disputes that later developed between their respective Houses, only five differences are recorded, but four are listed below, between Hillel and Shammai themselves. In the record of the Talmud alone, there are 316 issues on which they debated; the large number of their disputations led to the saying that one law has become two. The matters they debated included:

Admissions to Torah study. The House of Shammai believed only worthy students should be admitted to study Torah. The House of Hillel believed that Torah may be taught to anyone, in the expectation that they will repent and become worthy.

White lies. Whether one should tell an ugly bride that she is beautiful. Shammai said it was wrong to lie, and Hillel said that all brides are beautiful on their wedding day.

Divorce. The House of Shammai held that a man may only divorce his wife for a serious transgression, but the House of Hillel allowed divorce for even trivial offenses, such as burning a meal.

Hanukkah. The House of Shammai held that on the first night eight lights should be lit, and then they should decrease on each successive night, ending with one on the last night; while the House of Hillel held that one should start with one light and increase the number on each night, ending with eight.

In general, the House of Shammai's positions were stricter than those of the House of Hillel. On the few occasions when the opposite was true, the House of Hillel would sometimes later recant their position; similarly, though there are no records of the House of Shammai as a whole changing its stance, a few individuals from it are recorded as deserting a small number of the more stringent opinions of their school, in favor of the viewpoint of the House of Hillel.

The principles of the House of Shammai in relation to foreign policy were similar to those of the Zealots, among whom they, therefore, found support. As, over the course of the 1st century, public indignation against the Romans grew, the House of Shammai gradually gained the upper hand, and the gentle and conciliatory House of Hillel came to be ostracized, in other words; hated from the House of Shammai's public acts of prayer.

The **Zealots** were originally a political movement in 1st century Second Temple Judaism which sought to incite the people of Judaea Province to rebel against the Roman Empire and expel it from the Holy Land by force of arms, most notably during the First Jewish–Roman War (66-70). Zealotry was the term used by Josephus for a "fourth sect" during this period. The term "zealot", in Hebrew *kanai* (קנאי, frequently used in plural form, קנאים (*kana'im*)), means one who is zealous on behalf of God. The term derives from Greek ζηλωτής (*zelotes*), "emulator, zealous admirer or follower".

As the Jewish conflict with the Romans grew, the nations surrounding Judea (then part of Roman Judaea province) all sided with the Romans, causing the House of Shammai to propose that all commerce and communication between Jew and Gentile should be completely prohibited. The House of Hillel disagreed, but when the Sanhedrin convened to discuss the matter, the Zealots sided with the House of Shammai.

Subsequently Eleazar ben Ananias, the Temple captain and a leader of the militant Zealots, invited the students of both schools to meet at his house. Eleazar placed armed men at the door, and instructed them to let no-one leave the meeting. During the discussions many of the House of Hillel was killed; meaning that those present from the House of Shammai were able to force all the remaining individuals to adopt a radically restrictive set of rules known as The Eighteen Articles; later Jewish history came to look back on the occasion as a day of misfortune.

However, the fortunes of the House of Hillel improved after the First Jewish–Roman War, which had resulted in destruction of the Jewish Temple. Jewish leaders no longer had an appetite for war. Under Gamaliel II, the Sanhedrin, which was reconstituted in Yavne, reviewed all the points disputed by the House of Hillel; and this time it was their opinions which won the Sanhedrin's support. On most issues, it was said that whenever the House of Shammai had disputed the opinion of the House of Hillel, the House of Shammai's opinion was now null and void.

In the first century BCE, Babylonian born Hillel (later known as Hillel the Elder) migrated to the Land of Israel to study and worked as a woodcutter, eventually becoming the most influential force in Jewish life. Hillel is said to have lived in such great poverty that he was sometimes unable to pay the admission fee to study Torah, and because of him that fee was abolished.

Hillel was known for his kindness, gentleness, concern for humanity. One of his most famous sayings, recorded in Pirkei Avot (Ethics of the Fathers, a tractate of the Mishnah), is "If I am not for myself, then who will be for me? And if I am only for myself, then what am I? And if not now, when?"

The Hillel organization, a network of Jewish college student organizations, is named for him. Hillel and his descendants established academies of learning and were the leaders of the Jewish community in the Land of Israel for several centuries. The Hillel dynasty ended with the death of Hillel II in 365 CE.

Hillel the Elder's friendly adversary was Shammai, a native of the Land of Israel that was a builder, known for the strictness of his views. He was reputed to be dour, quick-tempered and impatient. Both lived during the reign of King Herod (37-4 BCE), an oppressive period in Jewish history because of the Roman occupation of the Land of Israel. Shammai was concerned that if Jews had too much contact with the Romans, the Jewish community would be weakened; and this attitude was reflected in his strict interpretation of Jewish law. Hillel did not share Shammai's fear and therefore was more liberal in his view of law.

Hillel was the more popular of the two scholars, and he was chosen by the Sanhedrin, the supreme Jewish court, to serve as its president. While Hillel and Shammai themselves did not differ on a great many basic issues of Jewish law, their disciples were often in conflict. The Talmud records over 300 differences of opinion between Beit Hillel (the House of Hillel) and Beit Shammai (the House of Shammai). The Rabbis of the Talmud generally sided with the rulings of the School of Hillel, although the Sages believed that both views were valid. Sixteenth-century kabbalist Rabbi Isaac Luria (the "Ari") said that not only are both the words of the House of Shammai and the House of Hillel enduring on the conceptual level, but each has its time and place on the pragmatic level as well.

In our present world, we follow the rulings of the House of Hillel, but in the era of Messiah, the majority opinion will shift in favor of the House of Shammai, and their rulings will then be implemented. The Ari believed that in our present reality, where divine commandments must be imposed upon an imperfect world, the rulings of the House of Hillel represent the ultimate in conformity to the divine will, while the rulings of the House of Shammai represent an ideal that is too lofty for our present state (which is why we perceive them as "stricter" and more confining), and can only be realized on the conceptual level. In the era of Messiah, the situation will be reversed: a perfected world will embrace the more exacting application of Torah law expressed by the House of Shammai, while the Hillelian school of interpretation will endure only conceptually.

Hillel's rulings were often based on concern for the welfare of the individual. For example with regard to the remarriage of an *aguna*, whose husband is not known with certainty to be alive or dead, the view of Hillel (and most of his colleagues) was that she can remarry even on the basis of indirect evidence of the husband's death. Bet Shammai required that witnesses come forth with direct testimony before she was permitted to remarry.

Another example of his leniency as compared with Shammai involves converts; Hillel favored the admission of proselytes into Judaism even when they made unreasonable demands, such as one did by demanding that the whole Torah be taught to him quickly "while standing on one foot." Hillel accepted this person as eligible for conversion, whereas Shammai dismissed him as not serious about Judaism.

"Who were the Sadducees and the Pharisees?"

The Gospels refer often to the Sadducees and Pharisees, as Jesus was in constant conflict with them. The Sadducees and Pharisees comprised the ruling class of Israel. There are many similarities between the two groups but important differences between them as well.

The Sadducees: During the time of Christ and the New Testament era, the Sadducees were aristocrats. They tended to be wealthy and held powerful positions, including that of chief priests and high priest, and they held the majority of the 70 seats of the ruling council called the Sanhedrin. They worked hard to keep the peace by agreeing with the decisions of Rome (Israel at this time was under Roman control), and they seemed to be more concerned with politics than religion. Because they were accommodating to Rome and were the wealthy upper class, they did not relate well to the common man, nor did the common man hold them in high opinion. The common man related better to those who belonged to the party of the Pharisees. Though the Sadducees held the majority of seats in the Sanhedrin, history indicates that much of the time they had to go along with the ideas of the Pharisaic minority, because the Pharisees were popular with the masses.

Religiously, the Sadducees were more conservative in one main area of doctrine. The Pharisees gave oral tradition equal authority to the written Word of God, while the Sadducees considered only the written Word to be from God. The Sadducees preserved the authority of the written Word of God, especially the books of Moses (Genesis through Deuteronomy). While they could be commended for this, they definitely were not perfect in their doctrinal views. The following is a brief list of beliefs they held that contradict Scripture:

1. They were extremely self-sufficient to the point of denying God's involvement in everyday life.

2. They denied any resurrection of the dead (Matthew 22:23; Mark 12:18-27; Acts 23:8).

3. They denied any afterlife, holding that the soul perished at death, and therefore denying any penalty or reward after the earthly life.

4. They denied the existence of a spiritual world; for example: angels and demons (Acts 23:8).

Because the Sadducees were more concerned with politics than religion, they were unconcerned with Jesus until they became afraid He might bring unwanted Roman attention. It was at this point that the Sadducees and Pharisees united and conspired to put Christ to death (John 11:48-50; Mark 14:53; 15:1). Other mentions of the Sadducees are found in Acts 4:1 and Acts 5:17, and the Sadducees are implicated in the death of James by the historian Josephus (Acts 12:1-2).

The Sadducees ceased to exist in A.D. 70. Since this party existed because of their political and priestly ties, when Rome destroyed Jerusalem and the temple in A.D. 70, the Sadducees were also destroyed.

The Pharisees: In contrast to the Sadducees, the Pharisees were mostly middle-class businessmen, and therefore were in contact with the common man. The Pharisees were held in much higher esteem by the common man than the Sadducees. Though they were a minority in the Sanhedrin and held a minority number of positions as priests, they seemed to control the decision making of the Sanhedrin far more than the Sadducees did, again because they had the support of the people.

Religiously, they accepted the written Word as inspired by God. At the time of Christ's earthly ministry, this would have been what our Old Testament is, now. But they also gave equal authority to oral tradition and attempted to defend this position by saying it went all the way back to Moses. Evolving over the centuries, these traditions added to God's Word, which is forbidden (Deuteronomy 4:2), and the Pharisees sought to strictly obey these traditions along with the Old Testament. The Gospels abound with examples of the Pharisees treating these traditions as equal to God's Word (Matthew 9:14; 15:1-9; 23:5; 23:16, 23, Mark 7:1-23; Luke 11:42). However, they did remain true to God's Word in reference to certain other important doctrines. In contrast to the Sadducees, they believed the following:

1. They believed that God controlled all things, yet decisions made by individuals also contributed to the course of a person's life.

2. They believed in the resurrection of the dead (Acts 23:6).

3. They believed in an afterlife, with appropriate reward and punishment on an individual basis.

4. They believed in the existence of angels and demons (Acts 23:8).

Though the Pharisees were rivals of the Sadducees, they managed to set aside their differences on one occasion; the trial of Christ. It was at this point that the Sadducees and Pharisees united to put Christ to death (Mark 14:53; 15:1; John 11:48-50).

While the Sadducees ceased to exist after the destruction of Jerusalem, the Pharisees, who were more concerned with religion than politics, continued to exist. In fact, the Pharisees were against the rebellion that brought on Jerusalem's destruction in A.D. 70, and they were the first to make peace with the Romans afterward. The Pharisees were also responsible for the compilation of the Mishnah, an important document with reference to the continuation of Judaism beyond the destruction of the temple.

Both the Pharisees and the Sadducees earned numerous rebukes from Jesus. Perhaps the best lesson we can learn from the Pharisees and Sadducees is to not be like them. Unlike the Sadducees, we are to believe everything the Bible says, including the miraculous and the afterlife. Unlike the Pharisees, we are not to treat traditions as having equal authority as Scripture, and we are not to allow our relationship with God to be reduced to a legalistic list of rules and rituals.

The Psychosomatic illness caused by the family breakdown.

The family breakdown has caused many unprecedented social and physical ills, in which has created unloving parents. Parents are the key, although God, El Elyon, the "Most High" is the source, in any family relationship. Unloving parents cause many mental illnesses and disorders. We will talk about the psychosomatic illness that stems from unloving parents. Based on research, about 85% of all health problems are related to psychosomatic.

Psychosomatic means that a physical condition is caused or greatly influenced by psychological; mental or emotional factors. The psychosomatic approach to health views illness as a form of communication between the conscious and the unconscious mind through the body. Illness is a person's way of adapting to the environment. It is a message that communicates a need for change. However, very few people interpret their illness as a form of communication or symptom of deeper problems. The most common solution of relieving the pain or the struggles that one faces is by medication and therapy, instead of seeking God for healing and deliverance.

Examples of psychosomatic illness

- Illness is a legitimate way to **avoid something unpleasant**. Illness can be a subconscious mechanism of defense. There are many situations that people would rather avoid rather than deal with.
- **Love and attention**. When people get sick, they receive attention; love and warmth from family members or friends.
- **Purpose crisis**. There is a point in time when people begin to ask the question; what is the purpose of my life? Unable to answer this question, some people turn their illness into their purpose in life. Everything begins to revolve around the illness; their self-known purpose, not God's purpose.

To add, when dealing with psychological issues, the unhappiness weakens the immune system which causes all types of physical diseases. Based on research, some physical diseases are thought to be particularly prone to be made worse by mental factors such as stress and anxiety stemming from the psychological state of mind; for example, psoriasis, eczema, stomach ulcers, high blood pressure and heart disease. It is thought that the actual physical part of the illness, the extent of a rash, the level of the blood pressure, can be affected by mental factors.

Also, some people also use the term psychosomatic disorder as a physical disease that is thought to be caused or made worse by mental factors; when mental factors cause physical symptoms, although, there is no physical disease. For example, a chest pain may be caused by stress and no physical disease can be found.

The #1 cause of emotional trauma is a dysfunctional family foundation.

The definitions of family placed on us by society are:
1. The traditional family is a basic social unit consisting of parents and their children, considered as a group, whether dwelling together or not:
2.   A single-parent family is social unit consisting of one or more adults together with the children they care for:

Now, allow us to go into depth based on the Biblical Family.

"How does the Bible define a good Christian family?"

A good Christian family is one which lines up with biblical principles; and one in which each member understands and fulfills his or her God-given role. The family is not an institution designed by man. It was created by God, and man has been given the responsibility of stewardship over it. The basic biblical family unit is comprised of one man, one woman, his spouse, and their offspring or adopted children. The extended family can include relatives by blood or marriage such as grandparents, nieces, nephews, cousins, aunts and uncles. One of the primary principles of the family unit is that it involves a commitment ordained by God for the lifetime of the members. The husband and wife are responsible for holding it together, the current attitude of our culture, notwithstanding. Although divorce is sought and granted much too easily in our society, the Bible tells us that God hates divorce.

"For the man who does not love his wife but divorces her, says the LORD, the God of Israel, covers his garment with violence, says the LORD of hosts. So guard yourselves in your spirit, and do not be faithless." (Malachi 2:16, ESV)

Ephesians 5:22-26 provide the guidelines for husbands and wives in a good Christian family. The husband is required to love his wife as Christ loved the church, and a wife should respect her husband and willingly submit to his leadership in the family. The husband's leadership role should start with spiritual matters and then flow to instructing and teaching both his wife and their offspring scriptural values, leading the family into biblical truth. Of course, the first requirement for the members of a good Christian family is that they all be Christians, having a true relationship with Jesus Christ as their Lord and Savior.

Fathers are instructed to bring up their children in the training and instruction of the Lord (Ephesians 6:4). A father is also to provide for his family. If he does not, he *"denies the faith and is worse than an unbeliever"* (1Timothy 5:8). So a man who makes no effort to provide for his family cannot rightly call himself a Christian. This does not mean that the wife cannot assist in supporting the family. While, Proverbs 31 demonstrates that a godly wife may surely do so, but providing for the family is not primarily her responsibility; it is her husband's.

Woman was given to man for the purpose of being her husband's helper (Genesis 2:18-20) and to bear children. Husband and wife are to remain faithful to one another for a lifetime. This eliminates the cultural view that divorce, living together without being married and same-sex marriage is acceptable in God's eyes. Sexuality expressed according to biblical standards is a beautiful expression of love and commitment. Outside of marriage, it is sin. God declares equality of worth in that all people, men and women, are created in God's image and likeness, and are therefore equally valuable in His eyes. This does not mean, however, that men and women have identical roles in life. Women are more adept at nurturing and caring for the young, while men are better equipped to provide for and protect the family. **Thus, they are equal in status, but**

each has a different role to play.

Children are given two primary responsibilities in the family: to obey their parents and to honor them, as stated in Ephesians 6:1-3. Obeying (which is do as you are told), parents is the duty of children until they reach adulthood; but we are to honor, which is respect, our parents for a lifetime. God promises His blessings on those who honor, with the highest respect, their parents.

When a husband, wife and children all fulfill their God-appointed roles in the family, when they have all committed their lives to Christ and to His service, then peace and harmony will reign in the home. But if we try to have a good Christian family without Christ as Head, or without adhering to the biblical principles the Lord has lovingly provided for us, we will fail.

The Key to a Successful Family is that family should model the institution designed by God; not man, with one husband and one wife and children.

Let us continue........

By the fathers turning against the children causes a spin off from Satan implied in 2 Timothy 3:1-4.." *1 But mark this: There will be terrible times in the last days. 2 People will be lovers of themselves, lovers of money, boastful, proud, abusive, <u>disobedient to their parents,</u> ungrateful, unholy, 3 without love, unforgiving, slanderous, without self-control, brutal, not lovers of the good, 4 treacherous, rash, conceited, lovers of pleasure rather than lovers of God—"*

The children behavior stated in 2 Timothy 3:1-4 is disobedient to parents, unthankful, unforgiving, without self-control, and headstrong. We have to remember we all are somebody's children. Therefore this does not rule out adults, which is 18 and over. This is for every person, child or adult, because we all have a father and a mother. For that purpose, "We" all are the children in 2 Timothy 3:1-4.

The breakdowns of family are caused by many factors, to name are few are: drug use, illegal sexual activity, the inability to secure gainful employment, jail sentences, and so forth.

Jebusites places a trodden down, "rejection" spirit, in an individual's mind. Rejection is the Spirit of the Mountain that must be disposed. Rejection is the refusal to accept, consider, and submit to authority of holiness and righteousness; which is God's principles and standards.

Why does rejection wound us so deeply?

Rejection attacks the very person that we are. It destroys our self-esteem, and attacks who we are and our purpose in life. This is why it is one of the most common tools the devil will use to destroy a person's life. God never wanted us to feel rejected or abandon. He desires for us to know who we really are; and realize how deeply He loves, accepts, and appreciates you, so that you can live out the fullness of what all "God has Chosen" you to be. God's Word tells us that without being rooted and grounded in the His love (and acceptance) and the love of Jesus, we cannot experience the fullness of God in our lives:

"And to know the love of Christ, which passeth knowledge, that ye might be filled with all the fulness of God. "Ephesians 3:19

Rejection has a way of destroying a person's life in a way of the person not knowing or understanding the attacks. The heartrending fact is that the number of people who are affected by rejection staggers in relationships; while putting the blame on the other person. If we want to be all that God has created us to be, then overcoming rejection and its effects are vital and absolutely essential.

The fruit of rejection

Many people who have faced rejection; especially the ones that were abused as a child, grew up with unresolved emotional wounds. Rejection causes emotional wounds, which if not cleansed and released, that will grow and fester into spiritual wounds, such as, unforgiveness, envy, blaming God, jealousy, etc. Those spiritual wounds open up to evil spirits, which find irresistible, to take advantage of the opportunity to invade us. The goal of the enemy is to build us up with destructive emotional baggage inside, such as, negative feelings towards others in our hearts, and against one another, ourselves, and God.

Rejection has a lot of unhealthy fruit which can widely vary from one person to another. Some of the common symptoms of rejection include:

- Rebellion in both children and adults
- Fabricated personalities (being somebody you are not, in order to be accepted)
- The tendency to reject others, so that you are not the first one to be rejected
- A tendency to always wonder if a person rejects or accepts you
- The need to fit in or be accepted by others and be a part of everything
- Self-pity where a person feels bad for themselves and tend to be all alone
- Inability to be corrected or receive constructive criticism
- Rejection creates an environment where you are starved for love or just do not fit in
- A tendency to blame God ("Why did He give me this big nose? Why did God make me so short?")
- A sense of pride that says, "How dare they reject me!"
- Opinionated personality and the need to be right about things
- Feelings of worthlessness, insecurity, or hopelessness
- Seeking a parent's approval is a sign that you are basing your identity upon what they think of you
- Envy, jealousy, and even hate can be rooted in rejection
- Fear of confrontation (because your identity is based upon what they think of you)

Counseling and medication cannot destroy the demon; only the Lord, YAHWEH-RAPHA, "the Lord who Heals" is able to, which is God's love penetrating into our hearts.

Rejections can easily be mis-interpreted by minor children. **For example: 1. Stern words or actions by parents.** Sometimes that "tough love" is damaging to our society because of the worldly activities and peer pressure that is already striking our young people in the face on a daily basis.

2. Comparing children to children. Example; you need to dress like your older sibling; your brother went to law-school, why don't you?

3. Divorce/Rejection on husband/wife. One may feel that they were not well-behaved enough in the marriage; which leads to personal self-esteem issues. Also, the kids may blame themselves for the divorce; especially the male children.

For example, the rejections by the children may be the thinking that they were not smart enough in school or made too many bad decisions at home, in school or in the community, which caused some heated arguments between the husband and wife.

To add, rejection by fathers develops sexual identity in boys and girls. Boys seek other males for approval, which leads to homosexuality. Girls never receive the flowers of being a woman; therefore, they will never seek a male for anything; which opens the door for lesbianism.

Who is the King of the Jebusites? The principality of the Jebusites is Baal. Baal means master, owner, lord. Once Baal takes precedents over God, subsequently, Jezebel enters in through Baal.

Jezebel (/ˈdʒɛzəbəl/, Hebrew: אִיזָבֶל / אִיזֶבֶל, Modern *Izével / Izável* Tiberian *ʾÎzéḇel / ʾÎzāḇel*) (fl. 9th century BCE) was a princess, identified in the Hebrew Book of Kings as the daughter of Ethbaal, King of Tyre (Lebanon/Phoenicia) and the wife of Ahab, king of northern Israel.

According to the biblical accounts, Jezebel incited her husband King Ahab to abandon the worship of Yahweh and encourage worship of the deities Baal and Asherah instead.

Also, Jezebel is said to have persecuted the prophets of Yahweh, and to have fabricated false evidence of blasphemy against an innocent landowner who refused to sell his property to King Ahab, causing the landowner to be put to death.

In addition, Jezebel became associated with false prophets. In some interpretations, her dressing in finery and putting on makeup led to the association, today, of the use of cosmetics with "painted women" or prostitutes.

For these transgressions against God and people of Israel, the Bible relates, Jezebel met a gruesome death, thrown out of a window by members of her own court retinue/entourage; and the flesh of her corpse eaten by stray dogs.

Jezebel is the Anglicized transliteration of the Hebrew לְבָזִיא ('Izevel/'Izavel). *The Oxford Guide to People & Places of the Bible* states that the name is "best understood as meaning 'Where is the Prince?'", a ritual cry from worship ceremonies in honor of Baal during periods of the year when the god was considered to be in the underworld.

Furthermore, Jebusites spirits enter through families in abortions.

--An abortion is the medical process of ending a pregnancy so it does not result in the birth of a baby.

--It is also sometimes known as a 'termination' or a 'termination of pregnancy'.

--Depending on how many weeks you have been pregnant, the pregnancy is ended either by taking medication or by having a surgical procedure.

An abortion is not the same as a <u>miscarriage</u>, which is where the pregnancy is lost or ends naturally. The loss starts without medical intervention, although medical or surgical treatment may be needed after a miscarriage has started to help empty the womb.

Many people use abortions for many other reasons. Some reason may seem valid; however, we must always allow God to take course in every pregnancy. Some people use abortions for **personal circumstance, in which we should still allow God to take the course;** including risk to the wellbeing of the unborn child or to the mother…

- a health risk to the mother
- a high chance the baby will have a serious abnormality; either genetic or physical

There are many selfish reasons that follow a "so-called unwanted pregnancy", such as, "We cannot afford another child." Once the thought of abortion or the act of the abortions, which leads to rejections from husband/wife, also, may create adulterous relationships, then confusion, then arguments, then trust issues and so forth.

We have to always remember when thinking of these "so-called" valid reasons, one is really entertaining the Jebusites mountain. Allow God to take control when a "so-called unwanted pregnancy" takes place.

Homosexuality, Lesbianism, and Abortions are the worshippers that strengthen the Baal. The church needs to not accept "homosexuality, lesbianism, nor abortions" in no form of fashion. These 3 types of sin/abomination need to stay at the altar, daily; not just on Sunday and Bible Study night.
.

What is our strategy in defeating the Jebusite Mountain?

The pastors play the biggest displacing authority on top of this mountain because pastors are the nurturers and caregivers.

Role of Pastors

Ephesians 2:20, *"Together, we are his house, built on the foundation of the apostles and the prophets. And the cornerstone is Christ Jesus himself."*
Pastors have to understand that they need the apostles and prophets in the churches for the foundations.

Pastors need to be very hands-on and sincere about God's mercy and grace. Pastors need to take on the one-on-one personal care of the Lord in providing care and nurturing for the sheep that are assigned to them; instead of the administration, teaching, and laying out the vision.

Women Pastors are very important in the church. Women Pastors are much more needed in destroying the Jebusites Mountain because they are more wired for intercession than men pastors. Women are more nurturing than men. Because of a woman's nurturing and caring instinct, they can better represent the heart of our Good Sheppard when comforting the Jebusites Mountain. Men and Women Pastors need to work closely together and delete the "so-called masculine" role gender that have seduced many churches around the world.

Marketplace Pastors

We need some marketplace Pastors. Marketplace Pastors need to be geared, with the anointing of God, showing healing, redemption, and acceptance of Christ. Marketplace Pastors should be on the jobs/businesses in the: front and back offices of establishments, warehouses, grocery stores, outside laboring jobs and so forth. Marketplace **Pastors need to reach the men first; then the women. Why? Men are head; enough said!!**

Government Service Pastors

The Department of Health and Human Services (HHS) is the United States government's principal agency for protecting the health of all Americans and providing essential human services. Each state has their own Department of the (HHS) principal agency. The Department of Children and Families is Florida agency.

Social workers bring their unique skills to helping two increasingly vulnerable groups: children and families. In all, about 16% of the country, half a million social workers work in child services while 12% work in family services.

A range of factors, which includes poverty, homelessness, alcohol and drug addiction, child abuse and neglect make today's families more susceptible than ever to splitting apart. In fact, less than half of America's children live in a traditional nuclear family, according to statistics.

The late George Murdock, an influential observer of families, offered an early description: The family is a social group characterized by common residence, economic cooperation and reproduction. It contains adults of both sexes, at least two of whom maintain a socially approved sexual relationship, and one or more children, own or adopted, of the sexually cohabiting adults.

Fortunately, social workers have a wide array of tools to help children and families to better cope with the normal stresses of life and to deal with systemic problems such as child abuse and homelessness through assessment, support, counseling, resource coordination and advocacy. Social workers:

- Counsel families to find better solutions to their problems;
- Place abused children in loving homes;
- Find employment and housing for homeless families;
- Help pregnant women, adoptive parents and adopted children navigate the adoption system; and
- Help children and families make best use of the welfare system.

In all of these arenas, social workers use systems and family-oriented approaches to helping families cope. The adoption system is a good example. Social workers counsel pregnant women, conduct home studies of potential adoptive parents, find suitable matches of adoptive parents and children and help adoptive parents deal with the struggles unique to adopted children. Increasingly, they also provide post-adoption counseling to help older adoptees deal with issues of self-identity, loss and self esteem, as well as, medical problems that may have a genetic component. What's more, adoption helps to reduce the act of abortions.

Social workers provide a wide range of services in the foster-care system as well. These services are critical as the number of children in foster care continues to rise. In this field of work, social workers assess at risk families to determine if a child needs placement. They evaluate potential foster homes, monitor the foster home during placement and help legal authorities and the family to determine an appropriate time to return the child to the family of origin.

A growing component of social work practice actually aims to make foster care services a thing of the past. Using a system known as family preservation services, social workers are key members of teams that work to keep families intact. Some of these interventions include helping stabilize immediate crises, maintaining and strengthening family relationships, increasing families coping skills and competencies and helping families to access useful services.

Social workers also help women and their children who are victims of domestic violence. In a typical case, a social worker at a shelter helped a battered woman and her two sons get back on their feet. She counseled the woman one-on-one, arranged for transportation to get the boys to and from school, and helped the woman develop goals and life skills so she could afford housing and child care once she and the boys left the shelter. The social worker also helped the woman find affordable housing and helped her contact a lawyer who specialized in abuse cases. Indeed, the social worker was essential to helping the woman develop a new and healthier life for herself and her boys....which is the many dedicated roles of a Social Worker.

I have search the pay grade for Social Workers, which is the job description for this positions. According to www.payscale.com, a U.S. survey, women account for the majority of Family Service Workers in the United States. The entire group has an average salary of $12.77 per hour. Earnings sit near $9.59 per hour on the lower side but can approach $17.05 on the higher side. Medical benefits are awarded to most; and a majority earns dental coverage. Most workers in this position report high levels of job satisfaction. The data for this snapshot was collected from individuals who took PayScale's salary survey.

- Assist in educating parents in behavior and life skills, individual and group classes.
- Assess quality of care by visiting home and residential sites.
- Act as a liaison with parents and treatment professionals.
- Manage caseload and follow-up care.

Though it's uncommon, some Family Service Workers move into roles as MSW Social Workers, where pay is an average $41K per year. Family Service Workers moving up in their careers tend to step into positions as Child, Family, or School Social Workers or Social Services Case Managers. The median paychecks in those roles are $5K higher and $2K higher, respectively.

We need more pastors in the field of Social Workers. There are many grants available to help with social programs. The pastors, whom are truly Sheppards of the flocks, are on this assignment not for pay, but, as a social infrastructure for our nation.

Judges Who Are Pastors

WE need judges that are Holy Spirit-filled and understand God's vision for the earth. We need the judges that are pastors, who know that God really considers them as pastors and are willing to bring His light into the judicial system without compromising.

Truth be told, it is not the faces on the mountains, but the laws that govern family relationships. We need pastors at the Supreme Court level to create the Christian based laws and ordinances that govern the "family". Pastors along with their congregations need a "Fighting Will of God's standards" to take on the "The Supreme Court" and the family legal issues of the nation. Also, Family Services agencies and programs need intercessors praying without ceasing:

1 Thessalonians 5:17 "….pray without ceasing,…….."

Top of the Jebusites Mountain—The Supreme Court
Middle of the Jebusites Mountain—Judges
Low Level of the Jebusites Mountain—Pastors

While we are battling on this mountain, we need to **Decree and Declare** in the Family Service programs, that the Lord, "Himself" is the "Father" of All Families. Our God is EL, ELOAH; God "mighty, strong, prominent" for all Families.

Psalm 68:5-6, "Father of the fatherless and protector of widows is God in his holy habitation……

He is the "Father of the fatherless". God already knew beforehand, that the earthly fathers would become weak and fail "family". The "Protector of the widows"……he knew there would be widows without husbands.

Now, we can better understand why God sent his Son, Jesus, which is a "male" to save the world. Jesus "male" is LOVED; there is Love in a "male" figure----that gave His life. Our father, God, which gave his only begotten son........LOVE in a "male"

EL, ELOAH, our God, mighty, strong, and prominent, I thank you for loving me like a father. I will no longer seek a father's love or comfort from any other outside source or earthly father. Rejection no longer holds me in bondage. I have been loved by the Savior of all my wrongs. Thank you, my Heavenly Father! In Jesus name. Amen.

Therefore, **Man**, you will no longer be bound by the spirit of homosexual, you are Loved by Jesus....**Woman**, you will no longer be bound by the spirit of lesbian, you are Loved by Jesus.....Parents you are no longer bound by the spirit of abortion....the Child is Loved by Jesus. **We no longer claim homosexuality, lesbianism, or abortions because we have found God that loves Us through Jesus; His only begotten Son that died on the cross for our sins!!**

WE need both prayer and actions as our strategy mechanism. Our Preventative Strategy is establishing and defending laws that strengthen family units. Our Redemptive Strategy is restoring, rebuilding and recovering families that have been lost.

"You shall not mistreat any widow or fatherless child. If you do mistreat them, and they cry out to me, I will surely hear their cry, and my wrath will burn, and I will kill you with the sword, and your wives shall become widows and your children fatherless."Exodus 22:22-24

The widows and the fatherless are the Champions at the Mountain of the Jebusites. WE need to forcefully reach them and tell them about Jesus; and His saving grace. Satan is no competition with the widows and the fatherless. I believe with all my heart that the ones that have been rejected through fatherlessness are the greatest "Warriors" for this mountain.

Oh, Lord I break the curse of fear off of every rejected fatherless child and widow in the mighty name of Jesus. I take authority of rejection, depression, fear, sexual deviances, addictions, anger, and violence due to unprecedented family breakdown. Your word says in Exodus 22:22,... **" that we shall not mistreat any widow or fatherless child".** *I speak restoration of a Fatherly love, Your Love and Kindness, in Jesus name. Amen.*

Enemy on the Mountain: Jebusites (represents rejection)
Significant Displacing Authority: Pastors
Basic Mission: Impact social systems so that the family unit is prioritized
Revelation 5:12 Key: Strength

When God blesses us with the millions, trillions, and billions, how will I help build the Kingdom of God concerning "The Family"?

"And the LORD answered me: "Write the vision; make it plain on tablets, so he may run who reads it." Habakkuk 2:2, ESV

_____

_____

_____

_____

_____

_____

_____

_____

_____

_____

_____

_____

_____

_____

_____

_____

_____

_____

_____

_____

_____

_____

_____

_____

Promised Land Seventeen
The Hivites
The Mountain of Celebration

The Mountain of Celebration includes art, music, sports, fashion, entertainment, and every other approach that we celebrate and enjoy life. All these types of celebrations move through the creativity and passion of people.

How powerful is the creativity of celebration through the passion and skillfulness of people? For example, through people and their passion, Christian music can revolve into secular music. I have experienced this in church. While the musician was playing a praise worship song, we were all (we thought) was high in the spirit, became a secular song by one change of keynote. Once church was over, my husband and daughter ask, "Did you hear when he changed the note to ---------", which was a club secular note. I was like, Oh my!!!!

Also, fashion designers may design provocative clothing for sales. We have some of the greatest fashion designers out there in the nation. But, if their sales are not where they want them, they start to compromise with the world to sale more clothing and; then, become a worldly household name for the rich and famous.

The Hivites Spirit counterfeit and imitate true celebration with corrupt substitutes and; wherein, opens the doors of the Jezebel spirit to enter in, which seduces people from the true pleasures and joy offered by God. In addition, this spirit of Jezebel prostitutes the good gifts of God.

"For He has strengthened the bars of your gates; He has blessed your sons within you." Psalm 147:13, NASB

"Father, I thank you for strengthened the bars of my gate where there will be no entrance for the Hivites Spirit to enter in as I celebrate You and Your goodness, In Jesus name. Amen."

Role of the prophets...

Prophets must see the roles of the deceptions of pop-culture and offer real and lasting alternative to society; especially designed for the youth and the teens of this generations.

This is where the Christian-based schools of music, drama, fashion, art, and the like, come into existence. These schools will allow the talent, skillfulness and creativeness to flow from spirituality, without the many disruptions of the world. Have you notice that many of the hip-hop stars have built music-based schools? The Music industry is the top leading stronghold on this mountain of Hivites. We are behind on the programme. God-fearing Christians we need to get in full circle with activities, for our crying nation, of young people.

Hivites mean "villager" or "dweller" in a small village or small town. Many of our top secular musician and singers come from small towns. Some of the top selling secular musicians appear from places we have never heard of before. The Hebrew root word is "**life** giver", "dweller in a life-giving village or town." The dwelling place is translated into a deceptive fraud using fleshly feelings and thoughts to satisfy the soul. One's deception is lured by illusions, delusions and sensual snares. These deceptions are placed in the mind and the mind is trapped in the imaginations of these snares. The snares or traps promise pleasures and prosperity at the expense of our "lives"; instead of seeking God's will for eternal value and reward.

The Hivites spirit comes in form of a magician's demon possessed delusion, that it is God's will for us to be rich/pleasure seekers. This type of delusion is created through self-will, self-seeking, pleasure of self, and idol worshipping. All of these types of delusions are a small amount of Satan's Promises of "Life" through pleasure seeking. The most common statement of all times, "You Only Live Once, Why Not Live!" translated into "The Bucket List".

Once the Hivite spirit has been uncovered and confronted, then many destructive mechanisms follow. The Hivites Spirit tries to clutch on to the flesh, the soul; as long as possible, through anger, hatred, temper, sometimes murder and divorcing of parents, causing destruction in the family structure.

Always remember this scripture, in Isaiah 54:17, when these signs develop, *"No weapon that is formed against you will prosper; And every tongue that accuses you in judgment you will condemn. This is the heritage of the servants of the LORD, And their vindication is from Me," declares the LORD."*

The weapons of the Hivites spirit may form, but they will not prosper…this is God promise, therefore, do not fear the attacks or the weapons; keep praying until there is full healing and deliverance from snares and traps of the enemy.

What are some other promises of the Hivites Mountain that keeps us entangled……..to name a few:

Bright lights, Loud music, Rock music, Las Vegas parties, Christian rock-music, world-wide tours with all the costumes and flashing background displaying drugs, alcohol, night clubs decorated in bright lights and so forth. These illusions attracts our attention and keeps us mesmerize; the "wow" how beautiful, gorgeous, exquisite and superb of the scenery. Once the beguile has taken control, then the "Living" life of taking a cigarette, alcohol, drugs, and sexual pleasures arises, whereas, the souls of God have become weaken and sold to the alluring power of Satan.

Seduction……Alluring Power…………..then Destruction!

"What does the Bible say about music?"

Music is an inherent part of every society. The unearthly sounds of throat-singing in Mongolia and Siberia are as important to their cultures as Bach is to European cultures or drum-driven song and dance are to Native American cultures. Since music is such an important part of life, it should not be surprising that the Bible says much about it; in fact, the longest book in the Bible is its song book; Psalms.

Psalms accounts for over 7 percent of the Old Testament. In addition to the Psalms are other song and poetry focused books such as Song of Solomon, Ecclesiastes, and others. In the New Testament, we have song lyrics recorded in

Revelation 5, 7, and 15; the mention of Jesus and the disciples singing in Matthew 26:30; and the example of the apostles' singing in Acts 16:25. Many people also consider Mary's *Magnificat* in Luke 1:46—55 and the angels' announcement in Luke 2:14 to be songs. The church is commanded to communicate with each other "with psalms, hymns, and songs from the Spirit. *"Sing and make music from your heart to the Lord"* (Ephesians 5:19).

Recorded musicians and music in the Old Testament:

The first reference to a musician in the Bible is in Genesis 4:21. Jubal was the fourth generation from Adam through Cain and is recorded as *"the father of all those who play the lyre and pipe."* Other early references to music include Exodus 15, which records Moses and the Israelites singing a song of victory after the overthrow of the Egyptian army in the Red Sea. At that time, Moses' sister, Miriam, led the Israelite women "with tambourines and dancing" as she sang. When Jephthah returned from battle, Jephthah's daughter met him with timbrels and dance in Judges 11:34. David's victories were also celebrated in song in 1 Samuel 18:6—7.

Two of the Old Testament's most important figures wrote songs: Moses and David. Moses has three songs recorded in the Bible: the song sung after the destruction of Pharaoh's army (Exodus 15:1–18); a song recounting the faithfulness of God and the rebelliousness of Israel, which he sang before all the people just before his death (Deuteronomy 32:1–43); and a prayer recorded in Psalm 90.

David, "the sweet psalmist of Israel" (2 Samuel 23:1), is credited with writing about half of the 150 songs recorded in Psalms, along with some in the historical books. He was the official musician in Saul's court (1 Samuel 16:14–23). During David's own reign, he organized the Levitical musicians, and 1 Chronicles 15:16 and 23:5 record that more than one in ten Levites in temple service were musicians.

Other musicians include Asaph (12 psalms), the sons of Korah (10 psalms), Solomon (two psalms and 1,005 other songs [1 Kings 4:32] and the Song of Solomon), Heman (one psalm), and Ethan (one psalm).

Music was used in conjunction with all manner of activities (Genesis 31:27; Exodus 32:17–18; Numbers 27:17; Judges 11:34, 35; Isaiah 16:10; Jeremiah 48:33). Music was used at coronations (1 Kings 1:39–40; 2 Kings 11:14; 2 Chronicles 13:14; 20:28), events in the royal court (2 Samuel 19:35; Ecclesiastes 2:8), and feasts (Isaiah 5:12; 24:8–9). It is interesting to note the connection between music and the supernatural: trumpets sounded when the walls of Jericho fell down (Joshua 6:1–20); and David played his harp to soothe Saul during demonic attacks (1 Samuel 16:14–23).

Recorded musicians and music in the New Testament:

Two of the Gospels mention the fact that Jesus and His disciples sang a hymn at the end of the Last Supper (Matthew 26:30 and Mark 14:26). Elsewhere in the Gospels, music is seen as part of mourning (Matthew 9:23) and celebration (Luke 15:25).

Paul gave instructions regarding the use of music during Christian gatherings in Ephesians 5:19 and Colossians 3:16.

"19 speaking to one another with psalms, hymns, and songs from the Spirit. Sing and make music from your heart to the Lord,"

"16 Let the message of Christ dwell among you richly as you teach and admonish one another with all wisdom through psalms, hymns, and songs from the Spirit, singing to God with gratitude in your hearts."

In Ephesians we see that addressing each other with hymns and songs is an indication of being Spirit-filled. In Colossians the same is an indication of being filled with the Word of Christ, and the songs come "from the Spirit." In James 5:13 we have this command: *"Is anyone cheerful? Let him sing praise."*

Music in the Bible

Both the Old and New Testaments address music and strongly support its use in worship. The extensive anthology of actual songs found in the Old Testament indicates the importance and value God places on creative musical expression. Music's use in worship in the church today is valuable and can honor God in a special way. Music is a communication tool, and a Spirit-filled Christian is a singing Christian. There are no New Testament instructions on the type of instruments to be used (or not used), and no particular "style" of music is recommended or forbidden. The simple command is to sing *"to God with gratitude in your hearts"* (Colossians 3:16).

The Hivites Mountain is very deceptive. The Hivites spirits accept Jesus and salvation. There is no fight against salvation; and the Hivites spirit is aware of the ex-slavery of the new covenant. On the contrary, the Hivites spirit moves in quickly to kill; and convince that it is alright to play or listen to secular music, because you are still healthy and it is harmless **and** it is satisfying to soul, in which is a lie…..it is truly satisfying to the flesh; not the soul.

Another deception is the "so-called mature" population of people is that "I Can Do this and it has not Affected my Work in the Church or My Praise and Worship in Church." I know I have been snared into this many and many times. Sometimes, as Christians, we hold onto the secular music not knowing that the "making-love" music is really making love to the devil. **The Old-school music, the non-violent secular music and music in the past with the "non-cussing" lyrics need to be thrown away**.

I rebuke you Satan, Demon of old music that has made me feel Good in the past to be remove from my present and future, in Jesus name. Amen!

The term, "Recording Artist" is a form of occultist through the music instead of the Holy Spirit. The term

"Recording Artist" is lead by the flesh and man; not by the Holy Spirit.

"I speak authority over the recording artist, the demon king of music; will no longer reign in my home, car, or atmosphere in Jesus name. Amen!"

If you are wondering why there is so much anger and strife in your home, find out what type of music is playing in our kid's rooms or in the garage. The atmospheres of our homes are experiencing demonic influence because it is comforted and soothed by the flesh of the secular music which creates anger, hatred, strife and jealousy.........

"I declare and decree that we will stop selling our souls to Satan, just as Esau did in Genesis25: 29-34:, while claiming that we are Christians that love God; in Jesus name. Amen."

The word "Hivite" is derived in Hebrew from the word *chavvah*, which means "life" or "living". In fact, chavvah is the original version of the name "Eve". This is why the Lord declares the following in Genesis:

"And Adam called his wife's name Eve; because she was the mother of all <u>living</u>." (Genesis 3:20)

Since the word "Hivite" is related to the concept of "life" in Hebrew, we can infer that the Hivites' vision of life is not one of limitation, poverty, and self-deprecation, as is the case with the Perizzites. On the contrary, Hivites love to "live it up".

Another interesting aspect can be derived from the only other appearance of the name "Eve" in the Old Testament:

"And Adam knew Eve his wife; and she conceived, and bare Cain, and said, I have gotten a man from the LORD." (Genesis 4:1)

The name "Cain" means, "possession". This is why Eve said, **"I have gotten a man from the Lord".** The name "Cain", therefore, refers to possessing an inheritance handed down by someone else. From this, we can infer in the Spirit that Hivites are people who have acquired some type of inheritance that allows them the "freedom" to live "la vida loca". This is why the Hivites spirit is so prevalent in the sons and daughters of wealthy millionaires. Obviously, this does not mean that all descendants of millionaires are Hivites, but, it does mean that, if they are not careful, they can easily fall under the influence of Hivites spirits.

We must now ask ourselves the following: what does all of the above have to do with being a "villager"? The answer is simple, if you observe Hivites carefully. Because of all the abundance and grace that surrounds them; they limit the vision of their lives to merely enjoying the wealth and fame built up by their parents or even themselves. Hivites turn into people with few ambitions in life; all they want to do is travel around the world and have a "good time". Some of you might be noticing that the Hivites spirit is very common in people who have retired. Such people are prone to believe that they have nothing else to do in life but relax and enjoy the wealth they have accumulated during their lives:

"13And one of the company said unto him, Master, speak to my brother, that he divide the inheritance with me. 14 And he said unto him, Man, who made me a judge or a divider over you? 15 And he said unto them, Take heed, and beware of covetousness: for a man's life consisteth not in the abundance of the things which he possesseth. 16 And he spake a parable unto them, saying, The ground of a certain rich man brought forth plentifully: 17And he thought within himself, saying, What shall I do, because I have no room where to bestow my fruits? 18And he said, This will I do: I will pull down my barns, and build greater; and there will I bestow all my fruits and my goods. 19 And I will say to my soul, Soul, thou hast much goods laid up for many years; take thine ease, eat, drink, and be merry. 20 But God said unto him, Thou fool, this night thy soul shall be required of thee: then whose shall those things be, which thou hast provided? 21So is he that layeth up treasure for himself, and is not rich toward God." (Luke 12:13-21)

Notice how verses 13 and 14 above speak of "inheritance" and "possessing", which are related to what we said above about Cain and Eve; and are therefore related to the Hivites spirit. Notice also that the rich man in the parable was not a lazy man:

"30 I went by the field of the slothful, and by the vineyard of the man void of understanding; 31 And, lo, it was all grown over with thorns, and nettles had covered the face thereof, and the stone wall thereof was broken down. 32 Then I saw, and considered it well: I looked upon it, and received instruction. 33 Yet a little sleep, a little slumber, a little folding of the hands to sleep: 34 So shall thy poverty come as one that travelleth; and thy want as an armed man." (Proverbs 24:30-34)

The rich man of Luke 12:16-21 was a hard-working man who took advantage of the fertile ground that he owned. He was a Girgashites workaholic motivated by "covetousness" or "greed", who longed to accumulate enough wealth so as to go into Hivites retirement where he could "eat, drink, and be merry" (Luke 12:19). Notice how the Lord Jesus ends the parable by declaring, in verse 21, that whosoever stores up treasure for himself is not rich in the eyes of God. This reveals another trait that is common to Hivites: they are self-centered people who only think about themselves. Hivites deceive themselves into thinking that the abundant grace that surrounds them is proof that the universe exists to serve them, instead of the other way around.

Enemy on the Mountain: Hivites (represents compromise)
Significant Displacing Authority: Prophets
Basic Mission: Model the greater creative works of God and prophesy through them
Revelation 5:12 Key: Glory

When God blesses us with the millions, trillions, and billions, how will I help build the Kingdom of God concerning "Celebration"?

"And the LORD answered me: "Write the vision; make it plain on tablets, so he may run who reads it." Habakkuk 2:2, ESV

_____
_____
_____
_____
_____
_____
_____
_____
_____
_____
_____
_____
_____
_____
_____
_____
_____
_____
_____
_____
_____
_____
_____
_____
_____

Promised Land Eighteen
The Girgashites
The Mountain of Government

Girgashites operates in the spirit of pride. This spirit is in the form of dwelling in clay soil. The spirits dwell in earthy desires and ambitions. The spirit is not defeated by practicing Christians, but by Christians that are not confessing Jesus, our Lord and Savior.

This Mountain of Government establishes laws and decrees like the President of the U.S.....The Girgashites Spirit function in these capacities.

1. Chief of State

This role requires a president to be an inspiring example for the American people. In some nations, the chief of state is a king or a queen who wears a crown on special occasions, celebrates national holidays, and stands for the highest values and ideals of the country. As the American Chief of State, the president is a living symbol of the nation. It is considered a great honor for any citizen to shake the president's hand.

Examples of Responsibilities:
- Awarding medals to the winners of college scholarships
- Congratulating astronauts on their journey into space
- Greeting visitors to the White House
- Making a patriotic speech on the Fourth of July

2. Chief Executive

The president is the "boss" for millions of government workers in the Executive Branch. He decides how the laws of the United States are to be enforced and chooses officials and advisers to help run the Executive Branch.

Examples of Responsibilities:
- Appointing someone to serve as head of the Central Intelligence Agency (CIA)

- Holding a Cabinet meeting to discuss government business
- Reading reports about problems of the Federal Bureau of Investigation (FBI)

3. Chief Diplomat

The president decides what American diplomats and ambassadors shall say to foreign governments. With the help of advisers, the president makes the foreign policy of the United States.
Examples of Responsibilities:
- Traveling to London to meet with British leaders
- Entertaining Japanese diplomats in the White House
- Writing a message or a letter to the leaders of the Soviet Union

4. Commander-In-Chief

The president is in charge of the U.S. armed forces: the Army, Navy, Air Force, and Marines. The president decides where troops shall be stationed, where ships shall be sent, and how weapons shall be used. All military generals and admirals take their orders from the President.
Examples of Responsibilities:
- Inspecting a Navy yard
- Deciding, in wartime, whether to bomb foreign cities
- Calling out troops to stop a riot

5. Chief Legislator

Only Congress has the actual power to make laws, but the Constitution gives the president power to influence Congress in its lawmaking. Presidents may urge Congress to pass new laws or veto bills that they do not favor.
Examples of Responsibilities:
- Inviting members of Congress to lunch in the White House
- Signing a bill of Congress

- Making a speech in Congress

6. Chief of Party

In this role, the president helps members of his political party get elected or appointed to office. The president campaigns for those members who have supported his policies. At the end of a term the president may campaign for reelection.
Examples of Responsibilities:
- Choosing leading party members to serve in the Cabinet
- Traveling to California to speak at a rally for a party nominee to the U.S. Senate

7. Chief Guardian of the Economy

In this role, the president is concerned with such things as unemployment, high prices, taxes, business profits, and the general prosperity of the country. The president does not control the economy, but is expected to help it run smoothly.
Examples of Responsibilities:
- Meeting with economic advisers to discuss ways to reduce unemployment
- Meeting with business and labor leaders to discuss their needs and problems

"Let every person be subject to the governing authorities. For there is no authority except from God, and those that exist have been instituted by God." Romans 13:1 (ESV)

Although these are the earthy duties of the President, we must understand that God is the authoritative government of the earth. His duties are service and humility, while Satan's government duties are manipulation and pride in the President's duties here on earth.

Lucifer, also known as the Girgashites leader, sits on the mountain as "prince" over the nations. This mountain is working to:
1. Destroy Israel

2. Destroy the next generation through abortions, wars and plagues
3. Destroy Christians
4. Destroy Man and Husbands
5. Suppress women and to release the spirit of Jezebel
6. Pervert sexual mores through homosexuality, lesbians, adultery, fornication and so forth.

Apostles are the individuals to take down the Girgashites Mountain. Apostles must have a low-profile. They must be low-key in appearance; not wanting to be seen in the public light. These group of apostles that are chosen, in high position, in the government must not be based on charisma; nor their money-making abilities, their networking skills, their personality types, their speaking ability. However, only their obedient response to the calling, the anointing and their intimacy with God is needed to do God's work.

God uses the "so-called" nobodies for His Kingdom work.

God has used nobodies to turn the world upside down. Peter was a red-neck fisherman..........Matthew 16:18, *"¹⁸ And I say also unto thee, That thou art Peter, and upon this rock I will build my church; and the gates of hell shall not prevail against it."*

God doesn't take the majority of His workers from the ranks of the wise, mighty or noble. First Corinthians 1:26 says, *"For you see your calling, brethren, that not many wise according to the flesh, not many mighty, not many noble, are called."*

Continuing in 1 Corinthians 1, verse 27, *"But God has chosen the foolish things of the world to put to shame the wise, and God has chosen the weak things of the world to put to shame the things which are mighty; and the base things of the world and the things which are despised God has chosen."*

Paul says to get His job completed; God uses things which are foolish, things which are weak, things which are base, things which are despised.

The Foolish

God is able to work through the non-intellectual things in this world. D. L. Moody was an uneducated and uncultured man. With no educational advantages, he established the Moody Press, Moody Bible Institute, the Moody radio stations, and the list goes on. He is an example that God's power is not resident in our wisdom. God uses the foolish things of the world to confound the wise.

The Weak

Weary, feeble, powerless... Sometimes when we feel physically or spiritually weak, we are tempted to take a "time-out," thinking that God will use us again when we are stronger. In Judges 6, we are introduced to Gideon who was taking a "time-out." It was wartime, and Gideon was hiding when an angel of the Lord appeared to tell him that he would be the one to save Israel. Imagine Gideon's astonishment: *"How can I save Israel? Lord, I come from a nobody family, and I'm the lowest nobody in my family. And You're going to use me?"*

After God enlisted the nobody, Gideon; He got a nobody army. **Then God took those nobodies and won the battle!** God takes us in our weak state and uses us so He alone can be glorified.

The Base

Of the four women in Christ's genealogy, one played the harlot, Tamar; another was a Gentile, Ruth; another an adulteress, the wife of Uriah; and the fourth a harlot named Rahab; living proof that God can and will use anyone, regardless of their past actions, class or occupation.

Why does God delight in using nobodies as His nobility?

The **first** reason is found in 1 Corinthians 1, verse 29: *"that no flesh should glory in His presence."* When we get to heaven, not one of us will be able to say we got there on our own merit. We are saved simply by the grace of God. The **second** reason is found in verse 31, *"He who glories, let him glory in the Lord."* If we operate in our own strength and not God's, we risk taking the glory and credit for ourselves. Scripture tells us that we must be weak and low enough in order for God to use us.

Adrian Rogers told a story about a woodpecker pecking on a tree. In the middle of his pecking, a bolt of lightning hit that tree, splitting it right down the middle. The woodpecker backed off, surveyed the situation, and flew away. Later that day he returned with nine other woodpeckers. Proudly he said, "There it is, gentlemen. Right there. That's what I did." (Taking the credit)

When we do as the woodpecker, as men and women, God shuts off the lightning. When you try to take credit for what God is doing, God shuts off the lightning and you are left with what you can do alone.

God wants to take us down to the very depths of ourselves to teach us that if there is any power, it is the power that is in God, and not in us. God doesn't need to make us into performers or superstars in order to use us. Instead, He is looking for men and women who have hearts that say, *"Lord, I am a nobody. I'm nothing without You. Will You use me?"* When God finds such a heart, something extraordinary happens; that nobody is promoted to the ranks of **God's nobility; His dignity; His graciousness; His goodness.**

So what qualified those men to be apostles? The truth is, it was not any intrinsic ability or outstanding talent of their own. They were Galileans. They were not the elite. Galileans were considered low-class, rural, uneducated people. They were commoners' nobodies. But those nobodies would become the preeminent leaders of the fledgling church; its very foundation.

Now when it comes to church leadership, there are some rather clear moral and spiritual qualifications that men must meet. The Bible sets the standard extremely high (see 1 Timothy 3:2-7; Titus 1:6-9; Hebrews 13:7).

But you know something? The standard is not any lower for the rest of the church. Leaders are to be examples for all others who strive to meet the same standard. **There is no such thing as an acceptable "lower" standard for rank-and-file**

church members. In fact, in Matthew 5:48, Jesus said to all believers, *"Be perfect, just as your Father in heaven is perfect."*

That is a tall order! Honestly, no one meets such a standard. Humanly speaking, no one "qualifies" when the standard is unqualified perfection. What joy there is in knowing that it is God Himself who must save sinners, sanctify them, and then transform the unqualified into instruments He can use.

The twelve were like the rest of us; they were selected from the unworthy and the unqualified. They were, like Elijah, men "with a nature like ours" (James 5:17). They did not rise to the highest usefulness because they were somehow different from us. Rather, their transformation into vessels of honor was a divine work and their incredible influence is a result of the divine message they preached.

Why God Chooses Us

Do you ever become discouraged and disheartened when your spiritual life and witness suffer because of personal sin or failure? We tend to think we are worthless nobodies; and left to ourselves, that would be true. But the encouraged worthless nobodies are just the kind of people God uses. If you think about it, that is all He has to work with.

Have you ever stopped to consider why that is true? God chooses the humble, the lowly, the meek, and the weak so that there is never any question about the source of power when their lives change the world. It is not the man; it is the truth of God and the power of God in the man. Next time you are studying the gospels or the book of Acts, take a few minutes to consider the work of God in the apostles. They were slow to believe, slow to understand, and had horrendous and ghastly memories. Sound familiar?

God Glorified in Nobodies. Do not worry any longer; that is perfectly consistent with the way the Lord always works. 1 Corinthians 1:20-21 says, *"Where is the wise? Where is the scribe? Where is the disputer of this age? Has not God made foolish the wisdom of this world? For since, in the wisdom of God, the world through wisdom did not know God, it pleased*

God through the foolishness of the message preached to save those who believe." That is the very reason why there were no philosophers, no brilliant writers, no famous debaters, no distinguished teachers, and no men who had ever distinguished themselves as great presenter among the twelve Christ chosen.

They became great spiritual leaders and great preachers under the power of the Holy Spirit, but it was not because of any innate lecturer skill, leadership abilities, or academic qualifications they had. Their influence is owing to one thing and one thing only: the power of God in the message they preached.

On a human level, the gospel was considered a foolish message and the apostles were deemed unsophisticated preachers. Their teaching was beneath the elite. They were mere fishermen and working-class nobodies. They were classified as peons; unskilled farm workers or rabbles, disorganized and disorderly group of people. That was the assessment of their contemporaries and that has been the majority opinion of the genuine church of Christ throughout history and to this very day.

"For you see your calling, brethren, that not many wise according to the flesh, not many mighty, not many noble, are called" (v. 26).

But think about this: *"God has chosen the foolish things of the world to put to shame the wise, and God has chosen the weak things of the world to put to shame the things which are mighty; and the base things of the world and the things which are despised God has chosen, and the things which are not, to bring to nothing the things that are, that no flesh should glory in His presence"* (vv. 27-29). God's favorite instruments are nobodies, so that no man can boast before God.

In other words, God chooses whom He chooses so He might receive the glory. He chooses weak instruments so no one will attribute the power to the instruments but rather to the God who exercises the instruments. Those who pursue their own glory will sadly find God's strategy unacceptable; and they will miss out on true glory and true joy.

With the notable exception of Judas, the apostles were not like that. They certainly struggled with pride and arrogance like every fallen human being. But the driving passion of their lives became the glory of Christ. And it was that passion, subjected to the influence of the Holy Spirit; not any innate skill or human talent that explains why they left such an unforgettable impact on the world.

Jesus, himself, came from a young maiden born in a manager. God did not choose a woman from the household of Caesar, of Herod, of a centurion, or any other prestigious leader; He chose a maiden to bore a man to save us from this evil world.

Caesar--- was a Roman general, statesman, and Consul.
Herod--- succeeded his father, Herod the Great, and served as tetrarch, appointed by the emperor Augustus to rule over one quarter of his father's kingdom.
Centurions--- were key officers in the armies of ancient Rome.

We have to keep in mind that Apostles have greater gifts, but must have GREAT HUMILITY that leads to GREAT POWER. The Humility brings untold thousands of angels to work with them to destroy Satan Kingdom. To add, territorial angels working with a "displacement" anointing.....because it is not about the title of the positions held, but the functions and anointing that needs to be restored.

How will we know when the Apostle has been set in place?

Everywhere an Apostle go, it will be known:
1. An Apostolic phenomenal takes place
2. Heaven and hell breaks loose where ever an Apostle set his feet.

Hebrews 3:1 NIV, *"Therefore, holy brothers and sisters, who share in the heavenly calling, fix your thoughts on Jesus, whom we acknowledge as our apostle and high priest."*

Apostle means "sent one." The Holy Spirit is an apostolic spirit. God's Spirit has been sent to us (**Galatians 4:6**).

Success Is Our Plan

Jesus Christ was sent by the Father. Jesus turned His disciples into apostles as He said, *"As the Father has sent Me, so send I you."* (**John 20:21**) This sending is not new.

Moses was called and sent. **Exodus 3:10** says, *"Come now therefore, and I will send you unto Pharaoh, that you may bring forth My people the children of Israel out of Egypt."* Moses had a call, and a commission. The apostolic anointing is, thus, a **sending anointing**. Moses turned to the bush. God called. God identified Himself. God expressed His concern for the situation. He had seen. He knows. The sending was purposeful and powerful.

The sending also involved warring. The apostolic anointing is a **warring anointing.** Moses would war against Pharaoh, against oppression. Moses wasn't anything special. He said, **"Who am I?"** But the power and authority would come from God. God not only called and commissioned and commanded. God committed Himself. God said, *"Certainly I will be with you; and this shall be a token unto you, that I have sent you..."* (Exodus 3:12) There would be signs and wonders and tokens that Moses would speak for God. (Exodus 3:20) This apostolic anointing is an anointing of signs and wonders and tokens.

Apostolic people are sent into an area to war against demons, to deliver people from bondage, and to serve God. But the apostolic anointing is also a **fathering anointing**. Moses would be as a father to the children of Israel. We saw Moses leading, nurturing, mentoring, disciplining, judging, and restoring God's people. Likewise, Moses governed. He provided direction and set things in order.

With this **governing anointing**, we also see a **building anointing**. Moses would go and gather the people, the elders. He would rally them around the Name and person of God. He would bring them out of bondage into their inheritance. He would build. With authority from God the people would be taken to a new place, to plant, to build, to make way for increase, and to bless. Moses would activate the changes in order to come into the order of God. He would be God's instrument to remove the hindrances to the destiny of God's people.

The apostolic anointing is also one of **favor**. God said, *"And I will give this people favor in the sight of the Egyptians: and it shall come to pass, that, when you go, you shall not go empty..."* (**Exodus 3:21**) God promised to be with Moses, and thus Moses, like Joseph, would have good success, along with, favor. This favor would then extend to God's people. By grace, by the glory of God, the people would come into a new place with a new order.

What God has purposed to do, those whom He has called, prepared, chosen, and commissioned, will receive grace to finish. There is with the apostolic anointing grace to focus on the task and execute what needs to be done. The anointing is a **finishing anointing.** As Paul would say many centuries later, *"But none of these things move me, neither count I my life dear unto myself, so that I might finish my course with joy, and the ministry, which I have received of the Lord Jesus, to testify the gospel of the grace of God."* (Acts 20:24) There is an anointing to labor more abundantly, with nothing stopping, barriers broken, relentless as it were, in order to finish.

The apostolic anointing is an **anointing for righteousness**. The Spirit of holiness comes forth with an anointing to break the power of hindering spirits and confusion. Apostolic people are sanctified to their Lord, separated to the task, sold out for God, having the battle lines clearly defined. They are on the Lord's side.

Who are apostolic people? They are believers in Jesus Christ, filled with the Holy Spirit, living in one accord with God, with His Word, and with others in the Body of Christ. They are relational and vibrant, not complacent or compromising; but hating corruption. They are glad, joyous, praising, enthusiastic, and passionate for the purpose and plan of God. Apostolic people have a holy fear of God (Acts 9:31) with an intense awareness of His presence and understanding that our God is a consuming fire. With reverence and a **"holy hush,"** they focus on the kingdom of God with singleness of vision.

[58] Therefore, my dear brothers and sisters, stand firm. Let nothing move you. Always give yourselves fully to the work of the Lord, because you know that your labor in the Lord is not in vain. (1 Corinthians 15:58)

Success Is Our Plan

Apostles submit to the Word, for their desire is holiness and the sound, healthy and correct doctrine of the truth of the gospel. They submit to the fire of God for cleansing, purging, and deliverance from evil.

Apostolic people desire to be steadfast, faithful, unselfish, caring for others, sharing, giving, and loving. The love of Christ constrains them. Aware of their destiny, they seek to glorify the One sending them forth. They enjoy God, looking up and out and forward.

Look Up to God, Out in Faith and Forward in Grace.

The apostolic anointing enables patience, the ability to endure suffering and keep going, to persevere, to inherit the promises through faith and patience. There is something attractive about this anointing; it is winsome, magnetic, and drawing people to Christ by the fragrance of a life dead to sin and alive to God.

Apostolic anointing brings boldness. People with this anointing clearly communicate the Word of God and are not ashamed of the gospel, or of Jesus Christ, or of His Blood, or of His Holy Spirit, or of His people. They keep in step with the Spirit, pressing forward on the front lines, and going for the glory. These people walk with a radiant grace, meeting God at En-Gedi (A Kid Spring); carrying the glory, bearing the brand mark of Jesus as servants of Jesus Christ. They are children of the resurrection, full of the power of the Holy Spirit, confident that God loves them and can be trusted with their very souls and spirits and lives.

The Holy Spirit wants men and women willing to be separated unto Him (Acts 13:2); sent out as ambassadors, servants walking in humility with a power and authority that comes from God the Holy Spirit, who is their Source, Supervisor, and Sealer. **Will you be one?**

It is not that we need the title of Apostles in the High places of the Girgashites mountain, but we need true Christians with the Apostle anointing that are called in the high places to be.....*"wise as serpents and harmless as doves."* (Matthew

10:16)

Christ's mandate to us that we become **"wise as serpents and harmless as doves"** implies that we must develop discernment, the ability to detect motivation and the spirits that motivate. The gift of discerning the spirits will become increasingly important as we approach the end of this age because deception will be the token of these extremely dangerous times. We have a clear warning from the apostle Paul that the battles we face on a daily basis cannot be won by conventional weapons that we can attain from the world. The weapons we must seek should be spiritual, having the power to destroy arguments and every false claim that sets itself up against the knowledge of God and God's Word..." *For though we walk in the flesh, we do not war after the flesh:*

10:4 (For the weapons of our warfare are not carnal, but mighty through God to the pulling down of strong holds;)

10:5 Casting down imaginations, and every high thing that exalteth itself against the knowledge of God, and bringing into captivity every thought to the obedience of Christ;" 2 Corinthians 10:3-5

Interpretation of Matthew 10:16, Sheep in the Midst of Wolves.

As he sends his disciples out, Jesus tells them that they will be *"as sheep in the midst of wolves."* The wolf is a horrendous beast of prey, known for its appetite, cunning, and fierceness. Sheep, on the other hand, are weak, witless, quiet and passive; surely no match for the strength and craftiness of the wolf. In the presence of wolves, sheep are in great danger because they have in themselves no effective means of defense.

The point of the analogy is the danger that the disciples will be in and their relative defenselessness against their powerful and malicious enemy. Jesus is not saying that his disciples are individually stupid, weak, or cowardly. Jesus is stating that in the mission of preaching the gospel of the kingdom, they will be opposed by the hostile powers that are in Israel and, at a later time, in the Roman Empire, and that they will not have the means for adequate defense against these powers.

Wise as Serpents

In view of these things, the disciples of Christ must act in a particular manner. It would be suicidal or wretched for Jesus' followers to conduct themselves during their mission without regard to the strong and vicious enemies who seek to devour them. Therefore, Jesus counsels them to be *"wise as serpents, and harmless as doves."* The circumstance of confessing Christ and his Word in a hostile setting requires wisdom and integrity.

The Greek word that is here translated "wise" refers to practical wisdom, prudence, cleverness, and discernment. One, who is "wise," in the sense of this term, is a person who shows presence of mind and has the understanding and sound judgment necessary to act prudently.

The *"serpent"* was typical of wisdom and cunning in the ancient world. The wisdom of the serpent is that of keen perception and cleverness; both in avoiding its enemies and catching its prey.

Therefore, to be *"wise as serpents"* refers to the ability of the disciples to avoid unnecessary contact or conflict with the *"wolves,"* and if such conflict or contact occurs, to know how to handle the situation in a way that minimizes the ability of the *"wolves"* to succeed in an attack. Jesus' disciples should not invite or provoke attacks from their enemies, but rather behave in such a fashion that frustrates the designs of the wicked against them.

As usual, Jesus himself sets the example. Throughout his ministry Jesus was wise as a serpent in regard to the "wolves" that were sent to destroy. He did not seek to provoke conflicts with them. If opposition to his ministry became too intense, he would leave the area for a time. He knew how to answer their attacks and at the same time expose their folly. A classic example of how Christ dealt with the cunning, crafty leaders of the Jews is found in Matthew 21:23-22:46.

Furthermore, Jesus understood that the "wolves" that sought his downfall were the religious leaders and not the common people (Mark. 12:37). By ministering to the needs of the people, he won their trust; and on various occasions, the support of the people protected Jesus from the leaders who were intent on destroying him (Mark 12:12; Luke. 19:47-48).

Harmless as Doves

But it is not enough to be *"wise as serpents."* The mission of serving Christ in the world also requires disciples to be *"harmless as doves."* The Greek word translated "harmless" means, literally, "unmixed," and was used to refer to such things as pure gold or unmixed wine. In the New Testament, it is employed figuratively of moral purity and integrity (Romans 16:19; Philippians 2:15).

In the ancient Near East, the dove was symbolic of purity, faithfulness, and guilelessness. The dove was, also, the only bird that could be offered as a sacrifice in the Old Testament.

To be *"harmless as doves"* expresses the need of Jesus' disciples to be above reproach in both conduct and speech. They must be clever and shrewd in dealing with their cunning wolf-like adversaries, but they must never stoop to the ethics of their enemies. They must be free from deceit and evil. Sin in the life and speech of the disciple gives his adversary an easy opening to discredit and neutralize his witness.

Jesus was pure as a dove. He could challenge his enemies, *"Which of you convinceth me of sin?"* (John. 8:46), and they were speechless. Those who hated him could never find anything in his life to discredit him. So, the only area left to attack was his teaching, or to make absurd charges that he broke the law by doing good, or that he performed miracles by the power of Satan. By making his enemies focus on his teaching, Jesus made his doctrine the focus of debate; this is exactly what he wanted.

Application of Matthew 10:16

Jesus' counsel in Matthew 10:16 instruct his followers on how to conduct themselves when faced with hostility towards their message. As such, the general principles taught in this text can be applied in any time, place, or sphere of life where Christians are persecuted for seeking to teach or live according to the Word of Christ. This would include the political sphere and the current anti-Christian sentiment displayed therein.

The following gives some suggestions on how Matthew 10:16 could be applied by Christians active in politics today.

1. The "wolves" with which Christians must contend in the political sphere are not the people but secular and worldly elite.

This should be kept firmly in mind, lest potential allies are mistaken for enemies. Gundry, commenting on Matthew 10:16, states: "The figure of sheep, which has recently represented the lost and shep-herdless people of Israel (9:36; 10:6), now, represents Jesus' missionaries, who are threatened by the wolf-like leaders of the people. Thus, certain solidarity exists between the persecuted missionaries and the harried people; both suffer from the same source."

How true this is today as well. The same secular elite that act in a wolf-like fashion against the followers of Christ are also troubling the people by their ungodly and foolish policies.

The secular elite, as represented in the media, academia, public policy and political action groups, and many public officials are the enemies; the wolves opposing Christian political principles. The common people have, in many ways, been targeted by these adversaries of Christ. But if Christians can demonstrate a better way, one of liberty and justice, they might just find widespread support from the people.

2. Christians in politics should avoid inviting or provoking unnecessary conflict with their enemies.

The meaning of *"wise as serpents,"* as explained above, needs to be directly applied to the political sphere. Conflict of one degree or another will be inevitable as Christians seek to apply the biblical principles of civil government to their society. But the point is that they should act discreetly, and sometimes work quietly, to keep from triggering unnecessary hostility and conflict. However, the fear of conflict must not be allowed to paralyze the Christian into inactivity and compromise. It is a travesty when a professed disciple of Jesus Christ uses Matthew 10:16 as a cloak for his own cowardice, or to hide his disobedience to Christ's command to bring all areas of life under the authority of the Word of God.

3. Christians in politics should be free from deceit and above reproach.

The sense of *"harmless as doves,"* as discussed earlier, needs to be carefully related to the political sphere. Christian politicians and activists must be known as men of faultless and un-impreachable integrity. They must be separate from all the guile, evil deception, corruption, meanness, deceit and scandal that so marks contemporary politics.

4. If Christians are to be effective in politics, they must have practical wisdom as to how politics works.

They should know the "ins and outs" and "nuts and bolts" of all aspects of the political process; from how to run a campaign, to the process of enacting proposed legislation into law. Christians should know how political parties operate, how to lobby legislators, the conventions of political protocol, etc. If Christians do not have fundamental knowledge on how things operate in politics, they cannot hope to be effective; and the wolves will devour them.

5. If Christians are to be effective in politics, they must have the practical knowledge to deal with the issues and problems of politics.

People are looking for solutions to the problems that plague their communities, cities, and states. Problems of education, taxation, crime, welfare, the economy, and so on. Christians need to be willing to roll up their sleeves and get to work serving the needs of the people in the socio-political sphere. But they need more than a willingness to work, they need knowledge, practical knowledge, and skill to understand and solve real-life problems to enhance the life and liberty of the people. Each political office requires a solid understanding of the duties of the office and the particular issues, and problems that need to be addressed.

As Christians serve their fellow citizens by actually making their lives better, the people will care less and less about how the "wolves" are painting Christians as public enemies and nuisances, but rather will be thankful to have Christian men governing them. A good biblical example of this is the case of Joseph. Egypt was faced with a grave national crisis. The need of the hour was for a wise and resourceful man who could provide the solutions to the problem and see the solutions carried out.

The man that was chosen was Joseph because he had a practical plan to meet the crisis. So Pharaoh appointed him to be governor over all the land, **even though he was a Hebrew and a slave!** Why was he chosen? Because as Pharaoh said, *"there is none so discreet and wise as thou art"* (Genesis 41:39).

7. If Christians are to be effective in politics, they need practical wisdom on how to conduct themselves in public.

Public office puts many strains on a man. He is constantly in situations where he must deal with others and respond to unexpected questions, circumstances, and attacks. If he does not know how to handle himself, he will discredit himself quickly; and the "wolves" will make fair game of him. Prudence, grace, and discernment in interacting with others and in managing stressful situations are essentials for the job.

A prime source for this kind of wisdom is the book of Proverbs. Proverbs is a gold mine of counsel on how to conduct oneself in public office and how to deal with people in any kind of situation. Anyone who aspires to political office ought to master the contents of Proverbs, paying particular attention to those texts that would specifically apply to the conduct of public office.

In the Septuagint (the Greek translation of the Old Testament), Proverbs employs in numerous texts the same word for "wise" that is used in Matthew 10:16. For example, the wise are those who know when to hold their peace (Proverbs. 11:12; 17:28); the wise seek out knowledge (Proverbs. 14:16, 18; 18:15); the wise hear reproof (Proverbs. 17:10; 19:25); the wise know how to turn away wrath with their answers (Proverbs. 15:1); the wise know how to draw counsel out of others (Proverbs. 20:5)

8. If Christians are to be wise and effective in politics, they need a comprehensive knowledge of God's law.

God's law will equip the Christian for the good work of civil governance. The law of God will make him wiser than his wolf-like enemies (Psalms 119:98).

"If you touch Israel, you touch the apple of the His eye",
Zechariah 2:8

Proverbs 29:2 (KJV), "*2 When the righteous are in authority, the people rejoice: but when the wicked beareth rule, the people mourn.*"

Lucifer is at the top of the mountain waiting to destroy the weak and use their power (man's power, which is useless) to take over the nation.

The fight at the top of the Girgashites Mountain is **National vs city vs region levels.** The battle is between the Natural Faces vs Ruling Powers. It is not the physical bodies of people that needs changing, but a secured, holiness and righteousness atmosphere, that amplify spirituality in the airwaves of Washington D.C. that is needed.

The people may vote an Apostle in the White House, but once the apostles are voted into the Washington, they may compromise with the evil of this world to remain in office for the second term. Therefore, the demonic atmosphere changes their influences, and then God's standard has fallen short. This is why it is important to amplify spirituality in the air waves of Washington D.C.

The governors, judges and mayors are the lower part of the Girgashites Mountain. This group of people:
1. Formulate foreign policy
2. Push budget reform

3. Law/Policies

We must be grounded in His Word, so when we come together as spiritual warriors, God's anointing may dominate the atmosphere; the airwaves. We have to understand that we carry the anointing that is needed to conquer the universe. Therefore, our anointing need not to be compromise and not tainted by the evils of this world.

I will shake all nations, and what is desired by all nations will come, and I will fill this house with glory,' says the LORD Almighty. Haggi 2:7

"For to us a child is born, to us a son is given, and the government will be on his shoulders. And he will be called Wonderful Counselor, Mighty God, Everlasting Father, Prince of Peace." Isaiah 9:6

As powerful spiritual warriors, we have to heap fire on every Girgashites, "evil settlers" on this earth. Some of their entrance to our souls and in this world are spying on individuals and collaborating with wicked forces outside, with hidden and ultimate aim of destroying or redirecting the destiny of the nations.

Most imperative, be aware of your surroundings. These Girgashites agents create "intelligent problems" that correctly observe times, seasons and so forth. They spy on you and try to steal your dreams. Agents are planted all over the the earth; some of the entrance comes in the form of:

Workers on your job
Babysitters
House-help/housekeepers
Professional colleagues…the ones that follow you after college
Neighbors
Family Relatives
Business associates

Lastly, the "near success syndrome" is developed. Psalm forty-nine is a meditation of David on the shortcomings and liabilities of wealth and success. In verses **six and seven** he says that those who boast in their wealth and success cannot redeem their soul with all their money. He says in **verse ten** that rich men and wise men die just like everyone else. He says in **verse eleven** that they think they can hold onto their wealth and make sure that it lasts, but they cannot.

Psalm 49 NIV:
1 Hear this, all you peoples; listen, all who live in this world,
2 both low and high, rich and poor alike:
3 My mouth will speak words of wisdom; the utterance from my heart will give understanding.
4 I will turn my ear to a proverb; with the harp I will expound my riddle:
5 Why should I fear when evil days come, when wicked deceivers surround me--
6 those who trust in their wealth and boast of their great riches?
7 No man can redeem the life of another or give to God a ransom for him--
8 the ransom for a life is costly, no payment is ever enough--
9 that he should live on forever and not see decay.
10 For all can see that wise men die; the foolish and the senseless alike perish and leave their wealth to others.
11 Their tombs will remain their houses forever, their dwellings for endless generations, though they had named lands after themselves.
12 But man, despite his riches, does not endure; he is like the beasts that perish.
13 This is the fate of those who trust in themselves, and of their followers, who approve their sayings. "Selah"
14 Like sheep they are destined for the grave, and death will feed on them. The upright will rule over them in the morning; their forms will decay in the grave, far from their princely mansions.
15 But God will redeem my life from the grave; he will surely take me to himself. "Selah"

16 Do not be overawed when a man grows rich, when the splendor of his house increases;
17 for he will take nothing with him when he dies, his splendor will not descend with him.
18 Though while he lived he counted himself blessed-- and men praise you when you prosper--
19 he will join the generation of his fathers, who will never see the light [of life].
20 A man who has riches without understanding is like the beasts that perish.

David was a highly motivated man, and I believe he was tempted to admire and imitate highly successful and wealthy men. This Psalm is a meditation on those things. In verse eighteen David said, *"Men will praise thee when thou doest well to thyself."*

Men tend to worship at the shrine of success. They praise those who have made good for themselves. The "near syndrome success" which I write about is seen in high school and college reunions when comparisons are openly made. "What do you do for a living?" "How much do you make a year?" High schools tend to promote this idea in their yearbooks by voting on who is "most likely to succeed."

Most men, even some Christian men, worship success. Little slogans like, "Take care of number one," "He's really done well for himself," and "Nothing succeeds like success" are common phrases from dads to their sons and even from leadership in churches. This is precisely what David meant when he said, *"Men will praise thee when thou doest well to thyself."*

Please do not misread my point here. God wants us to be successful. However, God's definition of success is not the same as the world's success. God's definition of success is to find His will for your life and do it. Money has nothing to do with success in God's eyes.

"This book of the law shall not depart out of thy mouth but thou shalt meditate therein day and night; that thou mayest observe to do according to all that is written therein; for then

thou shalt make thy way prosperous and then thou shalt have good success." Joshua 1:8

Success in the Bible has to do with our understanding and obedience to all the commands of God. This is not the same concept most people have who has been bitten by the "success bug". Through the years I have found some symptoms of the "near success syndrome."

1. Wrong Focus

When your eye is focused on results rather than on rewards, you may have the " near success syndrome."

Nowhere does God stress how many baptisms the church is to have a year, or how many souls to win, or how big the church is to be. God's focus is not on how much but on "what sort" (1 Corinthians 3:13-15). If the truth were known, many pastors and Christian workers in small churches are discouraged because in the conferences they go to, all they hear are preachers of large churches talking about *how much and how many.* "It is God's job to take care of the breadth of my ministry; it is my job to take care of the depth of my ministry."

But let us be careful that we do not jump off the deep end. God does say that we should produce and bring forth fruit. *Yes, primarily I am to be faithful; but I should desire also to be fruitful.*

If my eye is on the reward, my work will be guided by the Book. If my eye is on the result, my work will be guided by what succeeds.

If my eye is on the reward, my work with men provides things honest in the sight of all men. If my eye is on the result, my work tends to be manipulative and underhanded.

If my eye is on the reward, God gets the glory for anything achieved. If my eye is on the result, I often get the glory!

Success Is Our Plan

Where is your eyes focused?

2. Wrong Values

When what you do is more important than what you are, you may have been bitten by the "near success syndrome."

We must be careful what we emphasize in our churches and in our personal lives. Jesus emphasized that "**what we are**" is more important than "**what we do**." Our position is not all important, but the state of our heart and our integrity as a person is. Being a pastor is a great thing; however, being a man of integrity and godliness, as a pastor is a higher priority. Being the president of a company may be a desirable position, but being honest and a man of conviction is more important. If I must sacrifice one for the other, let me sacrifice my position. In fact, my success as a father, Solomon said, is based on my integrity more than anything else.

"The just man walketh in his integrity: his children are blessed after him." Proverbs 20:7

3. Wrong Emphasis

When the short-run is more important than the long-haul, it may be a symptom that the "near success syndrome" has bitten you.

For many, the one hundred yard dash has become more important than the cross country run. The ability to run fast has become more valued than to finish the race. But examine these verses:

"I have fought a good fight, I have finished my course"
2 Timothy 4:7

"It is finished." John 19:30

"These all died in faith" Hebrews 11:13

"Be thou faithful unto death and I will give thee the crown of life." Revelation 2:10

The Lord's emphasis is on finishing the race not on how fast you run in the race. For many years, I have desired to build job placement centers and training schools; and that desire has not left me, but my biggest desire now is to finish the race God has put me in, without being disqualified!

We all have many desires to help save the universe and many accomplishments to achieve; although our biggest desire should be to finish the race that God has put us in; without being disqualified!

4. Wrong Validation

When the praise of men is more important than the praise of God you have definitely been exposed to the "near success syndrome" virus.

Men will praise you when you do well for yourself, but then, every man praises according to his own standard of success; so the praise is no better than the man giving it. My highest desire must be to hear, *"Well done thou good and faithful servant."* Jesus said that the Pharisees loved the praise of men more than the praise of God.

As an example; *of young, but accomplished violinist, who after a concert was being applauded. He bowed to his audience but kept looking around. Someone asked him, "Who are you looking for?" He said, "My teacher, for only he really knows if I played according to the music."*

Only God really knows your life and it is **His praise** we must desire! **The praise of man is an inconsistent and weak assessment by which to judge our work. A great musician is more concerned with what his teacher thinks than with what his crowd thinks. A great football player is more interested in pleasing his coach than with pleasing the crowd, and a great Christian is more interested in pleasing the heavenly Father than with pleasing those around him.**

5. Wrong Fulfillment

When self fulfillment is more important than self denial, you may have the "near success syndrome."

We are living in the "me" generation and self fulfillment and happiness seems to be the goal of many sermons. But Jesus preached a message of self-denial; not self-fulfillment. He said, *"If any man will come after Me, let him deny himself, and take up his cross and follow Me."*

One reason the call to mission service and the ministry is no longer popular in America is the desire for self-fulfillment. The ministry does not seem to be the way to health, wealth, and happiness. Certainly, the call to the mission field or to Christian school ministry with its low pay, or to pastor, or be a pastor's wife is not seen as the American dream of success. But I am afraid that the American dream and God's dream (better stated God's will) are usually not one and the same.

The near success syndrome can be a deadly disease. So let us keep our eyes on the goal; God's goal. Success is finding the will of God for our life and doing it.

"I am thankful for Your Will God and My will is Your Will."

Enemy on the Mountain: Girgashites (represents corruption)
Significant Displacing Authority: Apostles
Basic Mission: Fill government positions with humble, servant, integrals' leaders.
Revelation 5:12 Key: Power

When God blesses us with the millions, trillions, and billions, how will I help build the Kingdom of God concerning "The Government"?

"And the LORD answered me: "Write the vision; make it plain on tablets, so he may run who reads it." Habakkuk 2:2, ESV

_____

Promised Land Nineteen
The Hittites
The Mountain of Media

Media is the prophetic voice of the nation. The mountain spirit behind media is designed to create fear, despair, and hopelessness; which is the cultural shaper of society.

Apollyon is the ruling spirit over the Hittites. Apollyon means destroyer and destruction. With the power of God, we are the destroyer and destructor of evil; and Satan tactics. Apollyon comes:

1. To promote fear and promote terror…Iraq and Afghanistan
2. To promote infighting and division…..throughout society in the form of hunger
3. To be a bearer of bad news

The pawn of Satan is to deliver and communicate fear and despair to the culture of mankind. There are demonic influences that cause deception, lack of telling the truth or telling partial truth and fear; in which operates at the Mountain of the Hittites.

The demonic influences…..

The first goal of demons is to prevent us from receiving salvation. If that fails, they work at preventing Christian maturity. They try to shut us down and make us ineffective. Their chief strategy is to try to get people to turn away from God. They do this through many forms of temptation, harassment, and also challenging God and His Word. Demons lie to us and work hard to have us lie to ourselves.

Forms of harassment are accusation and criticism. Demons will interject condemning thoughts into the minds of believers. They particularly like to stir up the past with thoughts of, "You really should have..." or "If only you had done (_____)differently". Demons are on a "seek and destroy" mission.

They work together and strategize. They take advantage

of our weaknesses and they love times when people are either physically and/or emotionally weak or vulnerable. They attempt to affect all areas of a person's body, soul, and spirit. The Hittites do not play fair.

There are several ways by which demons oppresses people. **Afflict:** To inflict something hard to endure. **Harass:** To annoy or disturb persistently, to wear out by frequent attacks. **Influence:** To exercise indirect power over in order to sway or affect. **Oppress:** To lower in spirit or mood. **Torment:** To cause severe suffering of body or mind. **Torture**: To punish or intimidate by inflicting excruciating pain. **Worry**: To disturb one or destroy one's peace of mind by repeated or persistent torment. **Wrong**: To inflict injury on another without justification.

We know that we are made up of body, soul and spirit. Again the soul in itself is made up of mind, will and emotions. Becoming a believer means we must surrender "our will" to the Lordship of Jesus Christ; our Savior. Although, the mind and emotions, we might not have fully surrendered to our Lord. In these circumstances either knowingly or unknowingly we are allowing the devil to have a legal hold on our mind or emotions. Psychic Power, Psychic Prayer, Mind Control, Mind Control Occult, Witchcraft and Soul Ties are some of circumstances that are knowingly and unknowingly. Briefly, we will focus on witchcraft and mind control.

WITCHCRAFT:

I Samuel 15:23. *"For rebellion is as the sin of witchcraft, and stubbornness is as iniquity and idolatry. Because thou hast rejected the Word of the Lord, He hath also rejected thee from being king."* When we turn away from God we are in witchcraft or in devil's territory. This is a most general statement in that we have given place to the devil and will live by the devil's rules and we have to understand the devil's mode of operation which is best described as witchcraft. That means we have surrendered our body, soul and spirit to the control, influence, or manipulation of the unseen forces of evil spirits.

The operation of the devil is only through the manipulation of evil spirits. If Satan wants one of his people in a higher position in a company, then he has to have an evil spirit in a person of authority to advance the preferred one. For example, if the devil wants to bring a preacher down, he might use an evil spirit of lust in a gorgeous young and well perfumed sweet thing to bring about a fall. This operation does not just have to be in a preacher because it works in all groups.

Witchcraft is the most effective weapon in the devil's arsenal to destroy and/or prevent any human being coming into the full power of God. Occult means unseen. Witchcraft and Occult go hand in hand. All these practices are hidden snares to involve humans in the devil's world and to make them think that they have it all.

The great conspiracy of Satan to control our mind reaches into the entertainment field through television and movies. Most of the actors and actresses on television today are either practicing witches or mixed up in witchcraft or seeking witchcraft or seeking the power of witchcraft. Most are in some way implicated in it.

Some authors, writers and script writers are absolutely polluted with witchcraft, as well. As a result they produced Star Wars, Jaws, Empire Strikes Back and many more. Many movies are the most horrible, grotesque, powerful, satanic, indescribable, treacherous, revolting productions. Words cannot describe the effects that witchcraft has had in our entertainment field. Filling the observer with fear and opening he/she up for demons to enter is the goal of each horror movie.

There is hardly a page of movie ads that are fit to read. We must remember that witchcraft includes the use of sex. The people who are plunging and dealing in witchcraft have no ability to develop any love such as the Scripture defined love. The only love they have is the sexual immoral activity. To them that is love. Sexual immoral activities and stimulation is not only used as a subverting factor, but as a counterfeit of true love and the sending forth of more powerful curses.

In witchcraft books they suggest that we go out in public with no clothes on except a raincoat and then take the coat off in an elevator to build up their energy or power. The braless and bikini looks have their roots in witchcraft. A look at a nude or indecently exposed body or pornographic material can be just as potent as the taking of a drug, in admitting or activating an evil spirit.

A believer must be aware that from every aspect of his life and activity, he is threatened constantly with the prospect of witchcraft being beamed at him/her by the enemy. These attacks come from unknown or unsuspecting sources. The snares of Satan are cleverly laid to trap the believer into a situation where Satan can have more control over his or her mind.

SATAN IS AFTER THE CONTROL OF OUR MIND

Mind control is the chief weapon of Satan to snare the believer. The Scriptures admonish us to **"bring every thought into captivity"**, II Corinthians 10:5. The Scriptures say that the spirit of a sound mind means a disciplined mind. It is absolutely essential for a person to keep a sound mind or a disciplined mind in order to become aware of the thoughts that are coming from the devil and the thoughts that are coming from the Lord. Many times a person will enter a world of fantasy and imagination, lusting after something, or covetousness, or of something they consider normal. Many times they will dwell on what to do in case of an accident. This is a great counterfeit when the devil will have you go over and over what to do in case of an accident. By accepting this and hearing this in our mind we are giving place to the devil for it to happen.

It is important to "capture our thoughts". By apprehending our thoughts, understanding our thoughts, and being able to look upon our own thoughts, we can bring every thought into captivity. Many times a split personality could stop the personality from changing by simply taking charge of his/her own thoughts. It is important to realize that things like Dungeons and Dragons, and other games of witchcraft, put the mind in gear for Satan. Then witchcraft activity becomes a common place. The casting of spells, the inducing of charms and the practicing of witchcraft takes over the entire mind and thus gives way to the mind control spirit, whereby, the mind can be controlled by the devil himself. This is also the reason for the psychedelic colors in the Rubik's cube, and the mind boggling disco lights and the lights that are sold as rhythm and colors. All these colors affect the mentality and aid in the taking over and controlling of the mind.

Mind Control is the prime root cause for failure to use the spiritual gifts for God's Glory. Beelzebub interferes with the correct operation of the gifts. We should ask the Lord to loose spirits of Joshua and Caleb and to help us to take full control, power and authority over Mind Control. Mind Occult will provide a powerful pulling force to readmit a demon who was cast out. Seal off this power with the Blood of Jesus.

STRONGHOLDS:

A stronghold is anything we hold onto that ends up holding us. Strongholds are toxic thoughts that can have an adverse affect on our thinking process. Strongholds of fear, worry, bitterness, anger, shame, control, etc. need to be replaced by Christ's thoughts. Ungodly beliefs are open doors, inviting Satan to come into our minds. If we do not reject Satan's lies, then we accept them as truth which is amounting to believing and trusting what Satan says about us more than what God says about us?

Ungodly beliefs are trying to put themselves above God. So those thoughts are not God's thoughts. Thoughts come from three sources: Ourselves, Satan or the demonic realm and God through the Holy Spirit. If we ever had an intrusive thought and we knew it was not ours and had a vain imagination attached to it, then it is from the devil. Usually it is the opposite of God's Word. They are spontaneous which are Negative and Destructive; line up with the names of Satan: Accuser, Father of Lies, Thief and Adversary

God's thoughts are also spontaneous which are Positive and Up building; line up with the names of the Holy Spirit: Comforter, Counselor, the Spirit of Truth, and the Convincer.

How do the Hittites get a foothold in the Media?

The number one entrance is Journalism, which is the activity of gathering, assessing, creating, and presenting news and information. It is also the "product" of these activities. Journalism can be distinguished from other activities and products by certain identifiable characteristics and practices. These elements not only separate journalism from other forms of communication, they are what make it indispensable to democratic societies. History reveals that the more democratic a society, the more news and information it tends to have.

Also, Journalism is a form of writing that tells people about things that really happened, like in movies or documentaries, but that they might not have known about already.

People who write journalism are called "journalists." They might work for the newspapers, magazines, and websites or for TV or radio stations. The most important characteristic shared by good journalists is curiosity. Good journalists love to read and want to find out as much as they can about the world around them. Journalism comes in several different forms:

I. News
   A. Breaking news: Telling about an event as it happens.
   B. Feature stories: A detailed look at something interesting that is not breaking news.
   C. Enterprise or Investigative stories: Stories that uncover information that few people knew.

II. The Opinions of Journalism
   A. Editorials: Unsigned articles that express a publication's opinion.
   B. Columns: Signed articles that express the writer's reporting and his conclusions.
   C. Reviews: Such as concert, restaurant or movie reviews.

Online, journalism can come in the forms listed above, as well as:
   Blogs: Online diaries kept by individuals or small groups.
   Discussion boards: Online question and answer pages where anyone can participate.
   Wikis: Articles that any reader can add to or change.

The best journalism is easy to read and just sounds like a nice and smart person telling you something interesting.

How do you get the facts for your news story? By reporting!

There are three main ways to gather information for a news story or opinion piece:

Interviews: Talking with people who know something about the story you are reporting.

Observation: Watching and listening where news is taking place.

Documents: Reading stories, reports, public records and other printed material.

The people or documents used by Journalist when reporting a story are called the "sources." In a journalism story, one always tells the readers what sources they have used. As a result, one must remember to get the exact spelling of all your sources' names. Journalist wants everything in their story to be accurate, including the names of the sources you quote.

Often, a person's name is not enough information to identify them in a news story. Lots of people have the same name, after all. Therefore, one will also want to write down the sources' ages, their hometowns, their jobs and any other information about them that is relevant to the story.

Whenever a journalist is interviewing someone, observing something happening or reading about something, they will write down the answers to the **"Five Ws"** about that source:

Who are they?
What were they doing?
Where were they doing it?
When they do it?
Why did they do it?

Many good reporters got their start by keeping a diary. Journalism has been trained in Ivey League Schools, such as, Harvard, Yale, and Columbia, which has the greatest impact on media. Despite Christian foundations, journalism has become the liberal education institution of the nation. WE have to take a stand at all Journalism schools to combat war against Satan and his "so-called" tactics of lies and deceptiveness.

There are many anti-Christians graduates; and we, as Jesus followers, need to take on high-level positions as professors, administrative, board members and so forth, at these prestige's universities that enrollments are majority anti-Christian, in which are in the journalism programs.

Prayer needs to be in a form of repentance for the entire earth. WE need to Reclaim the media…..Repent as believers for believers that have compromise in the Media…..Repent for the humanistic foundation that has been adopted…..Repent for the people that has taken God's role out of society…..Repent of propagating fear………Repent for inaccurate reporting about people and situation….Repent for lies that have been told based on non-circumstantial evidence.

WE need to Pray for air-waves to be filled with truth in reporting……righteousness in the way reports are being prepared….for stories of nobility, justice, truth, virtue and praiseworthy things.

According to Barna Research, 9% of journalism holds Christians biblical world view……………With this information, how do we expect to reach the media?   For one, Christians need to stop compromising once they are in position. This is why we need spiritual warriors in high places that do not want the fame or the spot light. God needs leaders that are not in the business of just making money; but saving lives. Leaders want to live comfortable, but not extravagant for the entire earth to notice them.

It is difficult for Christians in the media to recover when a Christian is the source of dishonesty or failure in integrity. The "Faith" has been tarnish, ammunition is developed and used………narrow and judgmental attitudes have been developed.

Journalism needs to follow a Christ-like agenda, which is to operate like a person with the love of God in their hearts.

Prayer strategies

-Church to regain biblical world-view.
-Journalist—biblical worldview to be manifested through the media and those who work in the media.
-Journalist must know what Christians believe in and model after.
-Adopt those in media----let the Journalist know we are praying for them. Christians need to adopt the "shake the enemy" effect, for example, send food baskets when major storms are breaking to comfort the media staff at the TV stations and Radio station.
-Stand in prayer for the media---prayer of repentance and the deception our of the secular media.
-Pray God will raise up new generation of godly representation in truth and righteousness.
-Bind the strongman that instills "fear" in people through the media.
-Bind the spirit that manipulate and report news that is untruthful or slanted to persuade inaccurate reporting.
-Pray for the spirit of Shadrach, Meshach, Abed-Nego who refuse to worship the god of Babylon.
-Pray for Nehemiah's to be raised up and rebuild the wall of the media of righteous reporting.
-Take an interest in journalism as people by going face to face, knocking on the doors, spreading the Good News of Jesus.
-Career doors are difficult unless someone has an inside family member or Ivy league connection...............Pray for doors to be opened to godly men and women in the media.
-Pray against the evil that resides in the Ivy League schools.
-Avoid name dropping.....serving those with high profile individuals must be done with great sensitivity.

Psalms 105:17-19, (NKJV) *"He sent a man before them—Joseph—who was sold as a slave.*
[18] They hurt his feet with fetters,
He was laid in irons.
[19] Until the time that his word came to pass,
The word of the LORD tested him.

God is doing a unique work around the world today. He is training and building up Josephs throughout the world. Some are still in the "pit" stage of their life, while others are heading toward fruitfulness.

What does it take for you to become a true Joseph? It takes years of preparation and testing to be a true Joseph. It takes what the psalmist says in Psalm 105: 16-20, *"He called down famine on the land and destroyed all their supplies of food; and he sent a man before them Joseph, sold as a slave. They bruised his feet with shackles, his neck was put in irons, till what he foretold came to pass, till the word of the Lord proved him true. The king sent and released him, the ruler of peoples set him free."*

A true Joseph is one who is a provider both spiritually and materially for those in the Body of Christ. It is a person who understands that he is simply a manager of all that God has entrusted to him. It is a person who has humility and a broken and contrite heart before God. But how does God prepare modern day Josephs?

Modern day Josephs are prepared through their own versions of bruised feet, with shackles and necks put in irons. It is often through the adversity of failed finances, failed marriages, failed relationships, and broken dreams. These are the things that try men the most. These are the things God uses to allow the Josephs of our day to be proven by the Word of the Lord. Once proven, God brings them out of their prisons and uses them mightily for God's purpose.

Joseph went through his own trials not because of any failure, but because of an incredible calling to save and provide for an entire nation. God had to prepare this man with 13 years of broken dreams and humble circumstances in order to break every ounce of pride and self-will in Joseph. God could not afford to have a 30 year old steeped in arrogance and pride running an entire nation. Are you willing to allow God to do whatever it takes for you to become a true Joseph? Ask the Lord today to do whatever is necessary to fully use your gifts and talents for His eternal Kingdom.

Success Is Our Plan

Now, I understand the closing down of the first business adventures, not working for over 4-years, staying in hotels, not being accepted, being denied of jobs; now, starting to the bottom in employment and working my way back to the palace. I understand now! The Joseph anointing must be place on the weak and humble; not the proud and self-center leaders.

As a group of meek and humbled Christians, we need to make an extraordinary commitment in:
-education
-training
-work hours required
-impacting on family life

To sum it all up, the Hittites "fear" and "terror" has made its way in the modern society through news and the media. The news and media focuses on negativity. What is happening in the media is that the non-Christians are deciding what is receiving the most airtime and headlines.

The principality of the mountain is Apollyon meaning "destroyer", which twists the news and enslaves people by magnifying their fears of living in peace on earth. WE need the true Evangelists to come forth and report the news accurately; even when it is bad. The true Evangelists need to find redemptive angles in every story; then, the words of the Evangelists will powerfully speak the "Will of God" throughout the earth.

Enemy on the Mountain: Hittites (represent bad news)
Significant Displacing Authority: Evangelists
Basic Mission: Fill the airwaves with "good news"
Revelation 5:12 Key: Blessing

When God blesses us with the millions, trillions, and billions, how will I help build the Kingdom of God concerning "The Media"?

"And the LORD answered me: "Write the vision; make it plain on tablets, so he may run who reads it." Habakkuk 2:2, ESV

Promised Land Twenty
The Perizzites
The Mountain of Religion

The Perizzite means "unwalled town or city or village"

Matthew 5:14, NLT *"You are the light of the world--like a city on a hilltop that cannot be hidden."*

The hedges of protection are moved when we practice:

Dissensions	immorality	enmities
Factions	impurity	strife
Envying	sensuality	jealousy
Drunkenness	idolatry outbursts of anger	
Carousing	sorcery	
Fleshly living	disputes	

All are found in Galations 5:19-21 AMP, "Galatians 5:19-21Amplified Bible (AMP)

[19] Now the doings (practices) of the flesh are clear (obvious): they are immorality, impurity, indecency, [20] Idolatry, sorcery, enmity, strife, jealousy, anger (ill temper), selfishness, divisions (dissensions), party spirit (factions, sects with peculiar opinions, heresies), [21] Envy, drunkenness, carousing, and the like. I warn you beforehand, just as I did previously, that those who do such things shall not inherit the kingdom of God.

Lord, I thank you that I am no longer a city without walls for the enemy to come in at its will. I plead the blood of Jesus around me and my family hedges. Surround your warring and mighty angels at the gates of marriages, families, churches, schools, government, jobs and businesses to strengthen the gates and bars, in Jesus name. Amen.

Proverbs 25:28, NLT *"A person without self-control is like a city with broken-down walls"*

The Perizzites Spirit uses the evil past of our lives with pressure and force to enter into our souls. We have to bind and rebuke our past daily. We have to let go of all hurt, pain and evil that torments us of the past.

By leaving our past, we first have to forgive ourselves, then our parents, our love ones; then, we can forgive everyone else that have or may cause harm to us.

WE definitely need to forgive our church members from the past, present and future, so that we may come together successfully to destroy the enemy camps at every level of the mountains that are set before us.........Hey God! My God!

It is not just saying "I forgive everybody", it is about calling each person out by name. Ask God to show you the people that you need to forgive. Create a list of names, groups, organizations, churches or church members, co-workers, business partners and ask for forgiveness on your behalf and their behalf. It may take for you to go to that person and say "I am sorry for holding the pain and hurt, even when they are the ones that hurt you."

Start your list right now:_____

_____
_____
_____
_____
_____
_____
_____
_____
_____
_____
_____
_____
_____
_____
_____

To overcome the Perizzites Mountain, we need "Forgiveness" to rise up like never before and be released into the atmosphere in this earth. The Perizzites spirit enters through un-forgiveness. With un-forgiveness there is separation.

Ezkiel 38:11-12, *"You will say, "I will invade a land of unwalled villages; I will attack a peaceful and unsuspecting people--all of them living without walls and without gates and bars."*

Perizzites comes from the Hebrew root word meaning "to separate". Separation from God is when we mediate on what we are going through or how bad it is for us. Then, we are separated from God and given over to what we have chosen to put our faith in; the hurt, the pain, the disappointments, the insults, the wounds and so on.

We have to continuously speak that God is in our "Rock, Strong Tower, Fortress, Shield, Hiding Place, Shelter and Refuge."

2 Samuel 22:2-3, AMP *"2 He said: The Lord is my Rock [of escape from Saul] and my Fortress [in the wilderness] and my Deliverer; 3 My God, my Rock, in Him will I take refuge; my Shield and the Horn of my salvation; my Stronghold and my Refuge, my Savior—You save me from violence."*

To add, Perizzites spirits are embedded in riches, money, and prosperity, and fleshy enjoyment of this world. The evil gates of the Perizzites are sickness, personal tragedies and financial difficulties to tear down the protected/strong walls of God.

The Perizzites spirit will use friends to condemn and criticize you. I understand there is something called "constructive criticism." But, we have to be very careful when using this term. When condemnation and criticism move towards your life, in the form of hurt; especially from leadership of the church, job, organization, and community…the Perizzites spirit has come into effect. You have to make sure your walls are up and guarded.

Perizzites were built on hills with no walls. A city built without walls will allow anyone to come in. Los Angeles has many homes built on top of mountains without walls..........The homes may look beautiful, but without walls the enemy can come in without notice or a phone call to rob, steal and destroy.

A city, Jacksonville, Florida, without "spiritual watchmen on the walls" is a city that is open to darkness. This is why the church need to focus more on spiritual forces of darkness; other than, peace obtained through prosperity, cars, homes and so forth.

Every church need to focus on being equipped to raise apostles, prophets, evangelists, intercessors, pastors and teachers, elders and deacons for spiritual warfare.

If we can come together in spiritual warfare to tear down the evil forces of murder, violence, sexual immorality, drugs, drug abuse, and so forth; then we can be a powerful church in helping to restore God's Kingdom of love, peace, commitment and servant hood.

The Mountain of Perizzites is taken down through the dynamic leading and power of the Holy Spirit. Since we all are filled with the Holy spirit , we all can come together to take down the Perizzites mountain.

-We will passionately be in love with the Lord
-We will refuse to practice a religion based on platitudes and principles
-WE will refuse to practices well-scheduled worship services and neat and tidy theology
-We will have supernatural experiences with God that defies the expectations and traditions of status quo Christianity.

In the mighty name of Jesus, we bind and cast out all family gods in trees, rocks, skulls, rivers, forests, sanctuaries shrine boxes, compounds and royal places, in Jesus name. Amen.

Enemy on the Mountain: Perizzites (represents idolatry)
Significant Displacing Authority: Holy Spirit

Basic Mission: Model a Holy Spirit infused life and ministry

Revelation 5:12 Key: Honor

When God blesses us with the millions, trillions, and billions, how will I help build the Kingdom of God concerning "The Media"?

"And the LORD answered me: "Write the vision; make it plain on tablets, so he may run who reads it." Habakkuk 2:2, ESV

Promised Land Twenty-One
Your Business Plan

You may be asking, "What is your business or school". Your answer is right in front of you. If you have been on somebody's job for at least 5 years that is your business. If you have worked at Wal-Mart for 5 years in the stocking department, you should have a business in merchandizing or a warehouse that holds all types of merchandise.

If you have worked at McDonald's for 5 years, you should have your own restaurant. If you have been a bank teller for 5 years, you should have your own bank by now. If you have worked in the hospital for 5 years, you should have your own clinic or hospital by now. If you have taught school for 5 years, you should have your own school or afterschool program.

If you have successful operated or worked on some else's job; you are already ahead of the game because you are already skilled and trained for the "calling" and purpose for building God's Kingdom.

Why do I need a business plan? Business plans help determine the best way to allocate scarce resources, such as budgets, inventory, and other assets. By projecting a company's financial vision, a business plan can help leaders avoid pitfalls that may lead to failures along the way.

10 Essential Components of a Business Plan:

1. Mission statement and/or vision statement so you articulate what you are trying to create;

2. Description of your company and product or service;

3. Description of how your product or service is different;

4. Market analysis that discusses the market you are trying to enter, competitors, where you fit, and what type of market share you believe you can secure;

5. Description of your management team, including the experience of key team members and previous successes;

6. How you plan to market the product or service;

7. Analysis of your company's strengths, weaknesses, opportunities, and threat, which will show that you are realistic and have considered opportunities and challenges;

8. Develop a cash flow statement so you understand what your needs are now and will be in the future (a cash flow statement also can help you consider how cash flow could impact growth);

9. Revenue projections; and

10. Summary/conclusion that wraps everything together (this also could be an executive summary at the beginning of the plan).

Write out your business plan with mission statements that will help build God's Kingdom.

Business/Mission Statement #1 (Education)

_____
_____
_____
_____
_____
_____
_____
_____

Business/Mission Statement #2 (Economy)

_____
_____
_____
_____

_____

_____

_____

Business/Mission Statement #3 (Family)

_____

_____

_____

_____

_____

_____

_____

Business/Mission Statement #4 (Celebration)

_____

_____

_____

_____

_____

_____

_____

Business/Mission Statement #5 (Government)

_____

_____

_____

_____

_____

_____

_____

Business/Mission Statement #6 (Media)

_____

_____

_____

_____
_____
_____
_____
_____
_____

Business/Mission Statement #7 (Religion)

_____
_____
_____
_____
_____
_____
_____
_____

Alright now, since we know our plans; let us create a business. Research the internet, go to your local library for sample business plans, contact your local business center or work center resources. Christians, Leaders, Professionals, Entrepreneurs; God's Kingdom Builders, let us get active in enthusiasm for building a Kingdom- minded atmosphere and move forward in God; to do His Will.

Promised Land Twenty-Two
Destroying the Triangle of Evil

1. **Genesis** is the apostolic, trailblazing book of the Torah (which God uses to get the Torah "started")
2. **Exodus** is the prophetic book of the Torah in which the prophet Moses and the prophetic calling of the Israelite people are manifested (Acts 3:22, Acts 7:37)
3. **Leviticus** is the evangelistic book of the Torah in which the inheritance-possessing people of Israel are manifested
4. **Numbers** is the pastoral book of the Torah where God the Shepherd counts His sheep
5. **Deuteronomy** is the teaching book of the Torah in which the Law is repeated, as when a teacher repeats a lesson to make sure that the students have learnt it correctly.

Promised Land Twenty-Three
The Triangle of Evil Bible Study

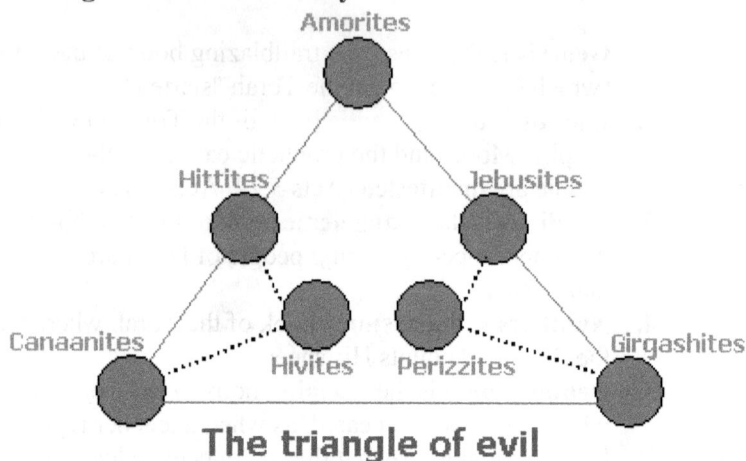

The triangle of evil

Now, let us search scriptures for clarification of these 7 evil spirits based on the format of the triangle of evil.

Revelation 2:26-27 KJV
26. And he that overcometh, and keepeth my works unto the end, to him will I give power over the nations:
27. *And he shall rule them with a rod of iron;* as the vessels of a potter shall they be broken to shivers: even as I received of my Father.
These be the Heathen Nations we are given POWER to rule over

The First Mountain ~ Amorites

Revelation 17:7-9 KJV
7. And the angel said unto me, Wherefore didst thou marvel? I will tell thee the mystery of the woman, and of the beast that carrieth her, which hath the seven heads and ten horns.
8. The beast that thou sawest was, and is not; and shall ascend

out of the bottomless pit, and go into perdition: and they that dwell on the earth shall wonder, whose names were not written in the book of life from the foundation of the world, when they behold the beast that was, and is not, and yet is.

9. And here is the mind which hath wisdom. The seven heads are seven mountains, on which the woman sitteth.

Exodus 23:23
23. For My Mal'ak shall go before thee, and bring thee in unto the Amorites, (HSN#567 'Emoriy) and the Hittites, and the Perizzites, and the Canaanites, and the Hivites, and the Jebusites: and I will cut them off.

Original Strong's Ref. #567
Romanized 'Emoriy
Pronounced em-o-ree'
probably a patronymic from an unused name derived from HSN0559 in the sense of publicity, i.e. prominence; thus, a mountaineer; an Emorite, one of the Canaanitish tribes: KJV--Amorite.

#1) The Amorite - 'Emoriy ~ Fornicators

There were Two Kings of the Amorites:
1) Sihon king of the Amorites who dwelt at Heshbon.
2) Og king of Bashan who dwelt at Ashtaroth in Edrei.

The two battles against these two kings were the first confrontations on the other side of the Jordan before crossing into the Promise Land. YHWH defeated both Sihon king of the Amorites, and Og king of Bashan, who was an Amorite and also a Giant.

Numbers 21:21-35 KJV
21. And Israel sent messengers unto Sihon king of the Amorites, saying,
22. Let me pass through thy land: we will not turn into the fields, or into the vineyards; we will not drink of the waters of the well: but we will go along by the king's high way, until we be past thy

borders.

23. And Sihon would not suffer Israel to pass through his border: but Sihon gathered all his people together, and went out against Israel into the wilderness: and he came to Jahaz, and fought against Israel.

24. And Israel smote him with the edge of the sword, and possessed his land from Arnon unto Jabbok, even unto the children of Ammon: for the border of the children of Ammon was strong.

25. And Israel took all these cities: and Israel dwelt in all the cities of the Amorites, in Heshbon, and in all the villages thereof.

26. For Heshbon was the city of Sihon the king of the Amorites, who had fought against the former king of Moab, and taken all his land out of his hand, even unto Arnon.

27. Wherefore they that speak in proverbs say, Come into Heshbon, let the city of Sihon be built and prepared:

28. For there is a fire gone out of Heshbon, a flame from the city of Sihon: it hath consumed Ar of Moab, and the lords of the high places of Arnon.

29. Woe to thee, Moab! thou art undone, O people of Chemosh: he hath given his sons that escaped, and his daughters, into captivity unto Sihon king of the Amorites.

30. We have shot at them; Heshbon is perished even unto Dibon, and we have laid them waste even unto Nophah, which reacheth unto Medeba.

31. Thus Israel dwelt in the land of the Amorites.

32. And Moses sent to spy out Jaazer, and they took the villages thereof, and drove out the Amorites that were there.

33. And they turned and went up by the way of Bashan: and Og the king of Bashan went out against them, he, and all his people, to the battle at Edrei.

34. And the Lord said unto Moses, Fear him not: for I have delivered him into thy hand, and all his people, and his land; and thou shalt do to him as thou didst unto Sihon king of the Amorites, which dwelt at Heshbon.

35. So they smote him, and his sons, and all his people, until there was none left him alive: and they possessed his land.

Deuteronomy 1:3-4 KJV

3. And it came to pass in the fortieth year, in the eleventh month, on the first day of the month, that Moses spake unto the children of Israel, according unto all that the Lord had given him in commandment unto them;

4. After he had slain Sihon the king of the Amorites, which dwelt in Heshbon, and Og the king of Bashan, which dwelt at Astaroth in Edrei:

Deuteronomy 3:1-11 KJV

1. Then we turned, and went up the way to Bashan: and Og the king of Bashan came out against us, he and all his people, to battle at Edrei.

2. And the Lord said unto me, Fear him not: for I will deliver him, and all his people, and his land, into thy hand; and thou shalt do unto him as thou didst unto Sihon king of the Amorites, which dwelt at Heshbon.

3. So the Lord our God delivered into our hands Og also, the king of Bashan, and all his people: and we smote him until none was left to him remaining.

4. And we took all his cities at that time, there was not a city which we took not from them, threescore cities, all the region of Argob, the kingdom of Og in Bashan.

5. All these cities were fenced with high walls, gates, and bars; beside unwalled towns a great many.

6. And we utterly destroyed them, as we did unto Sihon king of Heshbon, utterly destroying the men, women, and children, of every city.

7. But all the cattle, and the spoil of the cities, we took for a prey to ourselves.

8. And we took at that time out of the hand of the two kings of the Amorites the land that was on this side Jordan, from the river of Arnon unto mount Hermon;

9. (Which Hermon the Sidonians call Sirion; and the Amorites call it Shenir;)

10. All the cities of the plain, and all Gilead, and all Bashan, unto Salchah and Edrei, cities of the kingdom of Og in Bashan.

11. For only Og king of Bashan remained of the remnant of giants; behold his bedstead was a bedstead of iron; is it not in Rabbath of the children of Ammon? nine cubits was the length

thereof, and four cubits the breadth of it, after the cubit of a man.

However, before all of this we read a curious statement recorded in Genesis 48 where Jacob-Israel states to Joseph that he took a portion out of the hand of the Amorite with his sword and his bow; yet nowhere else do we read of a battle between Jacob and the Amorites:

Genesis 48:20-22 KJV
20. And he blessed them that day, saying, In thee shall Israel bless, saying, God make thee as Ephraim and as Manasseh: and he set Ephraim before Manasseh.
21. And Israel said unto Joseph, Behold, I die: but God shall be with you, and bring you again unto the land of your fathers.
22. Moreover I have given to thee one portion above thy brethren, which I took out of the hand of the Amorite with my sword and with my bow.

WHO is "the Amorite" of which Israel speaks in Genesis 48:22?

Genesis 35:22 KJV
22. And it came to pass, when Israel dwelt in that land, that Reuben went and lay with Bilhah his father's concubine: and Israel heard it. Now the sons of Jacob were twelve:

Where did Jacob-Israel make war against "the Amorite" with his sword and his bow as he states in Genesis 48:22? His "sword and his bow" are the Truth, the Right, and the Righteous Judgment. He therefore calls his own firstborn son Reuben "the Amorite" because he could not control his own voracious sexual appetite. Reuben lost part of his full inheritance because he went in unto Bilhah the concubine of Jacob-Israel and slept with the concubine of his own father. The words of Jacob to Joseph are supernal: Jacob is naming Reuben an Amorite with the sexual deviance and appetite of a Giant. The same as were Sihon king of the Amorites of Heshbon and Og the king of Bashan whose bedstead, (possibly of a sexual connotation) was the bedstead of a Giant. Therefore took up Israel his supernal sword and bow, and divided the inheritance of Reuben, (a spiritual Amorite) and

Israel gave his Word-command and divided the inheritance unto the two sons of Joseph; that is to Ephraim and Manasseh, because Israel as the father had the Right, and because his firstborn son Reuben betrayed him like an Amorite.

Amorites are betrayers, adulterers, fornicators, whoremongers, sexual deviants, and typically would have the "sexual appetites" of Giants. The tribal allotments of Reuben, Gad, and Manasseh were also in the northeastern territories, mountains, and lands of the Giants:

Deuteronomy 3:11-17 KJV
11. For only Og king of Bashan remained of the remnant of giants; behold his bedstead was a bedstead of iron; is it not in Rabbath of the children of Ammon? nine cubits was the length thereof, and four cubits the breadth of it, after the cubit of a man.
12. And this land, which we possessed at that time, from Aroer, which is by the river Arnon, and half mount Gilead, and the cities thereof, gave I unto the Reubenites and to the Gadites.
13. And the rest of Gilead, and all Bashan, being the kingdom of Og, gave I unto the half tribe of Manasseh; all the region of Argob, with all Bashan, which was called the land of giants.
14. Jair the son of Manasseh took all the country of Argob unto the coasts of Geshuri and Maachathi; and called them after his own name, Bashanhavothjair, unto this day.
15. And I gave Gilead unto Machir.
16. And unto the Reubenites and unto the Gadites I gave from Gilead even unto the river Arnon half the valley, and the border even unto the river Jabbok, which is the border of the children of Ammon;
17. The plain also, and Jordan, and the coast thereof, from Chinnereth even unto the sea of the plain, even the salt sea, under Ashdothpisgah eastward.

The rebellion of Korah and the sons of Reuben:

Numbers 16:1-3 KJV
1. Now Korah, the son of Izhar, the son of Kohath, the son of Levi, and Dathan and Abiram, the sons of Eliab, and On, the son

of Peleth, sons of Reuben, took men:

2. And they rose up before Moses, with certain of the children of Israel, two hundred and fifty princes of the assembly, famous in the congregation, men of renown:

3. And they gathered themselves together against Moses and against Aaron, and said unto them, Ye take too much upon you, seeing all the congregation are holy, every one of them, and the Lord is among them: wherefore then lift ye up yourselves above the congregation of the Lord?

Numbers 26:5-10 KJV

5. Reuben, the eldest son of Israel: the children of Reuben; Hanoch, of whom cometh the family of the Hanochites: of Pallu, the family of the Palluites:

6. Of Hezron, the family of the Hezronites: of Carmi, the family of the Carmites.

7. These are the families of the Reubenites: and they that were numbered of them were forty and three thousand and seven hundred and thirty.

8. And the sons of Pallu; Eliab.

9. And the sons of Eliab; Nemuel, and Dathan, and Abiram. This is that Dathan and Abiram, which were famous in the congregation, who strove against Moses and against Aaron in the company of Korah, when they strove against the Lord:

10. And the earth opened her mouth, and swallowed them up together with Korah, when that company died, what time the fire devoured two hundred and fifty men: and they became a sign.

Genealogy of Reuben ~

1 Chronicles 5:1-12 KJV

1. Now the sons of Reuben the firstborn of Israel, (for he was the firstborn; but forasmuch as he defiled his father's bed, his birthright was given unto the sons of Joseph the son of Israel: and the genealogy is not to be reckoned after the birthright.

2. For Judah prevailed above his brethren, and of him came the chief ruler; but the birthright was Joseph's:)

3. The sons, I say, of Reuben the firstborn of Israel were, Hanoch, and Pallu, Hezron, and Carmi.

4. The sons of Joel; Shemaiah his son, Gog his son, Shimei his son,

5. Micah his son, Reaia his son, Baal his son,

6. Beerah his son, whom Tilgathpilneser king of Assyria carried away captive: he was prince of the Reubenites.

7. And his brethren by their families, when the genealogy of their generations was reckoned, were the chief, Jeiel, and Zechariah,

8. And Bela the son of Azaz, the son of Shema, the son of Joel, who dwelt in Aroer, even unto Nebo and Baalmeon:

9. And eastward he inhabited unto the entering in of the wilderness from the river Euphrates: because their cattle were multiplied in the land of Gilead.

10. And in the days of Saul they made war with the Hagarites, who fell by their hand: and they dwelt in their tents throughout all the east land of Gilead.

11. And the children of Gad dwelt over against them, in the land of Bashan unto Salchah:

12. Joel the chief, and Shapham the next, and Jaanai, and Shaphat in Bashan.

However, "the fullness of the Gentiles" ~ Amorites comes in at a later date respective to each individual person: toward the end; near the appointed time of the end.

Genesis 15:12-16 KJV

12. And when the sun was going down, a deep sleep fell upon Abram; and, lo, an horror of great darkness fell upon him.

13. And he said unto Abram, Know of a surety that thy seed shall be a stranger in a land that is not theirs, and shall serve them; and they shall afflict them four hundred years;

14. And also that nation, whom they shall serve, will I judge: and afterward shall they come out with great substance.

15. And thou shalt go to thy fathers in peace; thou shalt be buried in a good old age.

16. But in the fourth generation they shall come hither again: for the iniquity of the Amorites is not yet full.

The Second Mountain ~ Hittites

Revelation 17:7-9 KJV
7. And the angel said unto me, Wherefore didst thou marvel? I will tell thee the mystery of the woman, and of the beast that carrieth her, which hath the seven heads and ten horns.
8. The beast that thou sawest was, and is not; and shall ascend out of the bottomless pit, and go into perdition: and they that dwell on the earth shall wonder, whose names were not written in the book of life from the foundation of the world, when they behold the beast that was, and is not, and yet is.
9. And here is the mind which hath wisdom. The seven heads are seven mountains, on which the woman sitteth.

Exodus 23:23
23. For My Mal'ak shall go before thee, and bring thee in unto the Amorites, and the Hittites, (HSN#2850 Chittiy) and the Perizzites, and the Canaanites, and the Hivites, and the Jebusites: and I will cut them off.

Original Strong's Ref. #2850
Romanized Chittiy
Pronounced khit-tee'
patronymically from HSN2845; a Chittite, or descendant of Cheth:
KJV--Hittite, Hittities.

Original Strong's Ref. #2845
Romanized Cheth
Pronounced khayth
from HSN2865; terror; Cheth, an aboriginal Canaanite:
KJV--Heth.

#2) The Hittites - Chittiy - Daughters of Heth ~ The Flesh

Genesis 10:15 KJV
15. And Canaan begat Sidon his firstborn, and Heth,

Genesis 23:8-20 KJV

8. And he communed with them, saying, If it be your mind that I should bury my dead out of my sight; hear me, and intreat for me to Ephron the son of Zohar,

9. That he may give me the cave of Machpelah, which he hath, which is in the end of his field; for as much money as it is worth he shall give it me for a possession of a buryingplace amongst you.

10. And Ephron dwelt among the children of Heth: and Ephron the Hittite answered Abraham in the audience of the children of Heth, even of all that went in at the gate of his city, saying,

11. Nay, my lord, hear me: the field give I thee, and the cave that is therein, I give it thee; in the presence of the sons of my people give I it thee: bury thy dead.

12. And Abraham bowed down himself before the people of the land.

13. And he spake unto Ephron in the audience of the people of the land, saying, But if thou wilt give it, I pray thee, hear me: I will give thee money for the field; take it of me, and I will bury my dead there.

14. And Ephron answered Abraham, saying unto him,

15. My lord, hearken unto me: the land is worth four hundred shekels of silver; what is that betwixt me and thee? bury therefore thy dead.

16. And Abraham hearkened unto Ephron; and Abraham weighed to Ephron the silver, which he had named in the audience of the sons of Heth, four hundred shekels of silver, current money with the merchant.

17. And the field of Ephron which was in Machpelah, which was before Mamre, the field, and the cave which was therein, and all the trees that were in the field, that were in all the borders round about, were made sure

18. Unto Abraham for a possession in the presence of the children of Heth, before all that went in at the gate of his city.

19. And after this, Abraham buried Sarah his wife in the cave of the field of Machpelah before Mamre: the same is Hebron in the land of Canaan.

20. And the field, and the cave that is therein, were made sure unto Abraham for a possession of a buryingplace by the sons of

Heth.

Genesis 25:29-32 KJV
29. And Jacob sod pottage: and Esau came from the field, and he was faint:
30. And Esau said to Jacob, Feed me, I pray thee, with that same red pottage; for I am faint: therefore was his name called Edom.
31. And Jacob said, Sell me this day thy birthright.
32. And Esau said, Behold, I am at the point to die: and what profit shall this birthright do to me?

Genesis 36:1-3 KJV
1. Now these are the generations of Esau, who is Edom.
2. Esau took his wives of the daughters of Canaan; Adah the daughter of Elon the Hittite, and Aholibamah the daughter of Anah the daughter of Zibeon the Hivite;
3. And Bashemath Ishmael's daughter, sister of Nebajoth.

Genesis 26:34-35 KJV
34. And Esau was forty years old when he took to wife Judith the daughter of Beeri the Hittite, and Bashemath the daughter of Elon the Hittite:
35. Which were a grief of mind unto Isaac and to Rebekah.

Hittites are MURDEROUS in heart ~

Genesis 27:41-46 KJV
41. And Esau hated Jacob because of the blessing wherewith his father blessed him: and Esau said in his heart, The days of mourning for my father are at hand; then will I slay my brother Jacob.
42. And these words of Esau her elder son were told to Rebekah: and she sent and called Jacob her younger son, and said unto him, Behold, thy brother Esau, as touching thee, doth comfort himself, purposing to kill thee.
43. Now therefore, my son, obey my voice; and arise, flee thou to Laban my brother to Haran;
44. And tarry with him a few days, until thy brother's fury turn away;

45. Until thy brother's anger turn away from thee, and he forget that which thou hast done to him: then I will send, and fetch thee from thence: why should I be deprived also of you both in one day?
46. And Rebekah said to Isaac, I am weary of my life because of the daughters of Heth: if Jacob take a wife of the daughters of Heth, such as these which are of the daughters of the land, what good shall my life do me?

Jerusalem of Below ~
Hittites - Daughters of Heth "married" Esau ~ Terror and Murder

Ezekiel 16:1-3 KJV
1. Again the word of the Lord came unto me, saying,
2. Son of man, cause Jerusalem to know her abominations,
3. And say, Thus saith the Lord God unto Jerusalem; Thy birth and thy nativity is of the land of Canaan; thy father was an Amorite, and thy mother an Hittite.

Commandments and Doctrine of the Master ~

Exodus 20:13 KJV
13. Thou shalt not kill.

Matthew 5:21-26 KJV
21. Ye have heard that it was said by them of old time, Thou shalt not kill; and whosoever shall kill shall be in danger of the judgment:
22. But I say unto you, That whosoever is angry with his brother without a cause shall be in danger of the judgment: and whosoever shall say to his brother, Raca, shall be in danger of the council: but whosoever shall say, Thou fool, shall be in danger of hell fire.
23. Therefore if thou bring thy gift to the altar, and there rememberest that thy brother hath ought against thee;
24. Leave there thy gift before the altar, and go thy way; first be reconciled to thy brother, and then come and offer thy gift.
25. Agree with thine adversary quickly, whiles thou art in the way with him; lest at any time the adversary deliver thee to the

judge, and the judge deliver thee to the officer, and thou be cast into prison.
26. Verily I say unto thee, Thou shalt by no means come out thence, till thou hast paid the uttermost farthing.

1 John 3:11-15 KJV
11. For this is the message that ye heard from the beginning, that we should love one another.
12. Not as Cain, who was of that wicked one, and slew his brother. And wherefore slew he him? Because his own works were evil, and his brother's righteous.
13. Marvel not, my brethren, if the world hate you.
14. We know that we have passed from death unto life, because we love the brethren. He that loveth not his brother abideth in death.
15. Whosoever hateth his brother is a murderer: and ye know that no murderer hath eternal life abiding in him.

Jerusalem of Above ~

Revelation 22:14-15 ASV
14. Blessed are they that wash their robes, that they may have the right to come to the tree of life, and may enter in by the gates into the city.
15. Without are the dogs, and the sorcerers, and the fornicators, and the murderers, and the idolaters, and every one that loveth and maketh a lie.

Revelation 22:14-17 KJV
14. Blessed are they that do his commandments, that they may have right to the tree of life, and may enter in through the gates into the city.
15. For without are dogs, and sorcerers, and whoremongers, and murderers, and idolaters, and whosoever loveth and maketh a lie.
16. I Jesus have sent mine angel to testify unto you these things in the churches. I am the root and the offspring of David, and the bright and morning star.
17. And the Spirit and the bride say, Come. And let him that

heareth say, Come. And let him that is athirst come. And whosoever will, let him take the water of life freely.

The Third Mountain ~ Perizzites

Revelation 17:7-9 KJV
7. And the angel said unto me, Wherefore didst thou marvel? I will tell thee the mystery of the woman, and of the beast that carrieth her, which hath the seven heads and ten horns.
8. The beast that thou sawest was, and is not; and shall ascend out of the bottomless pit, and go into perdition: and they that dwell on the earth shall wonder, whose names were not written in the book of life from the foundation of the world, when they behold the beast that was, and is not, and yet is.
9. And here is the mind which hath wisdom. The seven heads are seven mountains, on which the woman sitteth.

Exodus 23:23
23. For My Mal'ak shall go before thee, and bring thee in unto the Amorites, and the Hittites, and the Perizzites, (HSN#6522 Prizziy) and the Canaanites, and the Hivites, and the Jebusites: and I will cut them off.

Original Strong's Ref. #6522
Romanized Prizziy
Pronounced per-iz-zee'
for HSN6521; inhabitant of the open country; a Perizzite, one of the Canaanitish tribes:
KJV--Perizzite.

#3) The Perizzites - Prizziy - Dividers ~ Rephaim Giants

When at first the Mal'ak of YHWH led me into the Promise Land there was great and plentiful fruit abounding, which I neither labored for, nor cultivated myself. And much fruit there was of the Perizzites, of which fruits I began to partake, and did indulge myself of their delicacies. The first of my tasting was, like so many others, a book of the fruit of the Land called "The Late Great Planet Earth" written by a mighty one of the Perizzite families. However, this fruit left me famished and wanting for more; and many more fruits of the Perizzite kind there were to be had, for they do abound plentifully in the Land; and there are many different books of the Perizzite genus. And so many more of these books did I consume: Until eventually I myself began to become as one of them. Yet some time later, in an appointed time, the Mal'ak of YHWH must needs cut them off; even with the Sword of his mouth; even with the Doctrine of the Word of YHWH.

These are the mighty ones of the Perizzites and Rephaims. The Rephaims are the Giants of the Land and the Perizzites are the clawed Dividers of the Land. What the Perizzites and Rephaim do not understand is that YHWH allows them to remain in their positions of stature for a time so as to separate a people unto himself. They are allowed their positions of high esteem for a purpose even though they Divide the Land for gain.

Perizzites and Rephaims ~ ha-Priziy ha-Rpa'iym (Genesis 15:20)
Dividers of the Land - Divisive - Schismatics (Heretics)

A true "heretic" is a schismatic or one causing division for personal gain:

Titus 3:10-11 KJV
10. A man that is an heretick (GSN#141 hairetikos) after the first and second admonition reject;
11. Knowing that he that is such is subverted, and sinneth, being condemned of himself.

Original Strong's Ref. #141
Romanized hairetikos
Pronounced hahee-ret-ee-kos'
from the same as GSN0140; a schismatic:
KJV--heretic [the Greek word itself].

Original Strong's Ref. #140
Romanized hairetizo

Pronounced hahee-ret-id'-zo
from a derivative of GSN0138; to make a choice:
KJV--choose.

Genesis 13:5-7 KJV
5. And Lot also, which went with Abram, had flocks, and herds, and tents.
6. And the land was not able to bear them, that they might dwell together: for their substance was great, so that they could not dwell together.
7. And there was a strife between the herdmen of Abram's cattle and the herdmen of Lot's cattle: and the Canaanite and the Perizzite dwelled then (HSN#227 'az - thus, therefore) in the land.

Original Strong's Ref. #227
Romanized 'az
Pronounced awz
a demonstrative adverb; at that time or place; also as a conjunction, therefore:
KJV--beginning, for, from, hitherto, now, of old, once, since, then, at which time, yet.

"And there was a strife between the herdmen of Abram's cattle and the herdmen of Lot's cattle: and THUS-FROM THERE the Canaanite and the Perizzite dwelled in the Land"...

Genesis 13:8-12 KJV
8. And Abram said unto Lot, Let there be no strife, I pray thee, between me and thee, and between my herdmen and thy herdmen; for we be brethren.
9. Is not the whole land before thee? separate thyself, I pray thee, from me: if thou wilt take the left hand, then I will go to the right; or if thou depart to the right hand, then I will go to the left.
10. And Lot lifted up his eyes, and beheld all the plain of Jordan, that it was well watered every where, before the Lord destroyed Sodom and Gomorrah, even as the garden of the Lord, like the land of Egypt, as thou comest unto Zoar.
11. Then Lot chose him all the plain of Jordan; and Lot

journeyed east: and they separated themselves the one from the other.
12. Abram dwelled in the land of Canaan, and Lot dwelled in the cities of the plain, and pitched his tent toward Sodom.

The Perizzites are from the opposite side of the Jordan, the mountains, (symbolic of stature) even to the base of Mount Hermon from whence the Watchers descended in Enoch. The Perizzites and the Rephaim-Giants work together to Divide the Land for gain.

Genesis 15:18-21 KJV
18. In the same day the Lord made a covenant with Abram, saying, Unto thy seed have I given this land, from the river of Egypt unto the great river, the river Euphrates:
19. The Kenites, and the Kenizzites, and the Kadmonites,
20. And the Hittites, and the Perizzites, (HSN#6522 Prizziy) and the Rephaims, (HSN#7497 rapha')
21. And the Amorites, and the Canaanites, and the Girgashites, and the Jebusites.

Original Strong's Ref. #7497
Romanized rapha'
Pronounced raw-faw'
or raphah {raw-faw'}; from HSN7495 in the sense of invigorating; a giant:
KJV--giant, Rapha, Rephaim(-s). See also HSN1051.

Joshua 17:15 KJV
15. And Joshua answered them, If thou be a great people, then get thee up to the wood country, and cut down for thyself there in the land of the Perizzites (HSN#6522 Prizziy) and of the giants, (HSN#7497 rapha') if mount Ephraim be too narrow for thee.

The two names from Joshua 17:15 are the same names from Genesis 15:20; namely the Perizzites and the Rephaim-Giants. The Perizzites are connected to Parac-Persia and the DIVIDED empire of the Medes and the Persians, (silver chest plate and shoulders-arms).

Leviticus 11:13-14
13. And these are they which ye shall have in abomination among the fowls; they shall not be eaten, they are an abomination: the eagle, (nesher-Babylon) and the ossifrage, (Perec-Parac-Persia) and the ospray, (`Azniyah-Yavan "Countenance of `Az").

Leviticus 11:13 TUA (Transliterated Unaccented)
13. W'et- 'eleh tshaqtsuw min- ha`owp ; lo' ye'akluw --sheqets hem: 'Et- hanesher w'et- haperec w'et ha`azniyah

Original Strong's Ref. #6538
Romanized perec
Pronounced peh'-res
from HSN6536; a claw; also a kind of eagle:
KJV--claw, ossifrage.

Original Strong's Ref. #6536
Romanized parac
Pronounced paw-ras'
a primitive root; to break in pieces, i.e. (usually without violence) to split, distribute:
KJV--deal, divide, have hoofs, part, tear.

Perec-Parac is the "clawed divider" eagle-vulture. The root of Perec is Parac (pronounced "Paras" as in Persia). Perec is the same Aramaic Peres-Perez of Daniel chapter five.

Daniel 5:24-28 KJV
24. Then was the part of the hand sent from him; and this writing was written.
25. And this is the writing that was written, Mene, Mene, Tekel, Upharsin.
26. This is the interpretation of the thing: Mene; God hath numbered thy kingdom, and finished it.
27. Tekel; Thou art weighed in the balances, and art found wanting.

28. Peres; (HSN#6537 prac) Thy kingdom is divided, and given to the Medes and Persians (HSN#6540 Parac).

Original Strong's Ref. #6537
Romanized prac
Pronounced per-as'
(Aramaic) corresponding to HSN6536; to split up:
KJV--divide, [U-]pharsin.

Original Strong's Ref. #6540
Romanized Parac
Pronounced paw-ras'
(Aramaic) corresponding to HSN6539:
KJV--Persia, Persians.

Original Strong's Ref. #6539
Romanized Parac
Pronounced paw-ras'
of foreign origin; Paras (i.e. Persia), an Eastern country, including its inhabitants:
KJV--Persia, Persians.

Daniel 11:39 KJV
39. Thus shall he do in the most strong holds with a strange god, whom he shall acknowledge and increase with glory: and he shall cause them to rule over many, and shall divide the land for gain.

They are as the mighty ones of old time, the ancients of `owlam, men of the named and men of renown: Giants among the people and respecters of person, speaking evil of those things which they know not: but rather only what they know naturally, as brute beasts, and in those things they corrupt themselves. Woe unto them; having gone in the way of Cain, running greedily after the error of Balaam for reward, and perishing in the gainsaying of Korah. These are hidden stones in the feasts of charity, feasting with the saints, feeding themselves without fear: clouds without water, carried about with the wind; autumn trees which have passed their appointed times, yet without fruit, twice dead, plucked up by the roots; Raging waves of the sea, foaming out their own shame; wandering stars, to whom is reserved the blackness of darkness forever. And Enoch also, the seventh from Adam, prophesied of these, saying, Behold, the Lord cometh with ten thousands of his saints, To execute judgment upon all, and to convince all that are ungodly among them of all their ungodly deeds which they have ungodly committed, and of all their hard speeches which ungodly sinners have spoken against him. They are murmurers, complainers, walking after their own lusts; and their mouth speaketh great swelling words, having men's persons in admiration because of advantage, (Ref. Epistle of Jude).

Perizzites and Rephaim Giants they are …
Mighty ones lording themselves over the flocks of YHWH …
daq:
The Fourth Mountain ~ Canaanites

Revelation 17:7-9 KJV
7. And the angel said unto me, Wherefore didst thou marvel? I will tell thee the mystery of the woman, and of the beast that carrieth her, which hath the seven heads and ten horns.
8. The beast that thou sawest was, and is not; and shall ascend out of the bottomless pit, and go into perdition: and they that dwell on the earth shall wonder, whose names were not written in the book of life from the foundation of the world, when they behold the beast that was, and is not, and yet is.
9. And here is the mind which hath wisdom. The seven heads are seven mountains, on which the woman sitteth.

Exodus 23:23
23. For My Mal'ak shall go before thee, and bring thee in unto the Amorites, and the Hittites, and the Perizzites, and the Canaanites, (HSN#3669 Kna`aniy) and the Hivites, and the Jebusites: and I will cut them off.

Original Strong's Ref. #3669
Romanized Kna`aniy
Pronounced ken-ah-an-ee'

patrial from HSN3667; a Kenaanite or inhabitant of Kenaan; by implication, a pedlar (the Canaanites standing for their neighbors the Ishmaelites, who conducted mercantile caravans): KJV--Canaanite, merchant, trafficker.

Original Strong's Ref. #3667
Romanized Kna`an
Pronounced ken-ah'-an
from HSN3665; humiliated; Kenaan, a son a Ham; also the country inhabited by him:
KJV--Canaan, merchant, traffick.

#4) The Canaanites - Kna`aniy ~ All of the Transgressors
-- a) All of the transgressions of the sinners of the Heathen
-- b) A woman of abomination in her impurity (Revelation 17)
-- c) The Covenant through the eyes of the FLESH

Joshua 17:16-18 KJV
16. And the children of Joseph said, The hill is not enough for us: and all the Canaanites that dwell in the land of the valley have chariots of iron, both they who are of Bethshean and her towns, and they who are of the valley of Jezreel.
17. And Joshua spake unto the house of Joseph, even to Ephraim and to Manasseh, saying, Thou art a great people, and hast great power: thou shalt not have one lot only:
18. But the mountain shall be thine; for it is a wood, and thou shalt cut it down: and the outgoings of it shall be thine: for thou shalt drive out the Canaanites, though they have iron chariots, and though they be strong.

Judges 1:19 KJV
19. And the Lord was with Judah; and he drave out the inhabitants of the mountain; but could not drive out the inhabitants of the valley, because they had chariots of iron.

Judges 4:2-3 KJV
2. And the Lord sold them into the hand of Jabin king of Canaan that reigned in Hazor; the captain of whose host was Sisera, which dwelt in Harosheth of the Gentiles.

3. And the children of Israel cried unto the Lord: for he had nine hundred chariots of iron; and twenty years he mightily oppressed the children of Israel.

The Canaanites have chariots of IRON and this is a bad thing. There are two types of iron as in all things supernal in the Scripture. Iron is spirit whether for the good or for the bad. Just as the saints, who overcome, do rule the nations with a rod of iron; so also do the Canaanites have their iron war chariots. The good and bad connotations are first displayed in the typology of Torah. Notice in the two following passages the position of the metals changes between heaven and earth, iron and brass, (brass is judgment) and the latter is progressively worse. The iron as the earth below, of Deuteronomy 28:23, is probably what the Nebuchadnezzar image statue dream of Daniel 2 references. That being that the ten toes of iron and miry clay represent unclean spirit, (the iron) mingled with the seed of man, (potters' clay).

Leviticus 26:18-19 KJV
18. And if ye will not yet for all this hearken unto me, then I will punish you seven times more for your sins.
19. And I will break the pride of your power; and I will make your heaven as iron, and your earth as brass:

Deuteronomy 28:23-24 KJV
23. And thy heaven that is over thy head shall be brass, and the earth that is under thee shall be iron.
24. The Lord shall make the rain of thy land powder and dust: from heaven shall it come down upon thee, until thou be destroyed.

Deuteronomy 3:11 KJV
11. For only Og king of Bashan remained of the remnant of giants; behold his bedstead was a bedstead of iron; is it not in Rabbath of the children of Ammon? nine cubits was the length thereof, and four cubits the breadth of it, after the cubit of a man.

However, there is a good iron which is portrayed in a curious event recorded in the times of the prophet Elisha where the good iron swims; and it just so happens to be the head of an axe.

2 Kings 6:4-6 KJV
4. So he went with them. And when they came to Jordan, they cut down wood.
5. But as one was felling a beam, the axe head fell into the water: and he cried, and said, Alas, master! for it was borrowed.
6. And the man of God said, Where fell it? And he shewed him the place. And he cut down a stick, and cast it in thither; and the iron did swim.

The Jordan is symbolic of the baptismal waters of the River of Life. The "axe head" is iron which is spirit-supernal; if it is of the "good iron" kind then it will come to life and swim to the surface when the Great Shepherd causes his staff to Passover it. Pray that ye may be able to swim to the surface of the waters in that day; that ye may be found worthy to stand before the Son of Man: upon a Brazen Sea of glass having been mingled with baptismal fire.

Salvation even unto the Canaanitish peoples ~

THE GREATEST EXAMPLE OF THE ALL ISRAEL OF YHWH is the inclusion of the Gentiles found in the Matthew 15 account concerning the Canaanite woman of the coasts of Tyre and Sidon. She was grafted into the Olive Tree of YHWH by FAITH, (and then one is no more a "Gentile"). The Canaanite woman of Tyre was grafted into the Israelite family BY FAITH after Yeshua had made it extremely clear that he was sent ONLY to "the lost sheep of the house of Israel". The woman was required to change her own mindset; and she was willing to do so, spiritually hungry, and was saved. She was willing to become "a dog" sitting at the feet of the Master waiting for crumbs to fall from the table of the Master, (like Mary sitting at his feet and soaking up his doctrine). The same was true for even Nicodemus, a master-teacher of Israel, (meaning he probably had all of Torah memorized from his youth). Nicodemus realized in the end that he was nothing more than "Lazarus the poor beggar" and a spiritual "leper" coming secretly in the night; begging the true Master for crumbs of understanding.

Matthew 15:21-28 KJV
21. Then Jesus went thence, and departed into the coasts of Tyre and Sidon.
22. And, behold, a woman of Canaan came out of the same coasts, and cried unto him, saying, Have mercy on me, O Lord, thou Son of David; my daughter is grievously vexed with a devil.
23. But he answered her not a word. And his disciples came and besought him, saying, Send her away; for she crieth after us.
24. But he answered and said, I am not sent but unto the lost sheep of the house of Israel.
25. Then came she and worshipped him, saying, Lord, help me.
26. But he answered and said, It is not meet to take the children's bread, and to cast it to dogs.
27. And she said, Truth, Lord: yet the dogs eat of the crumbs which fall from their masters' table.
28. Then Jesus answered and said unto her, O woman, great is thy faith: be it unto thee even as thou wilt. And [Also] her daughter was made whole from that very hour.

NOTICE THAT WORSHIP WAS NOT ENOUGH ~ A change in mindset is first necessary and then the worship will be in Spirit and in Truth. Nowhere in the Scripture is the statement of Matthew 15:24 rescinded or modified and neither shall it ever be. Yeshua will not be changing his mind or his statement: so then it is we who MUST change our thinking, perspectives, and mindset. And looking at some of the other translations the statement is the same and even more pronounced. Nowhere does Yeshua say that he speaks of any fleshly seed line of "the lost sheep of the house of Israel" or a "dispensational timeline" for Jews and Israelites being separate from the Ekklesia-Church Age. Moreover, the northern tribes of the House of Israel had gone into captivity in 722BC which was ¾ of a millennium or about 750 years before the statement of Matthew 15:24.

Matthew 15:24 ASV (American Standard)
24. But he answered and said, I was not sent but unto the lost sheep of the house of Israel.

Matthew 15:24 RSV (Revised Standard)
24. He answered, "I was sent only to the lost sheep of the house of Israel."

Matthew 15:24 YGB (YLT Young's Literal Bible)
24. and he answering said, 'I was not sent except to the lost sheep of the house of Israel.'

Matthew 15:24 WEY (Weymouth's New Testament)
24. "I have only been sent to the lost sheep of the house of Israel," He replied.

If Yeshua was sent ONLY to the Lost Sheep of the House of Israel then it means THE ALL ISRAEL OF YHWH. Therefore if one is not willing to become an Israelite, and be grafted into the Jeremiah 11 - Romans 11 Olive Tree of YHWH, then Yeshua the Root and Vine states that he was not sent to that person.

Jeremiah 11:16-17 KJV
16. The Lord called thy name, A green olive tree, fair, and of goodly fruit: with the noise of a great tumult he hath kindled fire upon it, and the branches of it are broken.
17. For the Lord of hosts, that planted thee, hath pronounced evil against thee, for the evil of the house of Israel and of the house of Judah, which they have done against themselves to provoke me to anger in offering incense unto Baal.

Romans 11:16-17 KJV
16. For if the firstfruit be holy, the lump is also holy: and if the root be holy, so are the branches.
17. And if some of the branches be broken off, and thou, being a wild olive tree, wert graffed in among them, and with them partakest of the root and fatness of the olive tree;

And the New Covenant consists of the same Two Houses ~

Jeremiah 31:31-33 KJV
31. Behold, the days come, saith the Lord, that I will make a new

covenant with the house of Israel, and with the house of Judah:
32. Not according to the covenant that I made with their fathers in the day that I took them by the hand to bring them out of the land of Egypt; which my covenant they brake, although I was an husband unto them, saith the Lord:
33. But this shall be the covenant that I will make with the house of Israel; After those days, saith the Lord, I will put my law in their inward parts, and write it in their hearts; and will be their God, and they shall be my people.

Hebrews 8:8-12 KJV
8. For finding fault with them, he saith, Behold, the days come, saith the Lord, when I will make a new covenant with the house of Israel and with the house of Judah:
9. Not according to the covenant that I made with their fathers in the day when I took them by the hand to lead them out of the land of Egypt; because they continued not in my covenant, and I regarded them not, saith the Lord.
10. For this is the covenant that I will make with the house of Israel after those days, saith the Lord; I will put my laws into their mind, and write them in their hearts: and I will be to them a God, and they shall be to me a people:

Are not both Houses now the One Rod of Ezekiel 37:19 in His hand?

The Canaanite woman of Tyre was grafted into the Olive Tree BY FAITH. However, it was not until she was finally willing to eat whatsoever crumbs fell from the table of the Master; and that is when she was grafted into the Household of YHWH through Christ Yeshua in his Doctrine.

And the final words of Zechariah came true for the Canaanite woman:

Zechariah 14:21 KJV
21. Yea, every pot in Jerusalem and in Judah shall be holiness unto the Lord of hosts: and all they that sacrifice shall come and take of them, and seethe therein: and in that day there shall be no

more the Canaanite in the house of the Lord of hosts.

The Matthew 15:21-28 account of the woman of Tyre is one of the keys that will lead one into a deeper understanding of Zechariah 14. YHWH himself paid a visit to Tyre, just as was prophesied in Isaiah 23, and the fulfillment of that prophecy eventually led to the dispensing of the Gospel to the Gentiles through the ministry of Paul.

Isaiah 23:13-15 KJV
13. Behold the land of the Chaldeans; this people was not, till the Assyrian founded it for them that dwell in the wilderness: they set up the towers thereof, they raised up the palaces thereof; and he brought it to ruin.
14. Howl, ye ships of Tarshish: for your strength is laid waste.
15. And it shall come to pass in that day, that Tyre shall be forgotten seventy years, according to the days of one king: after the end of seventy years shall Tyre sing as an harlot.

Nebuchadnezzar leveled the city of Tyre, (then again later it was destroyed by Alexander). Yet Tyre was forgotten for seventy years. However, one will probably not find this seventy years in history because it was not meant in that way to begin with. The seventy years are found only where YHWH himself says it was forgotten; and that comes through a proper understanding of the Word. However, that proper understanding generally comes only by true faith, (believe it or not we learn the hard way that it takes much faith to simply believe what the Scripture says over our own teachers, historians, and traditions which are according to the knowledge of man). When Judah returned from the Babylonian captivity Tyre was paid in advance for building supplies to begin building the Temple. However, only the foundation was laid by Zerubbabel and the project was halted for seventy years, (491BC-421BC).

Ezra 3:6-7 KJV
6. From the first day of the seventh month began they to offer burnt offerings unto the Lord. But the foundation of the temple of the Lord was not yet laid.

7. They gave money also unto the masons, and to the carpenters; and meat, and drink, and oil, unto them of Zidon, and to them of Tyre, to bring cedar trees from Lebanon to the sea of Joppa, according to the grant that they had of Cyrus king of Persia.

Re: Ezra 4 Chronology

Not only does Ezra 4 reveal these things but the fact that the building of the Temple, (House of YHWH) was postponed seventy years is also mentioned in Zechariah 1:12-16.

Zechariah 1:12-16 KJV
12. Then the angel of the Lord answered and said, O Lord of hosts, how long wilt thou not have mercy on Jerusalem and on the cities of Judah, against which thou hast had indignation these threescore and ten years?
13. And the Lord answered the angel that talked with me with good words and comfortable words.
14. So the angel that communed with me said unto me, Cry thou, saying, Thus saith the Lord of hosts; I am jealous for Jerusalem and for Zion with a great jealousy.
15. And I am very sore displeased with the heathen that are at ease: for I was but a little displeased, and they helped forward the affliction.
16. Therefore thus saith the Lord; I am returned to Jerusalem with mercies: my house shall be built in it, saith the Lord of hosts, and a line shall be stretched forth upon Jerusalem.

So Tyre was forgotten those seventy years even though they had been paid in advance for the building supplies for the Temple in Jerusalem. Then Isaiah says that Tyre will once again play the harlot, (building supplies for the Temple delivered). Then after that seventy years period, at a later date, YHWH himself would pay her a visit and once more AGAIN she would return to her hire but the last time her merchandise would be holiness to YHWH, and not be treasured nor laid up: but for them that dwell before YHWH, to eat sufficiently, and for durable clothing.

Isaiah 23:16-18 KJV

16. Take an harp, go about the city, thou harlot that hast been forgotten; make sweet melody, sing many songs, that thou mayest be remembered.

17. And it shall come to pass after the end of seventy years, that the Lord (YHWH) will visit Tyre, and she shall turn to her hire, and shall commit fornication with all the kingdoms of the world upon the face of the earth.

18. And her merchandise and her hire shall be holiness to the Lord: it shall not be treasured nor laid up; for her merchandise shall be for them that dwell before the Lord, (YHWH) to eat sufficiently, and for durable clothing.

SO YESHUA PAYS A VISIT TO TYRE:
AND THE SPIRIT OF THE THEOU RESTS UPON HIM ~

Matthew 3:16
16. And having been immersed, the Yeshua straightway ascended out of the water: and, lo, the heavens were opened unto him, and he saw the Spirit of the Theou descending like a dove, and lighting upon him:

THUS THE FEET OF YHWH ALREADY STOOD UPON MOUNT OLIVET
And so the city of Tyre returns to her hire but unto the Holiness of YHWH ~

Acts 21:3-7 KJV
3. Now when we had discovered Cyprus, we left it on the left hand, and sailed into Syria, and landed at Tyre: for there the ship was to unlade her burden.

4. And finding disciples, we tarried there seven days: who said to Paul through the Spirit, that he should not go up to Jerusalem.

5. And when we had accomplished those days, we departed and went our way; and they all brought us on our way, with wives and children, till we were out of the city: and we kneeled down on the shore, and prayed.

6. And when we had taken our leave one of another, we took ship; and they returned home again.

7. And when we had finished our course from Tyre, we came to

Ptolemais, and saluted the brethren, and abode with them one day.

The great sea-port city of Tyre had returned to her hire; yet this time it was used of Paul to spread the Gospel to the Gentiles in at least one of his missionary journeys if not all. And this time the merchandise of Tyre was used for them that dwell before YHWH, to eat sufficiently, and for durable clothing! I wonder if that same Matthew 15 woman of Tyre was a part of that group kneeling on the shoreline; praying Paul and his companions in the Book of the Acts? For the Master once said of her: "O woman, great is thy faith!"...

And the woman of Tyre and Sidon was no more a Canaanite: For there shall be no more the Canaanite in the House of YHWH Sabaoth
Yet, each in his or her own appointed time ...

Fifth Mountain ~ The Hivites

Exodus 23:23
23. For My Mal'ak shall go before thee, and bring thee in unto the Amorites, and the Hittites, and the Perizzites, and the Canaanites, and the Hivites, (HSN#2340 Chivviy) and the Jebusites: and I will cut them off.

Original Strong's Ref. #2340
Romanized Chivviy
Pronounced khiv-vee'
perhaps from HSN2333; a villager; a Chivvite, one of the aboriginal tribes of Palestine:
KJV--Hivite.

Heathen Nation Head #5 ~ The Hivites - Chivviy - Beguilers and Wily Deceivers

Joshua 9:1-23 KJV

1. And it came to pass, when all the kings which were on this side Jordan, in the hills, and in the valleys, and in all the coasts of the great sea over against Lebanon, the Hittite, and the Amorite, the Canaanite, the Perizzite, the Hivite, and the Jebusite, heard thereof;

2. That they gathered themselves together, to fight with Joshua and with Israel, with one accord.

3. And when the inhabitants of Gibeon heard what Joshua had done unto Jericho and to Ai,

4. They did work wilily, and went and made as if they had been ambassadors, and took old sacks upon their asses, and wine bottles, old, and rent, and bound up;

5. And old shoes and clouted upon their feet, and old garments upon them; and all the bread of their provision was dry and mouldy.

6. And they went to Joshua unto the camp at Gilgal, and said unto him, and to the men of Israel, We be come from a far country: now therefore make ye a league with us.

7. And the men of Israel said unto the Hivites, Peradventure ye dwell among us; and how shall we make a league with you?

8. And they said unto Joshua, We are thy servants. And Joshua said unto them, Who are ye? and from whence come ye?

9. And they said unto him, From a very far country thy servants are come because of the name of the Lord thy God: for we have heard the fame of him, and all that he did in Egypt,

10. And all that he did to the two kings of the Amorites, that were beyond Jordan, to Sihon king of Heshbon, and to Og king of Bashan, which was at Ashtaroth.

11. Wherefore our elders and all the inhabitants of our country spake to us, saying, Take victuals with you for the journey, and go to meet them, and say unto them, We are your servants: therefore now make ye a league with us.

12. This our bread we took hot for our provision out of our houses on the day we came forth to go unto you; but now, behold, it is dry, and it is mouldy:

13. And these bottles of wine, which we filled, were new; and, behold, they be rent: and these our garments and our shoes are become old by reason of the very long journey.

14. And the men took of their victuals, and asked not counsel at the mouth of the Lord.

15. And Joshua made peace with them, and made a league with them, to let them live: and the princes of the congregation sware unto them.

16. And it came to pass at the end of three days after they had made a league with them, that they heard that they were their neighbours, and that they dwelt among them.

17. And the children of Israel journeyed, and came unto their cities on the third day. Now their cities were Gibeon, and Chephirah, and Beeroth, and Kirjathjearim.

18. And the children of Israel smote them not, because the princes of the congregation had sworn unto them by the Lord God of Israel. And all the congregation murmured against the princes.

19. But all the princes said unto all the congregation, We have sworn unto them by the Lord God of Israel: now therefore we may not touch them.

20. This we will do to them; we will even let them live, lest wrath be upon us, because of the oath which we sware unto them.

21. And the princes said unto them, Let them live; but let them be hewers of wood and drawers of water unto all the congregation; as the princes had promised them.

22. And Joshua called for them, and he spake unto them, saying, Wherefore have ye beguiled us, saying, We are very far from you; when ye dwell among us?

23. Now therefore ye are cursed, and there shall none of you be freed from being bondmen, and hewers of wood and drawers of water for the house of my God.

Shechem the Hivite ~ Fornicator - Thief - Rapist

Genesis 34:1-2 KJV
1. And Dinah the daughter of Leah, which she bare unto Jacob, went out to see the daughters of the land.
2. And when Shechem the son of Hamor the Hivite, prince of the country, saw her, he took her, and lay with her, and defiled her.

Proverbs 6:16-19
16. These six things doth YHWH hate: yea, seven are an abomination unto him:
17. A proud look, (Amorites) a lying tongue, (all "Cretans"-Canaanites) and hands that shed innocent blood, (Hittites-haters-murderers)
18. An heart that deviseth wicked imaginations, (wily-Hivites) feet that be swift in running to mischief, (Girgashites)
19. A false witness breathing lies, (Jebusites) and he that soweth discord among brethren (heretic-divider-Perizzites).

Sixth Mountain ~ The Jebusites

Exodus 23:23
23. For My Mal'ak shall go before thee, and bring thee in unto the Amorites, and the Hittites, and the Perizzites, and the Canaanites, and the Hivites, and the Jebusites: (HSN#2983 Ybuwciy) and I will cut them off.

Original Strong's Ref. #2983
Romanized Ybuwciy
Pronounced yeb-oo-see'
patrial from HSN2982; a Jebusite or inhabitant of Jebus:
KJV--Jebusite(-s).

Original Strong's Ref. #2982
Romanized Ybuwc
Pronounced yeb-oos'
from HSN0947; trodden, i.e. threshing-place; Jebus, the aboriginal name of Jerusalem:
KJV--Jebus.

Heathen Nation Head #6 ~ The Jebusites - Yebuciy - The Blind and Lame

2 Samuel 5:6-9 KJV
6. And the king and his men went to Jerusalem unto the Jebusites, the inhabitants of the land: which spake unto David,

saying, Except thou take away the blind and the lame, thou shalt
not come in hither: thinking, David cannot come in hither.
7. Nevertheless David took the strong hold of Zion: the same is
the city of David.
8. And David said on that day, Whosoever getteth up to the
gutter, and smiteth the Jebusites, and the lame and the blind that
are hated of David's soul, he shall be chief and captain.
Wherefore they said, The blind and the lame shall not come into
the house.
9. So David dwelt in the fort, and called it the city of David. And
David built round about from Millo and inward.

This devil is one of the smoothest and deceptive of them all. One
will notice that not much is spoken of the Jebusites in the
Scripture, especially concerning evil and ponerous things they
may have done, and this is probably because not much was
necessary to get the point across. They are the Sixth Mountain
and are the closest to the "natural man" without Messiah. They
inhabited the city called Jebus which is the ancient aboriginal
name for Jerusalem. They are imposters; posing as the faithful,
yet they hide behind the sick, the blind, and the hobbled, or lame.
However, in reality, they are no such thing but rather prefer to
feign one or more of the above maladies so that others will
sympathize with them to their own personal ends, and so that
they may escape any true accountability which leads to change
of mindset. A good example are the types who proclaim that
everything should be "kept simple" for the "unlearned" and
thereby they shun any deeper Biblical knowledge or growth
insomuch that they may be excused from learning or progressing
in a true walk with YHWH in Messiah. They will often quote the
passage stating "God is not the author of confusion" and then
proceed to accuse those with whom they disagree of speaking
confusing things which they cannot understand. The same types
love to reminisce over things such as the famous poster
"footprints in the sand" where only one set of footprints are
shown on a beach and the caption reads something to the affect
that it was one of the hard times when "Messiah carried me".
There is nothing wrong with the poster or its beautiful sentiments
but this type of imposter lives all of his life according to that

same philosophy. They refuse to accept any responsibility to holiness because "Messiah does everything for them" in their belief system. However, if one has no walk with YHWH in Messiah because he feigns "partial blindness" from the "deeper truths of Scripture" or because he claims to be "lame footed" or handicapped in his ability to walk forward into new things in Messiah then in reality the "footprints in the sand" that he imagines belonging to Yeshua are merely those of his own because he walks ALONE.

Probably for this reason the Scripture states that the blind and the lame were hated in the eyes of David. This is because David speaks in the spiritual and supernal. In other words it means the spiritually blind and the spiritually lame. The Jebusites attempted to hide behind the blind and the lame thinking to themselves that David would not approach them; and perhaps even out of sympathy, yet David saw through it. It is certainly not the physically blind or lame that David hated and the same is true for the Gospel accounts where Yeshua heals people of these types of physical maladies: certainly the healings are also spiritual and supernal in their meanings and that is surely the more important lesson. We have probably all known someone who might feign a sickness or an illness to gain sympathy; yet the same is true when it comes to the flock of YHWH: there are always those who claim one or more of these conditional reasons for why they are simply "not capable" of progressing in their walk with YHWH in Messiah; and neither do they feel the necessity of doing so because, after all, in their own mindset it is "not their job" to purify themselves or their garments. The sin of this reasoning begins with the lie of feigning something false concerning ones self in order to gain sympathy and remove any accountability to change of mindset through repentance, thus, an original lack of true repentance. The entire escapade stems from a hidden self righteousness which has never been truly examined or acknowledged on the part of the individual. And because of this internalized self righteousness they do not ultimately feel they need to change anything about themselves; for they are "perfect" inside of their own imagination; though they also feign humility, piousness, godliness, love, charity, and likewise the same ones love to quote those passages of Scripture. Yet when this genos-kind are unable to silence the truth or escape it they will eventually begin to murder and kill because the perfect self inside of them is more important than anything else in their kosmos.

Revelation 3:1-5 KJV
1. And unto the angel of the church in Sardis write; These things saith he that hath the seven Spirits of God, and the seven stars; I know thy works, that thou hast a name that thou livest, and art dead.
2. Be watchful, and strengthen the things which remain, that are ready to die: for I have not found thy works perfect before God.
3. Remember therefore how thou hast received and heard, and hold fast, and repent. If therefore thou shalt not watch, I will come on thee as a thief, and thou shalt not know what hour I will come upon thee.
4. Thou hast a few names even in Sardis which have not defiled their garments; and they shall walk with me in white: for they are worthy.
5. He that overcometh, the same shall be clothed in white raiment; and I will not blot out his name out of the book of life, but I will confess his name before my Father, and before his angels.

Matthew 9:27-29 KJV
27. And when Jesus departed thence, two blind men followed him, crying, and saying, Thou Son of David, have mercy on us.
28. And when he was come into the house, the blind men came to him: and Jesus saith unto them, Believe ye that I am able to do this? They said unto him, Yea, Lord.
29. Then touched he their eyes, saying, According to your faith be it unto you.

They called him "Thou Son of David" because of David and the Jebusites.

Matthew 12:22-23 KJV

22. Then was brought unto him one possessed with a devil, blind, and dumb: and he healed him, insomuch that the blind and dumb both spake and saw.
23. And all the people were amazed, and said, Is not this the son of David?

The crowd exclaims "Is this not the son of David?" for the same reason because it is a reference to the story of David and the Jebusites, recorded in II Samuel, and concerning the blind and lame.

Matthew 15:30-31 KJV
30. And great multitudes came unto him, having with them those that were lame, blind, dumb, maimed, and many others, and cast them down at Jesus' feet; (doctrine) and he healed them:
31. Insomuch that the multitude wondered, when they saw the dumb to speak, the maimed to be whole, the lame to walk, and the blind to see: and they glorified the God of Israel.

Mark 8:23-25 KJV
23. And he took the blind man by the hand, and led him out of the town; and when he had spit on his eyes, and put his hands upon him, he asked him if he saw ought.
24. And he looked up, and said, I see men as trees, walking. (every man has a fig tree-branch and a vine)
25. After that he put his hands again upon his eyes, and made him look up: and he was restored, and saw every man clearly. (for what a man truly consists of)

BE AWARE ~ FIVE ARE FALLEN ~ ONE IS

And the Jebusites are the typological Sixth Mountain. They seem harmless on the surface but these are the imposters of Jerusalem of Above, the same Jebusites who dwelt in Hebron, which stands for Heaven, and they dwelt in the hill of Zion before David took it from them. These same ones were still in control of Jerusalem of Below at the time when Yeshua arrived and commenced his Ministry; even these were the spiritually blind Pharisees, Sadducees, and Scribes, (blind, hobbled, and lame on the inside).

These slightly different blind kind were spiritually blinded because they believed that they already knew everything that was necessary to know, thus the sin of pride, and therefore the reason why they REMAINED blind.

Matthew 23:26-27 KJV
26. Thou blind Pharisee, cleanse first that which is within the cup and platter, that the outside of them may be clean also.
27. Woe unto you, scribes and Pharisees, hypocrites! for ye are like unto whited sepulchres, which indeed appear beautiful outward, but are within full of dead men's bones, and of all uncleanness.

Matthew 15:7-19 KJV
7. Ye hypocrites, well did Esaias prophesy of you, saying,
8. This people draweth nigh unto me with their mouth, and honoureth me with their lips; but their heart is far from me.
9. But in vain they do worship me, teaching for doctrines the commandments of men.
10. And he called the multitude, and said unto them, Hear, and understand:
11. Not that which goeth into the mouth defileth a man; but that which cometh out of the mouth, this defileth a man.
12. Then came his disciples, and said unto him, Knowest thou that the Pharisees were offended, after they heard this saying?
13. But he answered and said, Every plant, which my heavenly Father hath not planted, shall be rooted up.
14. Let them alone: they be blind leaders of the blind. And if the blind lead the blind, both shall fall into the ditch.
15. Then answered Peter and said unto him, Declare unto us this parable.
16. And Jesus said, Are ye also yet without understanding?
17. Do not ye yet understand, that whatsoever entereth in at the mouth goeth into the belly, and is cast out into the draught?
18. But those things which proceed out of the mouth come forth from the heart; and they defile the man.
19. For out of the heart proceed evil thoughts, murders, adulteries, fornications, thefts, false witness, blasphemies:

Revelation 3:17-18 KJV
17. Because thou sayest, I am rich, and increased with goods, and have need of nothing; and knowest not that thou art wretched, and miserable, and poor, and blind, and naked:
18. I counsel thee to buy of me gold tried in the fire, that thou mayest be rich; and white raiment, that thou mayest be clothed, and that the shame of thy nakedness do not appear; and anoint thine eyes with eyesalve, that thou mayest see.

The only reasonable "eyesalve" is the spittle from the MOUTH-DOCTRINE of Yeshua to cure the blind man ...

Seventh Mountain ~ The Girgashites

Deuteronomy 7:1-4 KJV
1. When the Lord thy God shall bring thee into the land whither thou goest to possess it, and hath cast out many nations before thee, the Hittites, and the Girgashites, (HSN#1622 Girgashiy) and the Amorites, and the Canaanites, and the Perizzites, and the Hivites, and the Jebusites, seven nations greater and mightier than thou;

Original Strong's Ref. #1622
Romanized Girgashiy
Pronounced ghir-gaw-shee'
patrial from an unused name [of uncertain derivation]; a Girgashite, one of the native tribes of Canaan:
KJV--Girgashite, Girgasite.

Heathen Nation Head #7 ~ The Girgashites - Mighty Ones - Legion

Matthew 8:28 KJV
28. And when he was come to the other side into the country of the Gergesenes, (GSN#1086 Gergesenos) there met him two possessed with devils, coming out of the tombs, exceeding fierce, so that no man might pass by that way.

The English translations could be slightly incorrect in that it is probably a single man possessed with "a double" or "duo"-two (in the Greek) as shown from the corresponding Gospel passages where they are cast out into the swine. The word translated "Gergesenos" is stated in the Original Strong's to be of Hebrew origin; the same which is the word employed for the Girgashites, HSN#1622 Girgashiy.

Original Strong's Ref. #1086
Romanized Gergesenos
Pronounced gher-ghes-ay-nos'
of Hebrew origin [HSN1622]; a Gergesene (i.e. Girgashite) or one of the aborigines of Palestine:
KJV--Gergesene.

In the Gospel of Mark we read that this double possessed man was dwelling among the tombs and in the MOUNTAINS. He had a Legion or double Legion of some 2000, or at least there were that many swine feeding on the hillside of the Mountain, yet the language of the passage simply and casually states that it was an "unclean spirit" (singular).

Mark 5:2-9 KJV
2. And when he was come out of the ship, immediately there met him out of the tombs a man with an unclean spirit,
3. Who had his dwelling among the tombs; and no man could bind him, no, not with chains:
4. Because that he had been often bound with fetters and chains, and the chains had been plucked asunder by him, and the fetters broken in pieces: neither could any man tame him.
5. And always, night and day, he was in the mountains, and in the tombs, crying, and cutting himself with stones.
6. But when he saw Jesus afar off, he ran and worshipped him,
7. And cried with a loud voice, and said, What have I to do with thee, Jesus, thou Son of the most high God? I adjure thee by God, that thou torment me not.
8. For he said unto him, Come out of the man, thou unclean spirit.

9. And he asked him, What is thy name? And he answered, saying, My name is Legion: for we are many.

Nothing could tame this one, nothing could hold him back, nothing could lock him up, not even chains and fetters could bind him, and nothing could deliver the poor soul of the man trapped inside along with the Legion in his midst. This kind cometh not out but by prayer and the great Famine of the Four Fasts of Zechariah 8:19. The body of the man had become his own cave, his own prison, his own tomb, that is, until Yeshua appeared. Revelation 6:13-14 is quoted from Isaiah 34. The "mixing" of symbolic animals or their seed is clearly stated to somehow concern the New Covenant of Jeremiah 31 which is quoted verbatim by the writer of Hebrews as the New Covenant.

Jeremiah 31:26-27 KJV
26. Upon this I awaked, and beheld; my sleep was sweet unto me.
27. Behold, the days come, saith the Lord, that I will sow the house of Israel and the house of Judah with the seed of man, and with the seed of beast.

BOTH Houses were to be "mixed" with the seed of man and with the seed of BEAST (the words are Spirit). The "wild beasts" are referenced throughout as in such places as Daniel 7 and Revelation 13. The lesser known, taught, and understood places are certain passages of Scripture which complete the understanding; such as Hosea 13.

Hosea 13:4-11 KJV
6. According to their pasture, so were they filled; they were filled, and their heart was exalted; therefore have they forgotten me.
7. Therefore I will be unto them as a lion: as a leopard by the way will I observe them:
8. I will meet them as a bear that is bereaved of her whelps, and will rend the caul of their heart, and there will I devour them like a lion: the wild beast shall tear them.
9. O Israel, thou hast destroyed thyself; but in me is thine help.

10. I will be thy king: where is any other that may save thee in all thy cities? and thy judges of whom thou saidst, Give me a king and princes?

11. I gave thee a king in mine anger, and took him away in my wrath.

They asked for a king instead of YHWH, and they got Saul who is also called "the Tsebiy-Gazelle of Israel" (which represents the "Beautiful Land" in the book of Daniel) and YHWH gave them and us much more than we bargained for, (kings of the Gentiles-Heathen). And YHWH takes them away in his fury, passion, wrath, and anger, which is to our Salvation. If we understand the symbolic meaning here then YHWH is stating that he will use our own sins, which symbolically turn us into evil beasts, and even he himself will be like the lion, the bear, and the leopard, and he will use them to REND THE CAUL-CHESTPLATE OF OUR HEARTS. And why? For our own good, to remove the "heart of stone" from inside "the chest plate of iron" so as to circumcise that heart of stone; putting it back inside ALIVE, and LIVING, and NEW IN MESSIAH. And according to Jeremiah 31 and Hebrews 8 this is all part of the New Covenant for everyone. It includes both Houses because YHWH has concluded all in unbelief, and in unrighteousness, so that he may bestow his great mercy upon all, showing also that he is no respecter of persons. Daniel 7 and many other passages concerning "wild beasts" apply to every one of us in ways we never imagined, whether we believe or acknowledge this fact or not.

Revelation 6:12-14

12. And I beheld when he had opened the sixth seal, and, lo, there was a great earthquake; and the sun became black as sackcloth of hair, and the moon became as blood;

13. And the stars of heaven fell into the earth, even as a fig tree casteth her untimely figs, when she is shaken of a mighty wind.

14. And the heaven departed as a scroll when it is rolled together; and every mountain and island were moved out of their places.

These stars are not the people of YHWH ...
And "the fullness of the Gentiles" has come in -~- for someone
...

Isaiah 34:4-8 KJV
4. And all the host of heaven shall be dissolved, and the heavens
shall be rolled together as a scroll: and all their host shall fall
down, as the leaf falleth off from the vine, and as a falling fig
from the fig tree.
5. For my sword shall be bathed in heaven: behold, it shall come
down upon Idumea, (Edom) and upon the people of my curse, to
judgment.
6. The sword of the Lord is filled with blood, it is made fat with
fatness, and with the blood of lambs and goats, with the fat of the
kidneys of rams: for the Lord hath a sacrifice in Bozrah, and a
great slaughter in the land of Idumea (Edom).
7. And the unicorns shall come down with them, and the
bullocks with the bulls; and their land shall be soaked with
blood, and their dust made fat with fatness.
8. For it is the day of the Lord's vengeance, and the year of
recompences for the controversy of Zion.

 1 Chronicles 5:3-4 KJV
3. The sons, I say, of (1) Reuben the firstborn of Israel were, (2)
Hanoch, and (3) Pallu, (4) Hezron, and (5) Carmi.
4. The sons of (6) Joel; (7) Shemaiah his son, (8) Gog his son,
Shimei his son.

Luke 11:24-26 KJV
24. When the unclean spirit is gone out of a man, he walketh
through dry places, seeking rest; and finding none, he saith, I
will return unto my house whence I came out.
25. And when he cometh, he findeth it swept and garnished.
26. Then goeth he, and taketh to him seven other spirits more
wicked than himself; and they enter in, and dwell there: and the
last state of that man is worse than the first.

Gog is the fullness of the Heathen come in, (Romans 11:25) that
is the fullness of the Seven Heathen Nations which the children

of Israel are commanded to rule over, even the iniquity of the Amorites having come to the full. It is the same typology as that of the scapegoat which is sent away into the wilderness with all the sins upon its head. That one is the original "old man" sin nature of which Paul writes. The same is the "unclean spirit" of which Yeshua speaks; the one which was cast out of the man, and yet returns, with "seven others more wicked than himself" seeking re-entry into his former house. The scapegoat is therefore "the eighth and of the seven" and he is Gog the Amorite which goeth into perdition in the End. The scapegoat theme is consistent throughout the Scripture concerning the cattle and even the unclean fowls, (the `oreb-raven is the eighth). YHWH says to Abraham that "the iniquity of the Amorites was not yet full" because the Amorite is the Eighth and of the Seven.

Romans 11:25-27
25. For I would not, brethren, that ye should be ignorant of this mystery, lest ye should be wise in your own conceits; that blindness in part is happened to Israel, until the fulness of the Gentiles be come in.
26. AND IN THIS MANNER shall all Israel be saved: as it is written, There shall come out of Zion the Deliverer, and shall turn away ungodliness from Jacob:
27. For this is my covenant unto them, when I shall take away their sins.

For whosoever shall call upon the name of the Lord shall be saved; yet each in his own appointed time; And it is appointed unto anthropon once to die: And none shall be alone in his appointed times O thou whole Palestina...

Heathen King #8 ~ Gog the Amorite - Ro'sh-Head - Nasiy' Prince

Ezekiel 38:1-7 KJV
1. And the word of the Lord came unto me, saying,
2. Son of man, set thy face against Gog, the land of Magog, the chief (HSN#7218 ro'sh) prince (HSN#5387 nasiy') of Meshech and Tubal, and prophesy against him,

3. And say, Thus saith the Lord God; Behold, I am against thee, O Gog, the chief (HSN#7218 ro'sh) prince (HSN#5387 nasiy') of Meshech and Tubal:
4. And I will turn thee back, and put hooks into thy jaws, and I will bring thee forth, and all thine army, horses and horsemen, all of them clothed with all sorts of armour, even a great company with bucklers and shields, all of them handling swords:
5. Persia, Ethiopia, and Libya with them; all of them with shield and helmet:
6. Gomer, and all his bands; the house of Togarmah of the north quarters, and all his bands: and many people with thee.
7. Be thou prepared, and prepare for thyself, thou, and all thy company that are assembled unto thee, and be thou a guard unto them.

Gog is the Rosh-Head builder and Watcher-Guardian of the Great Wall of the flesh encompassing all four quarters of the 'erets-land; And by the hook of 'Anak in his jaw he returns with the Nasiy-Rulers of the Rising Mist ...

Original Strong's Ref. #7218
Romanized ro'sh
Pronounced roshe
from an unused root apparently meaning to shake; the head (as most easily shaken), whether literal or figurative (in many applications, of place, time, rank, itc.):
KJV--band, beginning, captain, chapiter, chief(-est place, man, things), company, end, X every [man], excellent, first, forefront, ([be-])head, height, (on) high(-est part, [priest]), X lead, X poor, principal, ruler, sum, top.

Original Strong's Ref. #5387
Romanized nasiy'
Pronounced naw-see'
or nasi' {naw-see'}; from HSN5375; properly, an exalted one, i.e. a king or sheik; also a rising mist:
KJV--captain, chief, cloud, governor, prince, ruler, vapour.

Revelation 17:9-11 KJV

9. And here is the mind which hath wisdom. The seven heads are seven mountains, on which the woman sitteth.

10. And there are seven kings: five are fallen, and one is, and the other is not yet come; and when he cometh, he must continue a short space.

11. And the beast that was, and is not, even he is the eighth, and is of the seven, and goeth into perdition.

Promised Land Twenty-Four
Spiritual Warfare Prayer

"[11] To keep Satan from getting the advantage over us; for we are not ignorant of his wiles and intentions."

You Amorite spirit, I bind you and your power from operating against me and causing me to slander or to entice me to babble and rebel and talk about other people, in Jesus' name. You will cease and desist from sowing thoughts of discord and division into my mind. You will not bring condemnation to paralyze me in Jesus' name. I am free from your slander, from your babbling and talking and rebelling and bitterness and division and sowing discord, in Jesus' Name.

You Hittite spirit, I bind you and your powers from operating against me or to break me or to cause me to fear. The activities of doubt and unbelief are no longer bound in my life, in Jesus' name and I command you to loose me from the spirit of fear in loose my life and surroundings. And therefore I am free, in Jesus' name.

You Hivite spirit, I take authority over you in the name of Jesus. You will not bring deception or wickedness to me any longer. As a villager or deceitful friend, you will no longer disguise yourself as someone ordinary. You will not seduce me to part with my money or some get-rich-quick scheme or some wrong deal. I command you to cease your activity in my life, in Jesus' name and I claim back every dollar that I have spent or invested in schemes and wrong deals, in Jesus' name.

You Jebusite spirit, according to Matthew 11:28 30, I take authority over you. You spirit of heaviness, you will not operate against me any longer. You will no longer tread me under your feet or attack my emotions with negativity. You will not attempt to sap my confidence or my strength any longer. I command you to cease and desist from instigating the feeling of resignation or quitting in my life, in Jesus' name. Your powers are broken now, in the name of Jesus.

You Perizzite spirit, according to John 10:10, the thief cometh not but for to kill, to steal and to destroy. It says if I find a thief, he shall restore to me sevenfold. You have been found. You will no longer cause me to dwell in an un-walled city. You will no longer steal or dispossess from me what I have built up in Jesus' name. So I take back everything you have stolen in the name of Jesus and I declare that I am prospering and everything in the Book belongs to me. "Mammon is the spirit of money." You spirit of mammon, I bind you. I bind your powers against me from operating against me to steal from me or to block creative money -making ideas and to block creative thoughts from reaching me. I command you to loose every money-making thought that you have stolen from me or blocked from me, in the name of Jesus. Proverbs, chapter 6, verse 31 promised me that if the thief be found, he must repay sevenfold. I claim 7 ideas for every idea you stole from me and I bind you now, and I loose you from your attack, in Jesus' name. I prohibit satanic manifestations and I speak that divine "abortive" measures and "miscarriages" that occur in satanic wombs and incubators be destroyed in Jesus name.

Everything that Satan is trying to birth, I command a miscarriage. Now Father, you have given me a great work to accomplish. I war for the releasing of finances and all resources that belong to me. Everything prepared for me before the foundation of the world, that pertains to my life, my ministry, my calling and godliness, comes to me now. I shall not/will not be denied. I shall not/will not accept substitutes. I call in the resources necessary for me to fulfill God's original plan for my life and I command that it come to me without delay, in the name of Jesus.

I decree and declare that the wealth of the wicked is no longer laying up for me, but it is released now. Let those who hold on to my wealth longer than they should be shaken until they release it right now into my hands . I command you Satan, to "cough it up," spit it out, loose it, release it, and let it go, now ! In Jesus' name. Amen!

Father, I come in the Name of Jesus I repent for the sins and transgressions of my ancestors. I repent for all disobedience of Your commands by turning away and listening to the enemy or to other people. Father, I receive the redemption from the curse by the Blood of Jesus and ask you to break off all curses of poverty upon my family line and upon me. I declare that the blood of Jesus has broken every curse.

Lord, I repent for anyone in my family line who offered sacrifices that were not favorable and right. I repent for any withholding of the first fruits and the best portions; I repent for all wrong motives and attitudes of hearts. I repent for anger, resentment and bloodshed of my brother. Lord, please forgive any bloodshed and bring peace to the blood that cries out.

Lord, please break all Canaanite and Girgashite curses against me, as today I declare, I am my brother's keeper! Lord, please restore the ground to me and please restore Your promise of blessings and fruitfulness. Lord, please remove any marks on me and break the curse of wandering. Father, please allow my family to come into Your presence again as a chosen covenant people.

I repent for all my ancestors who denied justice to the poor, for all who held on to ill will, and for all who withheld forgiveness to a brother. I repent for shutting my ears to the poor, for exploitation of the poor, and for crushing them in court. I repent for all who did not forgive, but held grudges and became bitter against those who unjustly exploited them or crushed them.

Lord, please break all curses others have spoken against my ancestors or me because of the guilt of our sins and transgressions. Lord, please remove any curses that have put up walls of separation between You and me. Hear my prayers again and please open my eyes, ears, and heart. I repent for any generational dishonesty, even the smallest hidden, accepted, or self-justified dishonesty.

I repent for any of my ancestors who would not forgive debts in the Lord's timing and who ignored the poor. I repent for all hardheartedness, tightfistedness, and unforgiveness. Lord, please restore mercy and cheerful giving in my family line. Please bless me as You promised in Your Word.

Lord, I repent for generational idolatry, for disobedience, and for not following Your commands. I repent for not serving You joyfully and gladly in my time of prosperity.

Lord, please break all curses against us that send locusts and worms, Lord, please break all skies of bronze and ground of iron. Please release any captive sons or daughters and stop the destruction. Lord, please remove all iron yokes, all blindness, oppression, and spirits of robbery. Lord, please break the curses of hunger, nakedness, dire poverty, and slavery.

Lord, I repent for any of my ancestors who were unfaithful, greedy, disobedient, thieves or liars. I repent for breaking the covenant and coveting or keeping the things of the pagans and not totally destroying them as commanded.

Lord, please break any curses that have come on my family for the evil they did, especially the curse of destruction by fire.

I repent for all ancestors who were evil and tried to control and frustrate the poor. Lord I repent for any in my family line who put up security or pledges for another. Lord, please forgive any unfulfilled debts. I break all ungodly covenants, oaths, and alliances. Lord, please remove all traps or snares from the words of my mouth. Please break all sluggish and slumbering spirits from me and restore wisdom and ambition.

I repent for all my ancestors who unduly withheld from others and for all who trusted in riches rather than in God. I repent for all who ignored discipline and correction. I repent for all greed, bribes, and for idle talk and boasting. I repent for inaction, nonperformance, and not keeping my word.

Lord, please break all curses of injustice and shunning and please break any walls between me and others and between me and You. Please restore honor to our family.

Lord, I repent for myself and for all my ancestors for being liars, hasty, proud, arrogant, selfish and lovers of the world and its pleasures. I repent for our lack of diligence, oppression of the needy, exploitation, and favoritism. I repent for all rejection of God and any cursing or blasphemy of God.

Lord, I repent for all my family's sluggishness, laziness, neglect, and lack of judgment; I repent for anyone in my family who charged exorbitant interest. I repent for any and all family concealed sins. I repent for spiritual pride in those who would not repent.

I repent for any ancestors who chased fantasies because they were stingy and greedy. I repent for all who did not fight injustice, were unfair, and closed their ears to the cries of the poor and needy.

Lord, please break all poverty curses off of me and change my heart.

Lord, I repent for myself and anyone in my family who followed deceptive words and relied on social or religious identity for salvation. I repent for injustice, for oppressing the aliens, widows and the fatherless. I repent for any idolatry, for all ungodly sacrifices and worship, all innocent bloodshed, and for stealing, adultery, perjury and murder for myself and my family line. I repent for all our backsliding, rebellion, disobedience, pride, and spiritual pride. Lord, please break all connections and control that the queen of heaven has on my family and please restore in me wholeheartedness. Please make my heart pure, noble, faithful, and sensitive to You.

Lord, I repent for all generational idolatry and ask You to remove any spirit of prostitution in my heart. I repent for all corruption, guilt, sin, arrogance and unfaithfulness. Lord, I repent for all illegitimacy in my line.

Lord, please set me free from the enemies of moths, rot, lions, sickness, and sores. Please restore Your covenant as promised.

Lord, I repent for all my ancestors who were boastful and proud of their position, standing, and authority. I renounce all love of sin or iniquity. I repent for myself and for all in my family line who became comfortable, selfish hoarders and trusted in their wealth. I repent for all who sold their righteousness, for all who enslaved others, and for all who trampled the poor. I repent for all who were stingy and controlling of wealth.

Lord, please remove any curse that keeps me from enjoying the fruit of my labor. Please break off from me any poverty curses that have been passed on through my generational line, from Adam to me. Lord, please break off from me all curses "that there will never be enough." Lord, please restore to me a new purse without any holes. Please break off from me all curses of lack, shrinking, theft, loss, blight, mildew, and hail.

Lord, I repent for myself and for all those in my family line for being controlling, deceptive, and for putting ungodly burdens on others. I repent for trying to please man rather than God and for accepting praise, honor, worship, or ungodly authority and titles from men. I renounce all religious spirits, legalistic spirits, self-exaltation and hypocrisy. I repent for myself and my generational line for not entering the door to heaven and for shutting it on others. I repent for being a blind guide, and I ask You, Lord, to break all ungodly oaths, covenants, pledges, dedications, and alliances. I repent for all ungodly and insincere sacrifices or for any sacrifice on an unholy altar. I repent for being unjust, merciless, unfaithful, greedy, and self-indulgent. I repent for harboring sin or wickedness. I repent for myself and my family line for rejecting, mocking, cursing, or killing the prophets and the messengers from God. I renounce any spiritual pride that rebels against repentance, and I apply the blood of Jesus to all the roots of iniquity. I repent for all my ancestors who would not believe or declare that Jesus was Lord.

Lord, please give me the mind of Christ in the matters of finance.

I repent for myself and my ancestors who committed adultery with the queen of Babylon and enjoyed or benefited from her luxuries. Lord, please break all ungodly ties and connections with the queen of Babylon. Lord, please remove all consequences and plagues that were a result of any alliances with the queen of Babylon. Please remove all plagues of death, mourning, famine, and judgment fire.

Lord, please guide me by Your Spirit and Your Word in the godly use of wealth and teach me to be a faithful servant. In Jesus Name. Amen. Amen. Amen.

How will I help build the Kingdom of God?

Your Prayer:

Conclusion

When God blesses me with the millions how would I give it back the Kingdom of God? Will I build the Universities, will I invest in afterschool programs to educate and train politicians, or will I build employment centers and so forth?

I pray that this book was what you were looking for in order to start your business for the Kingdom of God; not man. If you have any questions or business ideas you want to share with me, send me an email, so we can come into agreement, at successisourplan@gmail.com.

I Love You Kingdom Builders, but God and His Son, Jesus Loves You More!!

Assignment

GIANT BATTLES IN LIFE

Ancient people had a simple approach to names. They would call people by an obvious trait. Even though a people in a city may have had different family names, their city was named after their reputation. For example, if it was a big city, its name might simply be *Big City*. If all the people in one city had a reputation for horsemanship, the city might be called *Horse City*. The seven nations that Israel had to defeat to subdue the Promised Land bore significant names. They are listed in Joshua 3:10.

CANAANITES

This name means *merchants who humiliate*. They were financial giants. The New Testament believer has to learn what God wants done in the area of finance. The devil would love to conquer the believer through bad financial decisions. How does God want us to be conquerors in our finances?

2. Note the following principles of Christian financial handling-

a) Proverbs 3:9

_____

b) Malachi 3:10

_____

c) Romans 13:8

_____

d) Proverbs 24:27

_____

Canaanites were motivated by greed and lust for material accumulation.

3. According to Jesus, what affect can a Canaanitish "spirit" have over the believer?

(Matthew 13:22)

_____

HITTITES

This name means *terror*. Hittites were giants who brought fear, confusion and discouragement. The believer today is challenged by the enemy's bombardment of fear, confusion and discouragement.

4. What were the Israelites told to do in the face of such opposition? (Numbers 14:9)

_____

5. What assurance of victory over fear, confusion, and discouragement do we have? (Matthew 28:20)

_____

(NB Joshua 1:5)

This giant wants to conquer us and hinder us from possessing our Promised Land. By looking to God in His Word rather than at the problem we face, we are assured of victory.

HIVITES

Hivites claimed to offer a good life by living their lifestyle. Many alternate philosophies and religions today offer to give their adherents "life". The enemy loves to lure people into lifestyles claiming to be the answer to that person's needs and desires. Lifestyles such as "swinging", "if it feels good-do it", "don't worry what other people think", "look out for number one", and "it is about time you did something just for yourself" can all lure people away from the lifestyle that God requires of them.

6. What lifestyle are we told to live? (NB Leviticus 20:23; Romans 8:4-5, 13; Philippians 3:17; 2Thessalonians 3:6)

_____

PERIZZITES

Perizzites were people who had been separated and lived in unprotected/unwalled villages. The enemy loves to separate us from God, and thus our protection.

7. How is God described in Psalm 61:3? (Psalm 9:9; Proverbs 18:10; 2Samuel 22:31)

_____

8. How does the enemy lure us away from God's protection?

_____

GIRGASHITES

Therefore, Girgashites are people who *go back* and are *earthy*. Backsliding and carnality. The believer must do battle with the spirit of backsliding and carnality. Girgashites battle by degrees. That is, by little compromises. The believer must learn to do battle with the little compromises that this enemy puts before them. No habit or sin is too great that you and God can not overcome it.

9. What does Hebrews 2:1 instruct us to do?

_____

AMORITES

Amorites were people who were arrogant and boastful in their speech, who always challenged. We too have a battle with our tongue.

10. What is the mark of a perfect person? (James 3:2)

_____

JEBUSITES

Jebusites were people who trod on others and polluted them. Power and defilement. Scripture speaks of two areas where people can be defiled: sexually (Genesis 34:5) and religiously (Leviticus 18:30; 20:3; Nehemiah 13:29). The Jebusite spirit seeks to destroy the believer in these two areas. We fight by observing God's Word.

11. First Thessalonians 4:3-7 speaks about this issue. What does it tell us to do?

_____

With God's help we are made more than overcomers! (1John. 5:4)

Amen.

References

http://archive.org/stream/BreakingFreeFromBondage_784/BeingRele
asedFromBondage_djvu.txt
http://bible.knowing-jesus.com/topics/Walking-In-The-
Spirit#sthash.AgQzcz3h.dpuf
http://www.legana.org/studies/conquer/study02.htm
http://www.whatchristianswanttoknow.com/bible-verses-about-trials-
20-scriptures-on-tribulations/#ixzz3Q37OxanL
http://www.whatchristianswanttoknow.com/bible-verses-about-trials-
20-scriptures-on-tribulations/#ixzz3Q37OP9O6
http://lifehopeandtruth.com/bible-questions/what/narrow-is-the-gate/
http://www.pottersministries.org/messages/html/CastingOutDemons.h
tml
https://sites.google.com/site/newlifebaptistchurchbosmont/7-tites
http://psychcentral.com/blog/archives/2008/04/15/6-difficult-types-
of-people-and-how-to-deal-with-them/
http://www.sheshbazzardaq.com/seven-mountains.html
http://shamah-elim.info/hittite.htm
http://www.desiringgod.org/articles/what-is-the-biblical-evidence-for-
original-sin
http://www.openheaven.com/forums/printer_friendly_posts.asp?TID=
40239
http://www.cnfministries.com/mountains5.pdf
http://historyeducationinfo.com/edu5.htm
http://en.wikipedia.org/wiki/Economy
http://en.wikipedia.org/wiki/John_Cotton_%28minister%29
http://en.wikipedia.org/wiki/College_of_William_%26_Mary
http://en.wikipedia.org/wiki/Yale_University
http://www.gotquestions.org/what-is-mammon.html
http://www.allaboutgod.com/goliath.htm
http://www.gotquestions.org/Christian-family.html#ixzz3ShoI0pRH
http://www.cnfministries.com/mountains5.pdf
http://www.gotquestions.org/Bible-music.html
http://en.wikipedia.org/wiki/John_Cotton_%28minister%29
http://www.gotquestions.org/Anglicans.html#ixzz3TlSymP82

Murdock, George Peter (1965) [1949]. *Social Structure*. New York: Free Press.

Robert H. Gundry, Matthew: A Commentary on His Literary and Theological Art (Grand Rapids: Eerdmans Publishing Company, 1982), p. 191.
http://ministry127.com/christian-living/5-symptoms-of-the-success-syndrome

Special Thanks for all my readers and supporters. Special Shout out to my team at Labor Ready, Jacksonville, Florida.

You can contact with Eureka Butler at
successisourplan@gmail.com
Website: www.hey-success.com

Social Media Accounts:

Facebook: http://www.facebook.com/eureka.butler5

Hey-God Book Series Facebook:
www.facebook.com/successisourplan

Twitter: EurekaButler5

Tumbler: eurekabutler5.tumblr.com

Other Books Authored by Eureka Butler

"Hey, I Choose To Be Successful"
Divorce Is Not An Option, It is a Stronghold
The Oil of Joy
A Steer Towards Success
18-Day Challenge for Every Man and Woman
Recipe for Success

Connect with me at: successisourplan@gmail.com
Website: www.hey-success.com